DEADLINE
FOR THE
MEDIA

Also by James Aronson

THE PRESS AND THE COLD WAR
PACKAGING THE NEWS

DEADLINE FOR THE MEDIA

Today's Challenges to Press, TV and Radio

James Aronson

THE BOBBS-MERRILL
COMPANY, INC.

INDIANAPOLIS / NEW YORK

THE BOBBS-MERRILL COMPANY, INC.
INDIANAPOLIS / NEW YORK

COPYRIGHT © 1972 BY JAMES ARONSON
ALL RIGHTS RESERVED
LIBRARY OF CONGRESS CATALOG CARD NUMBER 72-179640
DESIGNED BY JACK JAGET
MANUFACTURED IN THE UNITED STATES OF AMERICA

FOR CEDRIC BELFRAGE
A REBEL FOR LIFE

AUTHOR'S NOTE

FOR sharing with me their time, experiences and thoughts, my deep appreciation to Arthur Alpert of WRVR-FM, New York; Roldo Bartimole of *Point of View*, Cleveland; David Deitch of the *Boston Globe;* Ron Dorfman of the *Chicago Journalism Review;* Dan Georgakas of *Cineaste* magazine; Thomas A. Johnson of the *New York Times;* Nicholas A. Mottern of the late *Independent Man*, Providence; B.J. Phillips of *Time* magazine; and Andy Stapp and Terry Klug of the American Servicemen's Union.

For permitting me to test portions of this book in the *Antioch Review*, my special thanks to its editor, Lawrence Grauman, Jr.

For his sure and steady editorial guidance, my gratitude and respect to Alexander L. Crosby of Quakertown, Pennsylvania.

The best hope for the future of the media in America rests in the knowledge that journalists of such quality and integrity continue their work.

CONTENTS

INTRODUCTION

RARELY in the history of the United States have the news media made so much news themselves as in the early 1970s. This was extraordinary because the managers of newspapers—and television news, which joined the communications competition seriously in the late 1940s—have always been notoriously shy of publicly discussing their internal operations or any criticism of their operations.

The development was neither sudden nor uncalculated. Rather, it was cumulative, and several components helped bring it into being. The first rumblings came in surveys and public-opinion polls indicating that the general public in the last years of the 1960s was becoming skeptical of news and commentary in the daily press and was turning increasingly to television for its news. But overall, it was wary of both printed and televised news.

The skepticism paralleled a growing weariness with the war in Indochina. The credibility gap during the Johnson administration concerning news of the war, and America's role in the war, widened into a chasm of incredibility during the Nixon administration. The year 1968 seemed to mark a turning point for the communications media in their support of the war: there was a noticeable veering away in the editorial comment of the more responsible sectors of the media.

To dispel this atmosphere of healthy mistrust, President Nixon on November 3, 1969, launched an unhealthy appeal to the "silent majority" to rally round the flag in support of the war. Shortly thereafter Vice-President Spiro Agnew was spanked off on a voyage of the beagle to sniff out sedition in newspaper and television news-gathering apparatuses.

In a coordinated operation, Attorney General John Mitchell joined the hunt with grand-jury subpenas for newspapermen and women and television commentators, ostensibly to track down the sources of their information for evidence to assist government prosecution of defendants in criminal proceedings. In reality, it was a campaign of intimidation—to force the communications industry to mute its criticism as the White House sought a consensus for its foreign policy.

By the middle of 1970 the campaign had reached such proportions as to make it a Time of the Toad for the communications media. Agnew was still prowling the land on a long White House leash, and the number of subpenas was growing. Reporters and photographers were turning up as agents for the FBI in testimony at political trials. Army counterintelligence operatives were being accredited as newspaper reporters in Indochina to snoop on legitimate reporters. At demonstrations in Foley Square in New York or in Grant Park in Chicago, any experienced reporter could tell that the good-looking chap in the trench coat, looking frightfully Front Page behind his crisp new press badge, was one of J. Edgar Hoover's boys out for an airing, or the man from the local Red Squad. No one had ever seen him before or heard of the New Suburbia News Agency he allegedly represented.

The administration's pervasive campaign intimidated those newspapers and networks which had cautiously begun to reassume an adversary stance vis-à-vis government, and the administration's law-and-order demagoguery went largely unchallenged in the months before the 1970 elections.

The election results, however, demonstrated a persevering strain of common sense in the electorate. No significant changes were produced by the voting, because no genuine alternatives were offered, except in a few congressional contests; but it was clear that the law-and-order issue was perceived by a majority as a fraud. The people were concerned over real problems—the war, a failing economy and racism—and dissatisfaction with the administration's performance in all three areas was manifest.

The public common sense seemed to stiffen the flaccid resolve of the communications media and moved them finally to confront the clear and present danger being presented by the administration. In effect, the government, without recourse to legislative or judicial action, was well on the way to abrogating the freedom-of-the-press guarantees of the First Amendment, adopted precisely to protect this adversary role. Worried questions were raised in the communications industry about the unacknowledged but *de facto* partnership between government and the media—an arrangement which increased media profits and decreased media competition in return for services rendered—that is, for criticism withheld. Was it a partnership, after all, when one party to the arrangement put the squeeze on the other?

The situation unfortunately did not alarm the industry to the point where it was willing to examine its own largely uncritical support of government policy during the previous decade—let alone before. But it did move the owners and operators of the media to seek protective alliances among themselves and to enlist public support in their defense against the government's assault.

Increasingly, in the press and on television, and in the journals of journalism, the issues and the battle lines were laid out. There was even the unaccustomed suggestion that internal media reform, looking toward a greater sense of responsibility, might be the most effective recruiting agent for public support.

If the voices were faint in the executive suites of the industry, they were stronger and more persistent among the working staffs in the newsrooms. There the call was not only for self-examination, but for basic operational changes to permit a voice in policy and structural decisions for the men and women who actually handled the news.

Thus the communications industry at the managerial level seemed to be caught in a kind of pincers: one prong was the enormously powerful forces of government, insisting on even greater conformity and acquiescence by the media; the other prong was the far less powerful staffs of the newspapers and television networks, insisting on greater managerial independence of government and more internal democracy.

This stirring among the staffs had its origins in the tumultuous events of the 1960s—particularly the protests against war and racism—which in turn influenced the people who covered the events. In Europe, mainly in France and Germany, editorial staffs of influential publications had persuaded management during those years to share responsibility and profit, too. Sometimes agreement had been reached through quiet negotiations, sometimes only after bitter strife.

To the surprise and even grudging admiration of the European owners, newspapers and magazines thus affected showed not only increased circulation because of improved content, but improved profit sheets as well. The European experiment was being observed with great interest by American staffs, and proposals for similar arrangements in the United States were formulated. Preliminary discussions were begun in 1969, but at the end of 1971 they were still preliminary. Resistance, as expected, was vigorous, but the efforts were continuing.

A concomitance of these efforts was the beginning of realistic discussion and debate about traditional practices of journalism—the unwritten code of objectivity in the news and the trend toward "advocacy" journalism; the responsibility and activities of the working press both during and after working hours; the decline of investigative reporting, and changing style and language.

Much of this discussion was taking place in a new kind of publication—the journalism review—published, edited and written by newspapermen in the cities in which they worked and dealing with the newspapers and networks for which they worked. By the autumn of 1972, there were journalism reviews in 15 major cities, including, belatedly, New York. These publications vary in quality and degree of criticism, but their effect has been beneficial as an outlet for staff grievances, and as a means of exposing to the community at large the inner workings of the news-gathering process, something the owners of the media have always gone to great lengths to conceal.

The 1960s witnessed also the rise of the underground press, a misnamed entity which is almost entirely supraterranean and often visibly shocking in its expression of discontent with established American institutions in general and the news media in particular. From its psychedelic "subculture" beginnings in the mid-1960s, this iconoclastic medium has developed, often erratically, into a press of protest, largely political in approach and content, and focusing irreverently on the problems of American society. Some underground newspapers have developed into plump profit-making institutions whose sharp edges have been dulled by affluence. This factor, plus the persevering appeal of the underground press generally, has moved many establishment newspapers to modify their own style and content in the brisk scramble for circulation.

Another phenomenon of the 1960s was the rise of the black journalist within the establishment media, a development produced not so much by any civil righteous zeal on the part of white publishers as by sheer necessity. A lily-white approach to news gathering, advertising and entertainment information had become increasingly unacceptable in the black communities. Where the offense was not immediately discernible to some, its exposure was given a smart assist by the militant black freedom movement.

White reporters were not welcome in the black communities, and white products were resisted to the extent that the necessities of life permitted. These hard facts in the competition for news coverage and advertising revenue helped tumble the white walls of journalism and permit the entry of the black journalists. The result has been a revolutionary change in news coverage of black communities. But the change has created certain problems of identity for the black journalists themselves, and problems of survival for the black press and electronic media.

When the women's liberation movement was revived in the United States, after a long hiatus, the first reactions were predictable: suspicious gallantry in the executive offices, locker-room humor in the newsrooms and stories about liberation activities written with the grace and wit of a gentleman caller at a Kansas City parlor house.

But the mood changed at all levels when women on the staffs began to organize and put forward demands for equality in an industry notorious for its discrimination between the sexes. The demands were for fairness and respect not only for women working in the industry, but also in news presentation of women.

A significant area of establishment media largely unknown to the civilian population was vitally affected at the turn of the 1970s by the war in Indochina and the protest movement against it. This was the military media, a vast and interweaving network of newspapers, magazines, newsletters and radio and television stations covering an enormous section of the world in which the American military police patrols its beat.

As resistance to the war grew among the general public, there was a matching cadence within the armed forces, and the underground press in uniform had an important role in this resistance. From unsteady beginnings in the late 1960s, the GI press grew into an entity comprising two national newspapers and more than a hundred newspapers published on or near military bases on three continents.

This development brought into the open for enlisted men and women the same credibility gap in the regular military press that marked the regular civilian press. It also helped enormously to provide vital assistance and guidance not only for enlisted personnel, but also for draft resisters, conscientious objectors and deserters.

Meanwhile the communications industry was making astounding technological advances, with prospects both exhilarating and frightening. By satellite transmission men walked from the moon right into earthbound living rooms. Cable television was bringing urban culture into the most remote sections of the country. And cassettes were turning homes into compact film and theater libraries and auditoriums.

By mid-1971 there was hardly an area of the communications industry unaffected by these science-fiction devices, the ferment within the industry and the impact of all these developments upon the media, the government and the public—supposedly the master of both media and government.

Then, in June 1971, the mix exploded like an atomic device. The spark that set off the explosion, however, was not a derivative of plutonium but an eighteenth-century piece of parchment known as the Bill of Rights, and its First Amendment in particular. The immediate ingredient was the publication of documents concerning America's involvement in Indochina which came to be known as the "Pentagon Papers."

The New York Times took the lead in publishing this record of deception and prevarication by the government and within a matter of days was joined by 17 other newspapers. While many questions were involved—some of them still unanswered—in the publication of the papers, there was no question that it was a remarkable piece of journalistic public service.

The publication led to dramatic Supreme Court sessions, which, however, did not resolve the basic First Amendment issues fundamental to the case. It led also to a period of self-congratulation by the press, which neglected to consider one crucial factor: the communications media's own role during the period of deception.

Many correspondents and editors conceded in the days after publication of the Pentagon Papers that they had known many of the details and had made educated guesses about some. The *fact* of the publication, therefore, was an unacknowledged admission by the press that its own role in the 1960s had been inadequate at best and irresponsible at worst. Even more significantly, a basic question was left unanswered about the future role of newspapers and the television networks (which covered the controversy admirably and the fundamental issues miserably). The question was this: Would the communications media make public documents concerning current and ongoing events, if these documents demonstrated that government policy guiding these events was not in the public interest?

This was the overriding and decisive question confronting the communications media as the year 1971 ended. For the owners and operators of the media, the decision was whether to resist, individually and collectively, the government's direct encroachment upon the freedom of the press, and then to assert their responsibility in an adversary role to government; or to accede to the pressures and demands behind a dust storm of indignant rhetoric and double-talk.

For the men and women who work for the newspapers and the radio-television networks, the decision was the extent to which they would use their own collective power to persuade their employers to resist; and, if persuasion failed, the extent to which they would use this power to counter their employers' capitulation. The question that basically confronted the working staffs was this: If reform from within the industry failed, would there be an exodus from the established media and an effort to set up alternate media as an adversary to both government *and* the established media?

These questions were being asked in a time of increasing repression and economic distress—and confusion. The administration was dominated by a devious President and avaricious politicians in pursuit of power by any means. This was hardly a new phenomenon, but its gross presence in the Nixon administration was impossible to conceal. And nothing could hide the monumental mediocrity of the administration as a whole.

The regular opposition (in the Democratic party) had little to offer as alternative, and the intellectual administrators of the Kennedy-Johnson Cold War years—as represented by men such as Arthur Schlesinger, Jr.—were busily creating a new myth to excuse their own deceit: the inevitability of amorality in government.

For concerned and less calculating Americans, the assault by government against the communications industry represented a new McCarthyism. Yet this view was no more accurate than characterizing the repression of the 1950s as McCarthyism. The political intimidation could have succeeded in neither period without the blessing of the several administrations in power—Truman, Eisenhower, Kennedy, Johnson and Nixon—or without the general acquiescence of the media, however troubled that acquiescence may at times have been.

In a previous book, *The Press and the Cold War,* I sought to document the thesis that McCarthyism was not a by-product of the Cold War but an instrument of it. The repressive measures of the Nixon administration validate this thesis. And until the Cold War mythology is exposed, once and for all, for the gargantuan lie that it is, McCarthyism, Agnewism and Hooverism will remain the institutionalized methods of dealing with dissent, and the fragile parchment of the Bill of Rights will continue to crumble.

The communications media are a crucial part of the power complex which sets the course of life for the nation and, to an extent, for the peoples of the world. The media condition the citizen to think the thoughts that are preferred by government, industry, the military and the educational establishment—and by the media themselves. There is hardly an iota of difference among them.

This interlocking relationship was discussed in 1966 by an influential journalist employed by the nation's foremost newspaper, the *New York Times.* James Reston delivered the Elihu Root lectures,[1] sponsored by the Council on Foreign Relations, at the midpoint of the period covered by the Pentagon Papers.

Although Reston focused almost exclusively on foreign policy, he conceded a great influence by the press on domestic policy, and his basic ideas may be applied generally, particularly since dissent in the United States is so closely tied to foreign policy. He stated his theme thus:

> The rising power of the United States in world affairs, and particularly of the American President, requires not a more compliant press, but a relentless barrage of facts and criticism, as noisy but also as accurate as artillery fire. . . . Our job in this age, as I see it, is not to serve as cheerleaders for our side in the present world struggle, but to help the largest possible number of people to see the realities of the changing and convulsive world in which American policy must operate. It also means a redefinition of what is "news," with more attention to the *causes* rather than merely the *effects* of international strife. . . .

There can be no quarrel with Reston here, nor with his estimate of the increasing power of the Presidency since World War II, and of the declining influence of the Congress and the press in the same period. But there is much to quarrel with in Reston's subsequent estimate of what the role of the press should be and the degree to which it can make its power and influence felt in the public interest.

Contrary to official mythology, Reston said, "the people who write the news are not the enemies but the allies of officials." He noted that reporters are constantly used "to transmit to foreign governments, through press, radio, and television, those official views which the administration in Washington does not want to put in formal diplomatic communications."

There will always be times when officials will seek to conceal information, Reston said, and reporters will feel it their duty to publish this information, "but the area of conflict between them is narrowing and the area of cooperation is widening." The modern newspaper, he said, is searching for a new role, or should be: "That

---

[1] Published 1967 by Harper & Row as *The Artillery of the Press: Its Influence on American Foreign Policy.*

role, I believe, lies in the field of thoughtful explanation, which tends to make the reporter more of an ally of the government official than a competitor."

Reston quoted with approval Matthew Arnold's faith in America's "saving remnant," expressed more than 100 years ago, as against the "unsound majority" of the mass of the people. Reston found that this American remnant was growing in size, wealth, travel, voting constituency, and in its demand for more serious publications. He regarded this as an "increasingly influential factor in public affairs," but he was at the same time worried about the "resignation and even the surrender" of many of the best of this remnant—in the press, churches, universities, Congress and the executive branch of the government. He concluded:

> This, I believe, is the real danger. The responsible government official and the responsible reporter in the field of foreign affairs are not really in conflict 90 percent of the time. When they do their best work, they are allies with one another and with "the remnant" in the nation that wants to face, rather than evade, reality. Clever officials cannot "manipulate" reporters, and clever reporters cannot really "beat" the government. From both sides, they have more to gain by cooperating with one another, and with the rising minority of thoughtful people, than by regarding one another as "the enemy."

There is a startling contradiction between Reston's introduction to his lectures and the lectures themselves. In the introduction Reston advocated a noncompliant press laying down a constant artillery barrage of criticism directed at government to help "the largest possible number of people" understand the complexities of a changing world. In the lectures there was a persistent, almost fervent plea for an alliance between government and a press whose responsibility, according to Reston, was to explain the policies of government. All this would be done with the collaboration of an intelligent remnant resisting the simplistic solutions of an ignorant majority.

But it is precisely the government which has sought for a quarter of a century to enlist the active collaboration of the "silent majority" in support of its Cold War policies. And it is Reston's élitist remnant—men such as Walt W. Rostow, Robert F. McNamara, McGeorge Bundy and William P. Bundy, Roger Hilsman and

General Maxwell Taylor—who were largely responsible for the policy of calculated deceit revealed in the Pentagon Papers. Further, this "remnant" within government was most assiduous in seeking to silence even the loyalist opposition in the generally cooperating communications media. Far from facing reality, they sought to hide reality from the public. These are the men Reston described, in his comments immediately after the publication of the Pentagon Papers, as honorable men of the highest personal morality.

I have dwelt at length on Reston's views because I believe they represent the basic philosophy of the liberal press establishment: the section of the press which is regarded as the most enlightened and responsible. How enlightened and responsible it actually is will be a major concern of this book.

The encouragement of a cult of the élite in journalism in collaboration with government would discourage public enlightenment. What is desperately needed is public debate about American foreign and domestic policies. Yet this healthy exercise has been denied to the citizenry for generations.

I find entirely unacceptable the view that the public gets the news and information it wants, and the corollary notion that it gets what it deserves. How can the public know what it wants or deserves if successive national administrations in conjunction with the élite remnant do everything in their power to prevent it from understanding or even learning about the realities of policy?

No great national debate can be achieved unless there are radical changes in all areas of public life. One of the first essentials is a concentrated assault against the communications fortress which stands in the way of achieving these changes. I believe there are enough journalists of honesty and integrity to breach this fortress.

Part One

TURMOIL
AT THE TOP

CHAPTER I

THE PACKAGE
AS PRESIDENT

MOST students of American politics think Richard Milhous Nixon has never acted on impulse—at least publicly. They are wrong. He did once.

The great exception followed Nixon's defeat for the governorship of California by the incumbent Democrat, Edmund G. Brown, in November 1962. The scene was the Beverly Hilton Hotel in Beverly Hills, California, on election night.

Defeated candidates are invariably described as "haggard and unshaven," and Richard Nixon was all of that. But he was also engulfed in a black cloud of rage and frustration over what he regarded as unfair press treatment of his campaign. At this moment of defeat, newspaper reporters and television crews were waiting in the Cadoro Room below the Nixon suite for the customary appearance of the defeated candidate, his gracious acknowledgments and his magnanimous message of congratulations to the victor.[1]

But Nixon was resisting the pleas of his staff to make a statement. The press was impatient, said Herbert G. Klein, the San Diego newspaper editor who was Nixon's chief press adviser. "You've got to go down," Klein urged.

"Screw them," said Nixon. "*You* make the statement."

---

[1] A remarkably candid description of this episode is given in Jules Witcover's neglected *The Resurrection of Richard Nixon* (New York: G. P. Putnam's Sons, 1970).

3

Finally Klein went down. At the rear of the hotel a car was waiting to take Nixon home. As Klein was seeking to pacify correspondents irritated by the defeated candidate's snub, Nixon walked through the lobby of the hotel. But instead of going out the back door to his car, he marched into the Cadoro Room and grabbed the microphone from the astonished Klein.

"Good morning, gentlemen," he said. "Now that Mr. Klein has made his statement, and now that all the members of the press are so delighted that I have lost, I'd like to make a statement of my own."

What followed was a long, rambling, self-serving discourse, contradictory, bitter, at times almost incoherent. But for once there was revealed the unpackaged and spontaneous Richard Nixon for all the world to see. The heart of the statement was in these sentences:

> As I leave the press, all I can say is this: for sixteen years, ever since the Hiss case, you've had a lot of fun—a lot of fun—that you've had an opportunity to attack me and I think I've given as good as I've taken. I think it's time that our great newspapers have at least the same objectivity, the same fullness of coverage, that television has. And I can only say thank God for television and radio for keeping the newspapers a little more honest. . . . But as I leave you I want you to know— just think how much you're going to be missing. You won't have Nixon to kick around anymore, because, gentlemen, this is my last press conference.

The last assertion, like so many subsequent Nixon pronouncements, proved unfortunately to have no basis in fact. It might have remained a subject of high hilarity among newspaper people —if Madison Avenue alchemy and television technology had not proved so effective in the 1968 Presidential campaign.

It would, of course, be fanciful to trace the governmental assault against the communications media under the Nixon administration to Nixon's bitterness in 1962 (although this vindictive element surely was present). The campaign had far wider and more sinister implications. The fact that television—despite Nixon's 1962 gratitude—was a main target was a major clue. Television served its purpose well during the 1968 campaign, in which the electronic master mechanics in the Nixon entourage directed and stage-managed *every* Nixon appearance. After the election victory, however, except for the carefully contrived special message appearances, Nixon had to take his chances with television and the press, as all politicians do. His distaste for "live" televised press conferences soon became clear, and for good reason: his self-consciousness and uneasiness about coping with any situation not carefully prepared in advance.

A less suspicious President might have accepted the traditional Washington ground rules sanctioning a superficial application of the adversary relationship between President and press, and suffered a few sharp questions. And in the first few months of his administration Nixon did hold reasonably frequent press conferences which might have produced another episode of unpackaged spontaneity from Nixon (and enlightenment for the nation), but did not.

The White House correspondents, whose distaste for Nixon as a person is common knowledge, behaved more like governmental publicity men than inquiring reporters. Even this submissiveness, however, was not reassuring to Nixon, and, as time went on, the number of Presidential press conferences dwindled to a new low in the history of the modern Presidency. There was for a time some grumbling among the media about lack of contact with the President, and an occasional editorial in the *New York Times* or the *Washington Post* resulting in a hasty press conference; but even this protest petered out. Thus, because of Nixon's command of television time and his passion for the techniques of the 1968 campaign, the President was able almost completely to manipulate his television appearances as he wished. He became the first fully packaged President in American history.

The Nixon package, which extends to controlled relationship with newspapers and magazines also, is a combination of duplicity, fraud and polarizing pressures, all disguised in the slick formula which carried Nixon to the Presidency and all as self-seeking—and as dangerous—as the man himself and the interests for which he speaks.

There is no "new" or "old" Nixon. There has always been only one: calculating, anxious and supremely ambitious in the over-compensating manner of inadequate men. He has managed always, behind a facade of noxious sincerity, to pay off old scores when the power of office permitted. His relations with the press, to the degree that the amenities and the refinements of the Presidency permit, have followed this pattern. The administration's attacks on the media, however, must be analyzed not in the framework of personal Presidential politics, but of national and international policies.

The opening gun in the assault on the media was fired in typically reverse Nixon style—a sanctimonious disclaimer of what has happened or is about to happen—by Frank J. Shakespeare, director of the United States Information Agency and a former executive of the Columbia Broadcasting System. Speaking on September 26, 1969, nine months after Nixon took office, Shakespeare told the Radio-Television News Directors Association: "You must fight against any effort by any government that would make any effort (God knows I don't think the Nixon government would ever do it) to try to influence your judgments."

God knows the Nixon government did do it, just six weeks after Shakespeare's fervent pronouncement, in the first of a series of speeches by Vice-President Agnew, in Des Moines. It was directed primarily at Nixon's old friend, television, as the most vulnerable target of news management through intimidation (control of broadcasting licenses by the Federal Communications Commission). Agnew then proceeded to Birmingham to extend the assault to the press, primarily the *New York Times* and the *Washington Post,* both then increasingly critical of the administration's insistence on prolonging the war in Vietnam.

The speeches written for Agnew abounded in alliterative excess and calumny of alleged intellectualism—the kind of polemic that brings howls and whoops from selected audiences who salivate on cue. But accompanying the fundamentalist rhetoric was a purposeful threnody. Some direct excerpts from the speeches, delivered in measured, unemotional monotone, epitomize the basic theme:

President Nixon's words and policies [are subject] to instant analysis and querulous criticism.

We do know that to a man these [television] commentators and producers live and work in the geographical and intellectual confines of Washington, D.C., and New York City. . . . We can deduce that these men read the same newspapers. They draw their political and social views from the same sources.

Is it not fair and relevant to question [TV news] concentration in the hands of a tiny enclosed fraternity of privileged men elected by no one? . . . As with other American institutions, perhaps it is time that the networks were made more responsive to the views of the nation and more responsible to the people they serve.

A single company, in the nation's capital, holds control of the largest newspaper in Washington, D.C., and one of the four major television stations, and an all-news radio station, and one of the three major news magazines—all grinding out the same editorial line.

The day when network commentators and even the gentlemen of the *New York Times* enjoyed a form of diplomatic immunity from comment and criticism of what they said . . . is over. The time for blind acceptance of their opinions is past.

"I'm raising these questions," Agnew said, "so that the American people will become aware of—and think of the implications of—the growing monopoly that involves the voices of public opinion."

Agnew's charges, of course, contained some truths, but the speeches were largely demagoguery. The reference to "instant analysis" of the President's "words and policies" was a case in point. The direct reference was to Nixon's significant speech of November 3, 1969, seeking to rally the "silent majority" to support of administration policy in Indochina. Actually, the speech was in the hands of reporters two hours before it was delivered, and the White House correspondents in addition were briefed before the speech by Presidential adviser Henry Kissinger.

The attempt to mark the commentators and analysts as effete denizens of the Eastern shore was an appeal to "middle America" —as the real America—to reject this élite snobbery. "The views of this fraternity do not represent the views of America," Agnew said. The geographic origins of Agnew's main television targets were Missouri (Walter Cronkite), Montana (Chet Huntley) and North Carolina (David Brinkley). It was true that they worked mainly in Washington and New York, the main centers of news, just as the President and Vice-President work mainly in Washington, the center of government.

While Agnew was on solid ground in marking the growth of conglomerates in the news industry (his direct reference was to the Washington Post Company and its ownership of WTOP-TV Washington, its all-news radio station, and *Newsweek* magazine), he restricted his comments to monopolies lately critical of Nixon on Vietnam. He could have noted other and larger conglomerates —the *Chicago Tribune–New York Daily News* empire, for example, the Gannett chain and the Copley chain of newspapers. But these, of course, were supporters of the Nixon administration.

The Vice-President's alliterative flourishes were carefully fashioned, but so were his facts and figures, with just enough truth to score points in an unbalanced presentation. The calculation and timing of the assaults were just as careful, and they had a double purpose:

1. In the short range, to inhibit coverage of the November 15, 1969, antiwar mobilization in Washington and demonstrations for peace in general. The mobilization turned out to be the largest convocation against war in the nation's history—but there was no live coverage by any television network. *Variety*, the weekly newspaper of the entertainment and communications industry, reported that the networks had decided on their own in advance against live coverage. But the November 13 Agnew speech guaranteed that the decision would not be reversed by an industry not noted for courage.

2. In the long range, to achieve by pressure and threat of indirect control what the administration could not do by legislation. The First Amendment forbids enactment of legislation abridging freedom of the press, but governmental harassment and intimidation can achieve the same goals. It is significant that Agnew reminded the television networks that they were "enjoying a monopoly sanctioned and licensed by the government."

Was there a need for such administrative vehemence against the communications industry in view of the industry's general acquiescence to, and even anticipation of, governmental desires and preferences? For example, six weeks before the first Agnew speech, *TV Guide* (circulation 12 million) noted in its issue of

September 27, 1969, that television news and special-events programs were undergoing significant changes. They were shifting away from emphasis on the militant left, said the magazine, and toward the center and the right. All three networks would be "exploring middle and lower-middle class Americans."

In its issue of the same date, *Editor & Publisher*, the magazine of the newspaper industry, said: "The shift . . . is a reflection of the views of what is called 'the silent majority' who feel that television has devoted too much time to the role of the militant and the agitator and has given too little coverage to the quiet hard-working Americans of all races."

It was not until five weeks later, on November 3, 1969, that Nixon employed the phrase "the silent majority."

The Agnew attacks produced a flurry of indignant and defiant editorials—some of them of high quality—restating the constitutional guarantees of freedom of the press. There were statements by the heads of the television networks—of varying quality—declaring in essence that the networks would not be intimidated.

There was also a sandstorm of telephone calls, letters and telegrams (solicited by Agnew) indicating that the Nixon speech of November 3, followed ten days later by Agnew's first speech, had been effective. Overall, there was evidence, in the volume and "balance" of the coverage of the Agnew speeches and the reaction to them, that the administration had to a great extent succeeded in its purpose of intimidating the communications media.

"I think the industry as a whole has been intimidated," said CBS's Walter Cronkite. Norman E. Isaacs, then editor of the *Louisville Courier-Journal* and president of the American Society of Newspaper Editors, said he had been buried under an avalanche of "sick mail," including remarks about the "Jew-owned and Jew-dominated news media." (Ironically, the *Courier-Journal* is owned by the thoroughly WASPish Bingham family.) Significantly, half the mail from *editors* supported the Agnew position. It was Isaacs's opinion that Agnew's implied threat to the broadcast media had already penetrated.

In an interview with *Editor & Publisher* (August 22, 1970), John B. Oakes, editor of the editorial page of the *New York*

Times, conceded that Agnew's speeches had affected him and the *Times.* He said that perhaps without their realizing it, there had been a certain toning down, a hesitancy or reluctance in the quality of the *Times*'s dissent. The attitude of the Nixon administration, he said, had uglier overtones than those of previous administrations which had reacted sharply to criticism.

The full ugliness of the administration's intent was exhibited in a speech by Agnew six months after his opening blast—in Houston, on May 22, 1970. It came after the United States–Saigon invasion of Cambodia, which, together with the killing of students at Kent State University in Ohio and Jackson State in Mississippi, had provoked widespread demonstrations at universities across the country.

Agnew's audience was 500 Texans who had paid 500 dollars a head to raise money for the Republican National Committee. Gathered about the premises were an equal number of protesters, many newspaper reporters and numerous Secret Service agents, at least one of whom wore a press badge while two of his colleagues carried news cameras.

Sprinkled through a speech directed at some of the nation's leading newspapers and commentators were such phrases as "strident voices of liberalism" . . . "masters of sick invective" . . . and "hysterical view from the ivory tower." Agnew's chief complaint was that the offenders had been critical of the invasion of Cambodia and that some of them had ascribed the invasion and Nixon's callous denigration of campus protesters as contributing factors in the four deaths at Kent State.

Remarkably, the Vice-President had locked together in his pillory such diverse persons and institutions as Hugh Sidey of *Life* magazine, James Reston, Tom Wicker and Anthony Lewis of the *New York Times,* Carl T. Rowan, a black columnist for white newspapers, the *Atlanta Constitution,* the *Arkansas Gazette*— and I. F. Stone.

Stone's reaction was touching. "When I began publishing in the heyday of McCarthyism 18 years ago," he wrote in his *Bi-Weekly* of June 1, 1970, "I never dreamed that I would share the pillory with a Luce publication. In journalism at least Nixon has kept his pledge and brought us all together."

But Nixon and his number one polarizer had other things in

mind at the Shamrock-Hilton that night. The press was not the chief target but rather a convenient vehicle through which to strike at a more persistent and consistent group of dissenters—the university students and faculty members, whose unity in the aftermath of Cambodia and Kent State represented an immediate and direct threat to administration policy. After quoting at length from press clippings, Agnew got down to business:

> I have sworn I will uphold the Constitution against all enemies, foreign and domestic. Those who would tear our country apart or try to bring down its government are enemies, whether here or abroad, whether destroying libraries and classrooms on a college campus or firing at troops from a rice paddy in Southeast Asia.
>
> Nothing would be more pleasing to some of the editors and columnists I have quoted tonight than to have me simply shut up and disappear. Nothing would be more pleasing to those on the campus whose motives I have challenged. . . . They are . . . a small, hard core of hell raisers who want to overturn the system for the sake of chaos alone. . . . Unfortunately they are encouraged by an equally small number of faculty members who apparently cannot compete legitimately within the system, or choose not to do so.
>
> It is my honest opinion that this hard core of faculty and students should be identified and dismissed from the otherwise healthy body of the college community lest they, like a cancer, destroy it.

The press, according to Agnew, by criticizing the President, was encouraging the spread of malignant dissent in the universities. With the "isolationists" in the Senate who "seek at every turn to thwart the President's efforts" to prevent a Communist takeover in Southeast Asia, and "the electronic media," it comprised an unholy trinity in the service of Satan (communism) to destroy the American way of life.

Nixon and Agnew knew that the deepest-going dissent against administration policy was not in the media or in the Congress, but in the intellectual community. They knew that the dissenting students and teachers were ranging out from the universities seeking common cause with young labor unionists, the poor and the minorities in the inner cities.

This was the reason for the Hard Hat Uprising, when construction workers, blessed by Nixon and anointed by AFL-CIO President George Meany, smashed into peaceful students in New York protesting the invasion of Cambodia. And it was the reason for Agnew's invective at the Shamrock-Hilton. The White House strategists felt the time was not right for a direct confrontation with the university community, so the attack was indirect:

First, seek to intimidate the news media from giving space and voice to the new turn of dissent.

Second, discourage members of Congress by pressure and patronage from supporting the university community.

Third, if and when the first two missions are accomplished, come down hard on the dissenting students and faculty.

It was part of the carefully controlled strategy to put down dissent in every area of American life, and the nerve center of the campaign was in the White House. After the first Agnew speech, in Des Moines in November 1969, Clark Mollenhoff, then White House Deputy Counsel (in fact, the house detective), told the press: "The speech was developed in the White House. It represents White House concern about getting through to the public." And syndicated columnist Richard Wilson, a Nixon admirer, said of the Agnew line:

> This has been a bold and calculated move which can be seen in its true perspective as part of President Nixon's attempt to hold public opinion to his measured course of liquidating the Vietnam war at his own pace and then proceeding with broad domestic reforms and his own reelection in 1972. The move is bold and calculated beyond anything previously dared by a President.

That was a fairly sound analysis, even though the pace of domestic reform seemed to be cadenced by the pace of the turtle.

It has, of course, become almost a cliché to say that all administrations have sought to manage the news to advance their programs and policies. But the Nixon administration may be recorded as the first to *stage-manage* the news. The production was carefully synchronized under the direction of Herbert Klein, the first White House news coordinator and the man who was at Nixon's side that dark and dour night at the Beverly Hilton in November 1962. The campaign originated with Nixon himself and was based on the successful television series which packaged

Nixon into a product slightly more appetizing than Hubert H. Humphrey.

Since taking office, Nixon at his own choice, has addressed the nation by television, unencumbered by the press, with greater frequency than any past President to whom television was available. The use of live television at press conferences tends to inhibit the White House press corps, an already inhibited group whose unwillingness to ask penetrating questions has helped turn a once-exciting event into a half-hour soporific. It has also inhibited a self-conscious President for whom even innocuous questions opened his pores for copious perspiration. Spectator interest at televised Nixon press conferences thus has been reduced chiefly to clocking the number of mechanical gestures, shifting postures and sincere smiles the President can achieve before he is given his "Thank You, Mr. President" by the dean of the White House correspondents at a signal from a Presidential aide.

But in the news-managing machine in the windowless basement of the White House, the crisp directives left little chance for even the rare missed cue of the press conference. Jules Witcover of the *Los Angeles Times* presented an informed exposition of how the machinery was set in operation (Spring 1970 issue of the *Columbia Journalism Review*). The title of the article was "The Two Hats of Herbert Klein," one put on for the job of opening the executive branch of government, particularly at Cabinet level, to the press; the other for the job of sealing off the President from the press.

Like most publishers and network officials, Klein regarded the information media as a national business enterprise. Unlike the media executives, however, he rarely muffled his ideas and activities under a blanket of First Amendment platitudes. And he was a man who put the boss's desires into direct action.

Where earlier administrations transmitted their proposals and programs almost exclusively through the resident press corps in Washington (600 strong), the Klein way was to go directly to the country itself—to the 1,700 daily newspapers and the thousands of television and radio stations.

The Washington press corps, with a few exceptions, is not a boat-rocking crew. But they are professionals, and to a considerable extent they do strip the propaganda gloss off administration releases, which, for understaffed news bureaus, often serve in place of individual reporting enterprise. For the mechanistic minds in the Nixon administration, even this deglossing is unacceptable.

The Klein system was not to cut off the Washington press corps, but rather to go beyond it and in some cases to preempt it. Thus, the President's speeches and certain Cabinet pronouncements would be sent to the Washington press corps but also and immediately to newspapers and radio and TV stations throughout the country. On major proposals (postal reform, for example), briefing teams would be dispatched to newspaper editors and publishers (the Republican National Committee picked up the tab), and local public-relations firms would be engaged to smooth the way for the briefers.

It wasn't that the Washington press corps was not doing a good job, Klein explained, "but look at how many editorials are written around the country on the basis of an eight-inch wire service story" out of Washington. It was simply a more sensible informational approach, he said, and not at all a pressure campaign to persuade the managers of the communications industry to the administration's point of view. The local executives, Klein insisted, were not pushovers. "We have to take a chance that when they see our program they may disagree," he said.

The risks, however, were somewhat reduced by the briefers, who wined and dined the editors at the best local establishments, flattering them with the impression that they had a direct pipeline to the White House ("The President has asked me to tell you personally how highly he regards your editorial approach, even though he may not always agree with it. But he surely does appreciate your understanding how hard he is working to get this country going, and the difficulties he inevitably faces"). Such an approach has been known to round the heels of many an editor.

The guiding philosophy of this entire operation is the Spiro Agnew syndrome of distrust of the "Washington–New York news axis" (the word "axis" keeping alive the hateful connotation of the Berlin-Rome axis of World War II) and the "Eastern press" in general. The President himself participated in the process by in-viting editors and network officials to regional briefings at Washington, Chicago or the West Coast White House at San Clemente, California—pointedly excluding representatives of newspapers regarded as hostile—and by making well-publicized visits to the offices of newspapers supporting his policies.

One such visit in the summer of 1970 was to the *Daily News* in New York, an ardent Nixon supporter. The choice of the *News* was regarded as a pointed rebuke to the *New York Times*, the holy mosque for all visiting dignitaries. Although the *Daily News* complied with Agnew's specifications for the "conglomerate category" (circulation two million, TV station and radio outlet in New York), it did not qualify for his abuse. Actually, the *Daily News* is under the control of the Chicago Tribune Company, one of the nation's giant conglomerates. In addition to the *Daily News* and the *Chicago Tribune*, the company owns and operates the afternoon daily *Chicago Today*, broadcast facilities in four states, cable-television systems in two others and newspapers in Florida.

The problems posed for television news by the Presidential news-management offensive were somewhat different from those for newspapers, not only in the presentation of news, but also in the size of audiences and the threat of retaliation for criticism of government.

On presentation: What a President has to say is, of course, news. When the President wishes to appear before a national audience —even if his purpose is purely political—he requests time, which is free and usually at prime air time, preempting profitable income time for the networks. Thus the President commands television's "page one" without competition.

On the size of audience: Agnew in his November 1969 speeches pointed out that television audiences dwarfed those of newspapers. At that time, for example, the circulation of the *New York Times* was about 900,000, *Time* magazine four million and *Newsweek* 2.5 million. By contrast, the *CBS Evening News* (Walter Cronkite) audience was measured at 18.4 million daily, NBC (Huntley-Brinkley) 16.5 million and ABC (Frank Reynolds) four million. The ratios have since evened out among the networks, but the size remains constant.

On retaliation: Agnew noted significantly that the networks were not fully protected by First Amendment prohibition against governmental interference as were newspapers. What he did not have to say precisely was that television stations depend for their existence on licenses issued by an agency of the federal government, the Federal Communications Commission.

The accomplished media manipulators in the White House took full advantage of these circumstances, and in the process they were helped immeasurably by such media executives as Julian Goodman, president of the National Broadcasting Company, who said shortly after the first Agnew fusillades that he did not consider it proper for "political opponents" of the President to be interviewed immediately after he had spoken on the air.

This attitude of caution was assumed also by the Columbia Broadcasting System, which refused to *sell* an hour's worth of time to Senators George McGovern and Mark Hatfield to respond to Nixon's network speech in May 1970 justifying the United States invasion of Cambodia. The senators sought to present the case for the Church-Hatfield amendment designed to cut off appropriations for the Cambodian operation after a specific period of time—hardly a radical proposal. Senator McGovern said: "I am puzzled by a communications policy that presents the President's side of the issue and won't even sell us time."

The hour ultimately was purchased from NBC for 70,000 dollars, five days after Nixon's address. NBC President Goodman apparently found no impropriety in demanding and getting 70,000 dollars cash from "political opponents" of the President five days after the fact.

The White House attitude was bolstered also by the American Broadcasting Company, which, according to *Variety*, appointed a "happy news" producer early in 1970. He was dubbed by his colleagues the "Agnew's editor" because of Agnew's complaint that the media had been presenting only "bad news."

"Bad news" covers all factual news the White House finds unpalatable. Hence the administration strategy was to persuade the communications industry to feed the public good news, carefully edited to place the government in a favorable light. If this could be done, the public would not resist administration policy. Instead, it would vent its frustrations over the war and economic issues on the dissenters who knew the facts.

This strategy of obfuscation was the basis of the Republican law-and-order hoopla in the 1970 election campaign. The media, groggy from the Agnew rounds and wary of a direct confrontation with the administration, protested with little more than peeps and squeaks.

There were, of course, other ways to keep bad news from the public, and the ineffable Frank Shakespeare of the United States Information Agency, in his September 1969 speech already cited, had some guidance. Shakespeare expressed his concern about the prevalence of "liberals" on the network news staffs and the "liberal orientation" of television news. "I suppose," he said, "that it would be shocking to take into account a man's ideology when you hire him. . . . But if out of 50 or 100 men that you hire purely on the basis of ability, you are going to end up with a tremendous number on one side of the ideological fence rather than the other, then you are going to end up in a box. How are you going to handle it?"

He answered his own question: Do what newspapers do—the *New York Post*, for example, which publishes a column by Max Lerner and "a stable of liberal writers," *and* William F. Buckley. The *Post*, Shakespeare said, hired Buckley because he "represents the other point of view."

Aside from the question of how one defines the word "liberal" today (Max Lerner hardly falls into even that dubious category), the conservative point of view is overwhelmingly represented in the press and on the television networks. Buckley's column appears in 300 newspapers and he has for many years had his own television program. Indeed, the conservative point of view is the dominant one available in much of the local media west of the Hudson and south of the Potomac rivers. Further, on *basic* American foreign policy—that is, the policy of anticommunism—there has been little quarrel between liberals and conservatives since the end of World War II.

Both supported the Cold War aims of four consecutive national administrations, the liberals perhaps even more enthusiastically. And if some liberals in the first years of the 1970s turned squeamish about *aspects* of American foreign policy ("tactics" might be a more appropriate word), few have advocated a complete alteration of Washington's policy.

For Shakespeare (and for the publishers and the heads of the networks) there has been no acknowledgment that there is still another side deserving of a regular hearing in the marketplace of opinion, a side whose credentials ought to have gone up in value enormously with the media (but did not) in the aftermath of the revelations of the Pentagon Papers. That side is the radical point of view.

What would happen, for example, if a radical commentator, skilled in the printed or broadcast word, were to present himself as a candidate for regular appearance in a newspaper or on a television network as a "balance" to the saturating commentary of William F. Buckley? He almost certainly would not be hired.

The debate, therefore, between the government and the communications media was severely limited by this circumstance during and after the Agnew campaign. Unfortunately it has remained limited, despite a greater demonstration of courage and initiative by the communications industry after the 1970 elections. The public was not taken in by the law-and-order campaign and showed that it was not afraid of "bad news." On the contrary, it wanted to know why there was so much of it. It was this public manifestation of stubbornness that stiffened the resistance of the communications media.

The debate about the public's right to know (and desire to know) in the last analysis has never countenanced the entire spectrum of opinion and point of view, particularly in the areas of greatest concern to the young people of the nation. The debate has been further circumscribed by an identity of views on the part of the government (any administration) and the owners and operators of the means of communication. Limits have been set by a definition of the so-called national interest as identical with national policy.

The debate in the first years of the 1970s was significant but not fundamental. It could become basic, and the Nixon administration's single-minded campaign for a monolithic media could be defeated by an equally single-minded resistance by the media. But the directors of the media will not accept a direct challenge.

There was an ugly precedent for the Nixon media campaign. The manipulators of the press of Hitler's Third Reich succeeded in ridding the press of all dissent by a process called *Gleichschal-*

THE PACKAGE AS PRESIDENT 19

tung, most closely translated as "political coordination." The German names and strains in the Nixon administration provided an uncomfortable analogy with the propaganda efforts of the Third Reich, but the approach in Washington was made to appear American in style and practice. And some of the men in charge had no need for a German precedent. Attorney General Mitchell was a choice example.

CHAPTER II

A MATTER
OF PRIVILEGE

ANY confusion about the purpose of the Agnew assaults was dispelled by the great subpena crusade of Attorney General John Mitchell which followed. Mitchell's goal was not to encourage the nation's "silent majority" to speak but to silence the majority of the men and women who report, edit and broadcast the news and commentary. In this strategy (as will be shown later) there was special emphasis on silencing the growing number of black reporters in the general press, where, until the late 1960s, there had been "one-of-them" tokenism, or no blacks at all.

Involved in the subpena affair was the sharp debate taking place in the world of journalism about the question of "objectivity" in the news—whether in an increasingly complicated world an intelligent and even dispassionate reporter should confine himself to reporting the facts objectively, omitting opinions and evaluation or attributing them to unidentified sources (sometimes invented).

More and more, reporters were coming to believe that if the facts showed, for example, that racism was widespread in the United States or that the United States was engaged in a senseless, savage and illegal war in Southeast Asia, then it was the reporters' responsibility to present the facts supporting these conclusions and to state frankly and fairly the conclusions themselves. It would follow that it was the responsibility of the newspapers to print these facts and conclusions, and of the networks to broadcast and televise them. It would not be the reporters' responsibility to misrepresent the facts—that is, to "balance the news" with "good" and "bad," so that the facts would not appear to be so reprehensible.

There were, however, formidable obstacles to achieving this journalistic ideal, as Steve Knoll noted in *Variety* (December 31, 1969). His references were primarily to TV journalists, but they applied equally to all news gatherers and commentators. He wrote:

> As newsmen, it is their traditional role to view the words and actions of government officials with a healthy skepticism, and to act as "watchdog" in behalf of the public interest. Yet they serve broadcast stations and networks that function primarily as purveyors of entertainment rather than as news media, and they are part of large and diversified corporations, many of them major defense contractors. In short, they operate in an environment where the fruits of any tough investigative reporting may well run counter to the interests of their employers' employers.
>
> Agnew seemed to decry the power of the networks, but his principal target was the alleged power of the newsmen. His concern was not so much to diversify corporate control of the airwaves as to present news in a way more favorable to the administration's position. If this could be accomplished via corporate control, the Vice-President would probably have no objection at all.

Nor would Attorney General Mitchell—and that was the root issue in the subpena controversy.

It had been common practice for the government to request, and to receive, material from newspapers and radio-television networks under an arrangement best described as negotiated subpenas—that is, subpenas whose scope had been agreed upon by government and industry by consultation in advance.

These demands periodically produced a measure of grumbling but little publicity or public controversy until late in January 1970, when two federal agents served the CBS-TV network with a subpena to produce everything in CBS's possession involved in the making of a film about the Black Panthers on the West Coast —memos, notes, telephone calls, tapes and out-takes (tapes not edited or televised). CBS protested, announced its "total opposition to subpenas so broad in scope," and said it would not comply. That was January 26. On January 27, CBS said it *would* turn over the material to the Justice Department.

It became known, at the same time, that subpenas had been served in October 1969 on four Chicago newspapers, and on *Time, Life, Newsweek* and NBC News for unedited film, photographs, files and even notebooks of reporters who had covered the Weathermen's "Four Days of Rage" demonstrations in Chicago that month. *Time* and *Life* turned over their files. The newspapers and NBC News entered into negotiations with the Justice Department concerning what *Newsweek* called "the mechanics of submitting available material to all investigative agencies at one time."

Apparently what concerned media officials most about the transfers was cost in money, not in integrity. *Newsweek* submitted its files, but deleted the names of persons mentioned in them, after considerable staff pressure on management to use the scissors. CBS, vacillating further, announced that it would seek to narrow the scope of its subpena.

The government's demands brought to the fore a critical issue. For newspapermen and women privacy and confidence are essential conditions in treating with news sources. No source will continue to supply sensitive information if its origin might be revealed by a reporter, or if the information might turn up in court proceedings that could involve the source. Although no federal law protects this special relationship between reporter and informant, the confidential arrangement has long been accepted. Seventeen states do have laws protecting the right of reporters not to divulge their news sources, and in March 1970 legislation was introduced in the House of Representatives and in the Senate (the Newsmen's Privilege Act of 1970) to protect the working press from forced disclosures of confidential information. No action was taken.

(In April 1971, 33 members of the House joined to sponsor a new bill covering appearances by news personnel before federal courts, grand juries, congressional committees and governmental agencies, departments, and commissions. It had the support of the Freedom of Information Committee of the American Society of Newspaper Editors, which charged members of the government with using the subpena to try "to force the press to act as lawmen.")

As media managements and legal staffs sought a solution to the problem, the government tried a new tack. On February 2, 1970, it served a new kind of subpena—a personal one—on Earl Caldwell, a staff reporter of the *New York Times* stationed in San Francisco, ordering him to testify before a federal grand jury about the Black Panthers. Caldwell is black. Specifically he was ordered to bring tape recordings and notes of interviews with Panther leaders David Hilliard and Raymond Masai Hewitt.

Caldwell announced that he would refuse to appear. The *Times* assigned lawyers and company officials to advise him and pledged that it would use "all its resources to make sure that no judicial action violates the constitutional guarantees of a free press." But it did not say that it would instruct Caldwell not to appear.

The Caldwell case ignited a fuse among black journalists from coast to coast, because black reporters for white newspapers and the TV networks hold a special place in the black community. For generations the needs and desires of black people were non-news for the communications media. The only time they broke through in print or on the airwaves was when a human volcano erupted, generally as the result of police violence, which became incidental in the ensuing coverage.

But the impact of the black freedom movement in the middle 1960s forced the newspapers and networks into an awareness of racial news as never before. They discovered also that white reporters were not welcome in the black communities and that the only way they could cover these areas was with black reporters (see Chapter IX). So they began to hire blacks, and for the first time in the general media, news of black people took on a new dimension—a human one.

While there were conflicts among the black journalists with the white media about questions of professionalism and politics in their work, there was no conflict at all about their color or commitment to their people. This was reflected in the extraordinary confidence the black community placed in the black journalists. And it was precisely this link of commitment and confidence that the Nixon administration sought to smash, as part of its vote-pandering process among the most racist-minded sections of the electorate.

This strategy was discernible immediately to the black journalists, and they reacted quickly. A statement signed by 70 leading black writers appeared as a full-page advertisement in the *New York Amsterdam News* and the *New York Courier* (significantly the *New York Times* and the *Washington Post*, traditional repositories for attention-getting petitions, were bypassed). A full issue of the monthly *Ball & Chain*, published by the Black Journalists, an organization of media workers in the San Francisco Bay Area, was given over to the Caldwell case.

The statement of the 70 noted that the subpena had been served on Caldwell as an individual and that if a prison term was the penalty for refusing to comply, it would be Caldwell, not an official of the *New York Times*, who would go to prison. The signers said they believed Caldwell had been served because the government reasoned that as a black man he had special access to information in the black community. The statement said:

> The role of every black newsman and woman has been put into question—Are we government agents? Will we reveal confidential sources if subpenaed? Can our employers turn over our files, notes, or tapes if we object? We do not intend to be used as spies, informers, or undercover agents by anybody—period! We will protect our confidential sources, using every means at our disposal. . . . We are black journalists attempting to interpret, with as great understanding and truth as is possible, the nation's social revolutions.

To underscore the individual nature of his subpena, Caldwell engaged his own lawyer—Anthony Amsterdam, a professor of law at Stanford University Law School. Others took action, too. In New York a leaflet was distributed by network and newspaper employees who picketed the "Black Slab" (as the CBS structure is called). It said: "Employees of CBS and other media corporations can no longer ignore the fact that their executives are turning them into police agents." At the *Wall Street Journal* an overwhelming majority of the editorial staff petitioned the management not to turn over raw files to the government. On February 4 the *New York Times* said in an editorial:

> People whose jobs, associations or reputations are at stake cannot be expected to speak freely on an off-the-record basis if they have reason to fear that both their identity and the totality of their remarks will be turned over to the police. The attendant and even more serious danger

is that the entire process will create the impression that the press operates as an investigative agency for government rather than as an independent force dedicated to the unfettered flow of information to the
public.

Mitchell took note of the criticism and responded in a fashion
that had become standard for the Nixon administration: advance
two brash steps, take one step back (or seem to), and come out
ahead. The administration had learned well from Joe McCarthy's
mistakes: he could not even simulate a step backward.

In all previous cases, Mitchell said in what appeared to be a
mollifying mood, the media had been informed that the Justice
Department would be willing to modify its "request," and in subsequent negotiations this had been done. Unfortunately, in the
most recent flurry of subpenas this procedure had not been
followed, he said, and Justice Department personnel were being
instructed to adhere to past policies. The Attorney General understood the "peculiar problems" raised for the press by the subpenas
and offered to meet with media executives to reassure them in
relation to these problems.

Immediately after his statement, an indefinite postponement of
the Caldwell appearance was announced, but not before the
Times had informed the Justice Department that it would move
to quash the Caldwell subpena and make a test case if the department persisted. The argument would be that Caldwell's rights
were being infringed and his ability to function professionally
endangered.

Mitchell's seeming offer of conciliation was followed by a dis-
creet corporate pilgrimage to Washington. One of the pilgrims,
Julian Goodman, president of NBC, suggested that government
"restraint" would resolve the whole problem. He said he did not
regard a common corporate strategy against the subpenas as "practical" because of the highly competitive nature of the communications industry. This was a clear signal to Mitchell that united
media opposition was highly unlikely, in any case not between
newspapers and the networks (traditional rivals in the war for the
advertising dollar) and perhaps not even among the networks
themselves.

Having reassured the corporate media that the rash of subpenas had been simply a "failure of communications," Mitchell, in accordance with administration practice, then moved forward again. Two weeks later he issued a subpena to CBS correspondent Mike Wallace to testify before a grand jury in New Haven considering charges against a group of Black Panthers. "This is hardly the way to give us reassurance," said Richard Salant, the president of CBS News.

In the midst of the maneuverings, negotiations and cries of anguish, a member of the government's executive family itself sought to stiffen the flaccid resolve of the communications industry. It was not a new role for Nicholas Johnson, gadfly member of the Federal Communications Commission. In a speech before a meeting of Harvard's Nieman Fellows[1] in Washington, Johnson declared that the freedom and integrity of the press were in serious danger and that the owners and operators of the media were contributing to their own peril by not refusing absolutely to comply with the subpenas.

"It is shocking and saddening," he said, "that the establishment press is so willing to acquiesce. The media have vast financial and legal resources at their command. The country could only benefit if they were to resist government encroachment upon their independence and defend in court their absolute First Amendment right to refuse such subpenas."

Speaking specifically to the area of FCC concern, Johnson said that at the same time it was attacking TV-radio presentation of the news, the administration was charting policies to protect the economic interests of the networks. Whether or not there was an actual deal, he said, "the results are very much the same as if there were a government-media agreement that the media will take care of the administration's image if the government will take care of the media's balance sheets."

Deal or agreement, there was ample evidence that in the year 1970—and surely in the ten months preceding the 1970 elections

---

[1] The Nieman Fellows are newspapermen and women who have spent a year at Harvard, under the terms of the Nieman Foundation established in 1938. Each year a group of journalists is selected by a board of newspaper editors for a course of study at Harvard (the whole field of instruction is open to them) during which time they receive a salary equivalent to their newspaper salary. In addition, they meet with persons in government and public life at off-the-record sessions, and publish the quarterly *Nieman Reports*.

—criticism of the Nixon administration diminished in the communications media. "I think the industry as a whole has been intimidated," said CBS's Walter Cronkite on March 3, 1970. A political writer for a West Coast daily told *Time* magazine: "Buried in our subconscious is the thought, 'Be goddam careful. Don't start a beef.'"

Pat Carbine, then executive editor of *Look*, said on a television program that her magazine planned to reduce its files to a minimum, apparently to reduce the amount of material the government might demand. A panelist from *Life* on the same program said that his colleagues would destroy their files after a certain period of time. Sander Vanocur, then of NBC, exploded at that: "My God, is this Nazi Germany? Is this Communist Russia? I still think this is a free country. Why are we acting like this?"

A possible answer to Vanocur's question was contained in a presumptuous chiding (a favorite *New York Times* headline word) administered to Commissioner Johnson by the *Times*'s then television critic Jack Gould on March 15. Gould acknowledged Johnson's effectiveness in stirring the academic community to an awareness of the sins of the broadcast industry and in blocking questionable corporate deals with government; but he nonetheless implied that Johnson was a publicity seeker who would ultimately pay dearly for the influence he had achieved. "He will learn," the Gould sermon said, "that you can talk your heart out to the literate public, but that they represent only a minute fraction of the viewing audience and seldom respond consistently to your views."

More significantly, Gould said, "Johnson has mobilized the broadcasters against him, and when it comes to lobbying in Congress or around the White House, no eager citizen group is in their league." Gould predicted that the "refreshingly open-minded" new chairman of the FCC, Nixon's appointee Dean Burch, would draw the spotlight away from Johnson, who would tire of the game and not seek a second seven-year term with the FCC (Johnson's term was scheduled to expire in 1973).

To Johnson, Gould seemed to be saying, "Get back on the team and work with the agency." To the citizens' groups Johnson was encouraging, Gould seemed to be saying, "It is futile to try to buck the establishment, so you might as well come in off the streets and work through channels." But it was exactly the demonstrated futility of operating in this fashion that had moved Johnson to the public platform; and it was the powerful communications lobby in Washington which had consistently opposed a common front in the industry against government encroachment. As for the refreshing Dean Burch (who had been a director of Barry Goldwater's campaign for the Presidency in 1964), one of his first major actions in office was to request from all the networks transcripts of their commentaries immediately after Nixon's famous November 3, 1969, appeal to the silent majority.

Ironically, one day after the Gould comment appeared, Attorney General Mitchell pressed forward again. Gould's colleague Earl Caldwell was served with a second subpena to testify before a federal grand jury. The new summons did not require Caldwell to present his confidential notes, but it did require him to testify about his confidential relations with news sources.

There were indications that both Caldwell subpenas had been based on wiretapping by the government of Black Panther telephone calls and electronic surveillance of their quarters. There were further indications that the government might be seeking an indictment of the Black Panthers under the Smith Act on a charge of conspiracy to overthrow the government by force and violence. This, of course, had been the device used against the Communist party—and, by example, against all serious opposition to government policy—in the Smith Act trials of the 1950s.

The *Times* and Caldwell's attorney moved to quash both subpenas. In a decision on April 3, 1970, Federal District Judge Alfonso J. Zirpoli in San Francisco denied the motions. He ruled, however, that while Caldwell would have to appear before the jury, he could not be required to disclose confidential information unless there was "a compelling national interest that cannot be served by alternate means." This meant that the government would have to demonstrate *in advance* that the national interest was compelling and that the information could not be obtained from any other source.

The *Times*—and many authorities on constitutional law—regarded the Zirpoli ruling as a "landmark decision," and it was indeed the first time that any court had limited the government in this manner. But Caldwell, while willing to authenticate his published stories in open court, refused to become a party to secret testimony before a grand jury on the ground that it would make him appear to be an investigative arm of government. The *Times* was clearly disappointed by his position and did not associate itself with Caldwell's appeal from the Zirpoli decision.

The government opposed the appeal, which was rejected in May, and a new subpena was issued for Caldwell to appear before a new grand jury. Once again the *Times* came back into the picture (since the process was started all over again) and associated itself with Caldwell's effort to dismiss the new subpena —a move initiated by Caldwell's personal attorney, Anthony Amsterdam. The move failed, and on June 5 Caldwell was judged to be in contempt of court. Again he appealed, and since the only possible ruling on this appeal was whether Caldwell could be forced to appear, the *Times* again joined in. It noted that the conditions set by Judge Zirpoli would prevail and could be cited as precedent if other staff reporters—on the *Times* or elsewhere —were to be subpenaed.

During the waiting period for a further Caldwell ruling, there was little public activity on the subpena front in the early summer months of 1970; but Attorney General Mitchell had been busy behind the scenes. In August, after taking many soundings in the communications industry, he issued a set of "guidelines" for subpenas which seemed, as the *New York Times* expressed it, to "reflect a welcome, if belated, recognition of the dangers inherent in any governmental intrusion on the news-gathering process." In fact, the "new" guidelines were for the most part a reversion to the procedures prevailing before the contested subpenas had been issued.

Mitchell carefully selected the audience to receive the guidelines—the House of Delegates of the American Bar Association, meeting in St. Louis. First he urged the lawyers to conduct a thorough study of the conflict between the government's request for evidence in criminal cases, and the contention of the working press (and their employers) that their sources of information would dry up if they were revealed publicly. Then he listed his rules:

1. Recognizing that subpenas may limit the freedom of the press, the Justice Department must carefully weigh this factor against the public interest.

2. The required information should be obtained wherever possible from other sources, and requests to the press made as a last resort.

3. Before a subpena was issued, the government should negotiate with the media to limit its scope.

4. Each subpena must be authorized by the Attorney General himself.

5. Requests for authorization must demonstrate that the information is essential and unobtainable from other sources. In normal cases, subpenas would be limited to verification of published or broadcast information. But they could be extended into the area of unpublished and unbroadcast material. Here "great caution" should be used.

While Mitchell seemed to be taking his cue with respectful reasonableness from the Zirpoli ruling, a clue to his underlying attitude—which subsequently became manifest in all civil liberties questions—came in this part of his speech to the bar association:

> We will not permit an innocent man to be convicted or a guilty man to be freed because we decline to subpena a newsman who has information vital to the case. And we may be on the threshold of a much broader controversy because we are now heading for a number of legal confrontations which could seriously mutate fundamental relationships among the government, the bar, and the courts.

The Attorney General's powers were broad enough to permit many confrontations, and the guidelines were vague enough to allow him to interpret them according to his own bountiful prejudices. As for the reminder to his subordinates to exercise "great caution" in issuing subpenas, the temperance of his phrasing clashed abruptly with the character of the man himself.

This contradiction was demonstrated just five weeks after the Attorney General's speech to the bar association, in some remarks unencumbered by prepared text. Mitchell's own caution was nowhere in evidence in these further remarks. In a "candid and convivial mood," according to a United Press International dispatch in the *Boston Globe* of September 19, 1970, he was interviewed by a reporter for *Women's Wear Daily* at a cocktail buffet

at the Women's National Press Club in Washington. He characterized student and faculty dissidents as "these stupid bastards
who are ruining our educational institutions" and declared that
"this country is going so far right that you are not even going to
recognize it."

The *New York Times,* which had commented favorably on Mitchell's speech to the bar association, had no editorial comment on
this convivial prediction or on Mitchell's implied approval of the
rightward trend. The fact that the remarks may have been facilitated by several martinis made them perhaps more than less
significant, since they obviously represented the unrepressed
Mitchell. But the communications industry, a continuing target
of the Attorney General, was indulgently looking the other way.

A set of judges with a clear concept of the First Amendment,
however, was looking straight at the Attorney General in a decision
of utmost significance handed down on November 17, 1970, two
weeks after election day. The Ninth Circuit Court of Appeals in
San Francisco supported Caldwell's refusal to appear before the
grand jury and ruled that the government must show a pressing
need for evidence *before* ordering a journalist to testify in secret.
Demonstrating an unusual sensitivity to the relationship of black
militant groups to news reporters (the decision even referred to
"the 'establishment' press"), the court said:

> The very concept of a free press requires that the news media be
> accorded a measure of autonomy; that they should be free to pursue
> their own investigation to their own ends without fear of government
> interference, and that they should be able to protect their investigative
> processes.
>
> To convert news gatherers into Department of Justice investigators
> is to invade the autonomy of the press by imposing a governmental
> function upon them. To do so where the result is to diminish their
> future capacity as news gatherers is destructive of their public func-
> tion. To accomplish this where it has not been shown to be essential to
> the grand jury inquiry simply cannot be justified in the public interest.

The Ninth Circuit Court decision was not binding on any other
circuit court, but it clearly set limits to the scope of the government's power. Further, it related its findings to the turmoil of the

1960s and the special problems of news gatherers stemming from these concerns. The judges wrote:

> The need for an untrammeled press takes on special urgency in times of widespread protest and dissent. In such times the First Amendment protections exist to maintain communication with dissenting groups and to provide the public with a wide range of information about the nature of protest and heterodoxy.

While the judges warned that their ruling was a "narrow one," because of the sensitive position of the Panthers and Caldwell's relations with them, the United States attorney who had supervised the government's case was appropriately concerned with the "broad implications" of the decision. In fact, however, the very narrowness of the decision was what gave it broader implications.

In the past, in cases involving reporters' privileges in New York, Philadelphia, Portland and Honolulu, reporters have gone to jail as a result of decisions which were *general* in their approach and thus not consonant with a Supreme Court ruling in the case of *Barenblatt* v. *U.S.* In that case the Supreme Court declared: "Where First Amendment rights are asserted to bar governmental interrogation, resolution of the issue always involves a balancing by the courts of the competing private and public interests at stake in the *particular circumstances shown.*"

In the previous cases, the courts had ignored the "particular circumstances" of each case, and the Ninth Circuit Court seemed to be insisting that the courts return to the Supreme Court interpretation in the Barenblatt case. They were requiring the courts to consider precisely in each case whether there would be an infringement of First Amendment privileges; whether the reporter's refusal to testify would upset "fair administration of justice"; whether there was an alternate source of information; and whether compelled disclosure would have an adverse effect on the free flow of news and information.

The phrase "fair administration of justice" was bound to be repeated in a new proceeding in the Supreme Court of the United States as the result of a government petition for a reversal of the Ninth Circuit Court ruling in the Caldwell case, and two others— one involving a television reporter in New Bedford, Massachusetts, the other a newspaper reporter in Louisville, Kentucky. Interestingly, the author of the phrase "fair administration of justice" was Potter Stewart, now a Supreme Court justice, when he was a member of a Circuit Court of Appeals in 1958. Stewart's phrase occurred in a decision upholding the conviction of Marie Torre, a reporter for the *New York Herald Tribune*, for contempt of court for refusing to identify a television network executive who had allegedly made a slanderous remark about singer Judy Garland. Miss Torre spent 11 days in jail. In his lower-court opinion, Stewart said:

> Without question the exaction of this duty [to testify] impinges sometimes, if not always, upon the First Amendment freedoms of the witness. . . . If an additional First Amendment liberty—the freedom of the press—is here involved, we do not hesitate to conclude that it too must give place under the Constitution to a paramount public interest in the fair administration of justice.

The Supreme Court agreed in May 1971 to accept the Caldwell case and to hear appeals in the other two cases because of conflicting lower-court decisions—that of reporter Paul Pappas of New Bedford, also convicted for refusing to give information concerning the Black Panthers; and that of Paul M. Branzburg, of the *Louisville Courier-Journal*, who had refused to disclose the names of a group of young people allegedly involved in the manufacture and peddling of hashish. Both Pappas and Branzburg had been ordered—and had refused—to testify before grand juries.

Thus a test of tremendous significance was shaping up. The position of the government was that newsmen were no different from other citizens, that they had a duty to reveal information about an actual or potential crime and that they were, like other citizens, subject to subpena to testify before a grand jury. It set forth as the chief issue to be decided by the Supreme Court whether a reporter had an absolute right, under the First Amendment, to refuse to testify "unless the government first shows a compelling need for the information."

To require proof of such need, the government said, would impair seriously the investigative functions of the grand jury. In its brief, it spoke of the "firmly established policy of grand jury secrecy" and said that Caldwell's obstinacy had undermined the jury's "traditional" functions. It characterized Caldwell's fear that his testimony in secrecy would destroy the confidence of his sources as "imaginary and insubstantial, not real and appreciable."

In July 1971, Solicitor General Erwin N. Griswold, a former dean of the Harvard Law School, submitted an *amicus curiae* brief asserting that, if newspapermen were to be privileged to refuse grand jury testimony, then Congress should institute that privilege, not the Supreme Court. For almost two centuries, his brief said, news gatherers have obtained confidential information without a constitutional clause protecting them from having to disclose their sources if they were called to testify. Despite this lack of protection, he said, "the flow of confidential information to the media has increased significantly over the years." Reporters, Griswold's brief declared, "are claiming not merely the right to gather news, but the right to withhold news on the basis of promises that they, in their sole discretion, make to their informants."

As the government pressed its case, an impressive array of friends of the First Amendment lined up on the other side. After the Ninth Circuit Court ruling, Caldwell said he had been prepared to go to jail and stay there. "It's not just my victory," he said; "it's an essential victory for the whole communications business. Last February, I thought we could all throw away our notebooks and find another job. Now it doesn't look like that."

Others were more skeptical. Norman Isaacs, editor in residence at the Columbia University Graduate School of Journalism and a former editor of the *Louisville Courier-Journal,* said: "If the decision stands up in court, I think its effect on the independence of journalists will be excellent. I can't be too hopeful now. We're in for a year and a half or two years of court maneuverings before we'll know the true results of the ruling." Caldwell's attorney, Anthony Amsterdam, was almost equally guarded. He said: "The [Ninth Circuit] Court is laying down a general principle that will have to be developed in future cases."

To uphold Caldwell's principle, the Supreme Court would have to oppose Justice Stewart's principle that there must be a balance between the need for information and the deleterious effect upon the rights of news gatherers.

The lines thus were drawn between those who espoused an absolute interpretation of the First Amendment guarantee of freedom of the press—that there was an unqualified privilege against testifying—and those who said that the Constitution, under certain conditions, should be interpreted in a flexible manner.

Both points of view were reflected—sometimes surprisingly—in friends-of-the-court briefs filed with the Supreme Court in September 1971. There was general agreement that the widespread use of subpenas was a threat to freedom of the press, but considerable disagreement as to what the courts should do about it. What emerged clearly throughout the briefs was that the increase in subpenas had kept pace with the increase in radical political activity. The target was not in doubt. In two and a half years 124 subpenas had been served on the Columbia Broadcasting System, the National Broadcasting Company and their wholly owned subsidiaries—although some had been sought by defense lawyers seeking information for their clients.

Taking the absolute position on the First Amendment were the American Society of Newspaper Editors, Sigma Delta Chi, the professional journalism fraternity, the Dow Jones Company (publishers of the *Wall Street Journal* and the *National Observer*), the *Washington Post*, *Newsweek* magazine and the National Press Photographers Association.

The nonabsolutists were CBS, NBC, the American Broadcasting Company, the *Chicago Sun-Times*, the *Chicago Daily News*, the Associated Press Broadcast Association, the Association of American Publishers (books)—and the *New York Times*.

This latter brief was filed for the group by Alexander M. Bickel of the Yale Law School, who represented the *Times* in the litigation following the government's attempts to prevent publication of the Pentagon Papers. During the Pentagon Papers hearing before the Supreme Court, Bickel drew an abrupt implied rebuke from Justice Douglas on the issue of congressional legislation in the area of press freedom (see Chapter IV).

In the subpena brief, Bickel paraphrased the Ninth Circuit Court decision with his assertion that the government prosecutors were seeking to use news gatherers as "a springboard for investigation" and as an "investigative arm of the government." But he affirmed also that news personnel could be required to respond to grand jury subpenas if there first was a showing that they had probable knowledge of a specific crime, that the information could not be obtained from other sources and that the government had a compelling need for the information. Such compelling need, he said, could be justified in an investigation of a major crime—not in cases involving such activities as prostitution, narcotics and gambling offenses.

It was not surprising that the *New York Times* took a nonabsolutist position. In its own editorial columns as far back as the hearings before the Senate Internal Security Subcommittee in 1956 (in which it was directly involved), it had insisted that the press was not sacrosanct and was as subject to inquiry as any other institution, provided the inquiry was in good faith. It was this *Times* position which had moved Earl Caldwell to engage his own attorney from the beginning; and it was this position which obviously led the *Times* to engage Bickel, whose nonabsolutist views were well known, to present its position in the subpena case and in the Pentagon Papers case. What was more surprising was that the Newspaper Guild and the Authors League of America aligned themselves with the nonabsolutists in separate briefs.

Against this background of disagreement among the "friends of the court" and with the new conservative alignment in the Supreme Court, prospects for a favorable decision for the reporters involved in the litigation seemed dim. What they were seeking was a ruling that would go beyond even the Ninth Circuit Court insistence on "compelling need"; but it was conceivable that the Nixon Court would vacate even that unprecedented decision. If that happened, the warning signals would be vividly clear for radical groups to avoid confidential arrangements with the press —precisely what Attorney General Mitchell had sought to achieve in the first place.

And that is precisely what a majority of the Supreme Court did on June 29, 1972. In a 5-to-4 decision, with Justice Byron White joining the four Nixon appointees, it vacated the Ninth Circuit Court decision and ruled against Caldwell, Branzburg and Pappas. Justice White wrote in a majority opinion that "there is no First Amendment privilege to refuse to answer the relevant and material questions asked during a good-faith grand jury investigation." Newsmen, he said, have the same duty as other citizens to obey subpenas and give testimony.

Interestingly, Justice Stewart, whose earlier lower-court opinion in the Torre case was so crucial, voted with the minority. In a dissenting opinion, he described the Court's view of the First Amendment as "crabbed," and wrote: "Not only will this decision impair performance of the press's constitutionally protected functions, but it will, I am convinced, in the long run, harm rather than help the administration of justice."

Justice Douglas, the Court's remaining constitutional absolutist, wrote in a separate dissent: "Now that the fences of the law and the tradition that has protected the press are broken down, the people are the victims. The First Amendment, as I read it, was designed precisely to prevent that tragedy."

In the months during which the Caldwell case was moving through the courts, the Newspaper Guild had won agreements from newspaper publishers in California and New York (including the *New York Times*) pledging management's legal and financial support for any reporter or photographer facing government pressure to reveal the source of confidential information. The *Times* agreement stated that an employee "shall not suffer any loss of pay or other benefits" and "need not suffer financial loss even if he should go to jail."

But with the Supreme Court's reversal of the Ninth Circuit Court, the *Times*—and other newspapers—presumably would not support reporters financially or otherwise beyond the specific limits of the Supreme Court ruling. And the publishers would not be likely to keep up payments to a reporter who defied the Supreme Court and went to jail for his principled stand. Nor would the conditions be flourishing in the Congress for a law circumventing a Supreme Court decision.

In the last analysis, as Justice Black might well have stated, under the restrictions of the First Amendment Congress cannot legislate in the area of freedom of the press. In a time of heightened repression—sometimes, and particularly for black persons, creating a life-or-death situation—the relationship between a newspaper reporter and a confidential source ought to be as inviolable as the relationship between a doctor and his patient, or a lawyer and his client. Any decision to the contrary would mock both the democratic process and the guarantee of human rights.

There was another form of mockery prevalent in the country,

as the long policing and investigatory arms of government reached out to limit the democratic process. This was the practice of police and governmental agents masquerading as news reporters. The practice, as will be demonstrated, created fresh turmoil in the media, and this time among people in the media not usually given to indignant protest.

CHAPTER III

ON ASSIGNMENT
FROM WFBI

THE DATE was October 23, 1969. The witness stepped down from the courtroom stand, walked to the table where the defendants were seated and leveled an identifying finger at one of them. "That's quite a letdown, Louis. I'm really disappointed in you," another of the defendants said, more in hurt than anger.

The finger belonged to Louis Salzberg, a press photographer and a familiar figure at radical gatherings, who had just disclosed on the stand that he had been an agent of the Federal Bureau of Investigation since 1967. The voice was that of David Dellinger, the dean of the defendants in the Chicago conspiracy trial then in progress.

Others among the defendants were less charitable. They grunted "Oink! Oink!"—and seemed, with this sentiment, to be reflecting the opinion of a majority of newspaper and television reporters about the use of government and police agents as media informers.

The practice was not new, but had become increasingly widespread as disenchantment with the war in Southeast Asia had grown and the protest movement had become more effective. It had been accelerated also in an effort to hamper the black freedom movement, in both the black communities themselves and among black journalists in the white media.

Police and FBI agents, in fact, have been operating as "accredited" media reporters in cities from coast to coast, and Central Intelligence Agency and National Security Agency men have been

39

masquerading as correspondents in South Vietnam, Laos, Cambodia and other Free World bastions of American endeavor against the threat of the "international Communist conspiracy."

As the practice has increased, so has the protest against it by men and women of the media. After years of suffering the presence of known or suspected agents in their midst (and grumbling in private), the media people have finally begun to speak out, supported by the Newspaper Guild and other organizations of journalists. In many cases they have threatened to expose—and actually have exposed—agents on the spot. They have also sought by various means to force governmental agencies and police officials to adhere to stated policy against the practice. Such moves, however, have seldom discouraged it.

What troubles the media people about agents among them—aside from an instinctive revulsion against informers and spies in general—is the fact that their presence makes news sources suspicious of all media reporters. A source is not going to offer information if he suspects his questioner may be delivering his message to the FBI or the Chicago Red Squad, perhaps even verbatim on tape by means of a concealed recorder. Further, awareness of the practice of governmental infiltration tends to create hostility against all media personnel.

Even more perplexing than agency infiltration is the problem of the voluntary newspaperman-as-agent. This is the genuinely accredited reporter who, motivated by distorted patriotism or neurotic necessity or simple avarice, will offer himself as an instrument of espionage and deliver information not only about suspected radicals but also about his own colleagues who may not measure up to his or J. Edgar Hoover's standards of impeccable civic morality. A cop, after all, is a cop—federal, city or county—and his job is to be a cop. But a volunteer media agent is another bag of fish, and when the wrapping is removed, the odor is unmistakably that of red herring. Take the Chicago conspiracy trial.

Louis Salzberg was always around when "Movement" people were in the streets or in a meeting hall planning action in the streets. A nondescript man in his early forties, he was invariably accompanied by the press camera he used on assignment for *El Tiempo,* a Spanish-language New York daily.

Salzberg's faithful presence seemed to impress Movement leaders and followers to the extent that he was named to the steering committee of Veterans for Peace and the Fifth Avenue Parade Committee. He was also prominent among the Crazies, whose specialty was disruption. *Everybody* loved Louis.

What everybody did not know was that the loved one had since 1967 been working for the FBI under the cover of an accredited news photographer. When he was fired by *El Tiempo* in January 1969, the FBI helped him to establish his New York Press Service, an agency whose primary service was to take pictures of people at demonstrations for the files of the FBI. The FBI got thousands of photographs from him. Ironically, David Dellinger generously helped him get started with a letter of introduction for his press service.

Salzberg's own letter of introduction to prospective Movement clients was direct: "The next time your organization schedules a demonstration, let us know in advance. We'll cover it like a blanket and deliver a cost-free sample of our work to your office. No obligation to purchase, naturally." For the FBI the blanket sample was not cost-free: the purchase price to Salzberg had been guaranteed in advance. It amounted to 10,000 dollars in something less than three years, delivered at street corners, parking lots and zoos. Salzberg's code name was "Winston."

Salzberg's testimony at the Chicago trial demonstrated touchingly the FBI's protective attitude toward the morals of young America. In August 1968, Salzberg said, he had covered at a New York church a meeting of the Resistance, an antidraft group, addressed by Tom Hayden (a Chicago conspiracy co-defendant whose fingering by Salzberg had moved Dellinger to his regretful comment cited earlier). According to Salzberg, Hayden told the church audience that the purpose of forthcoming demonstrations in Chicago, coinciding with the Democratic National Convention, was to "fuck up the convention."

Defense Attorney William F. Kunstler repeatedly tried to elicit from Salzberg why the purported quote from Hayden had not appeared in a Salzberg report prepared by an FBI agent. Salzberg finally said: "I was told the reports could not have obscenities in them. They have very young girls as stenographers, and they did not want to subject them to that."

Salzberg insisted that he had not been motivated by money: "I personally feel that by any means necessary communism must be stopped." Then, in a comment which ought to generate at least a small measure of approbation for media executives, he added: "What surprises me is that newspaper editors have not called me up to congratulate me."

A week before the Salzberg testimony in Chicago, the government had produced as a witness a man named Carl Gilman, then twenty-seven, a cameraman and occasional reporter for KFMB-TV in San Diego. Gilman testified that he had come to regard events he had covered as a "threat to the security" and was therefore moved to volunteer his services to the FBI. His concern about security was enhanced by a 150-dollar monthly check from the FBI, for which he turned in reports about the antiwar movement and resistance to the draft.

Try as he would to keep his news work separate from his vigilance for the FBI, Gilman said, it became impossible because the FBI was increasingly demanding. When David Dellinger spoke at a rally at San Diego State College (before he became a Chicago defendant), Gilman covered the rally, not, he said, "as a newsman but to gather news for the FBI." He testified that Dellinger had urged his audience to burn draft cards and to "do anything to disrupt this insane war." Then, he reported, Dellinger shook an ominous "clenched fist" and said he'd see his audience in Chicago, or words to that effect. In what must be recorded as the most impressive understatement of the undercover year, Gilman then testified that Dellinger told his audience he expected there would be "problems in Chicago."

After his testimony, Gilman told an interviewer from *Time* (November 14, 1969), "I came back from the trial [to his job] prepared to be fired, but it's been two and a half weeks now and nothing has happened. I told the news director at the station that I didn't think that what I had done would affect my work." There was some criticism from Gilman's colleagues, but he was undeterred. "I would do it all over again," he said. And there seems little reason to doubt that he has.

Also testifying that day in Judge Julius Hoffman's courtroom was Dwayne Oklepek, who had been on the staff of *Chicago's American* (now called *Chicago Today* and still owned by the

Chicago Tribune). The prosecution had been seeking to prove that the defendants were the masterminds of planned disruptive demonstrations, but Oklepek was forced to concede that co-defendant Rennie Davis had expressed his distaste for "dictators." Oklepek did insist, however, that Tom Hayden was considered "violent by his own intimates and irrational at times." The testimony was, of course, hearsay and therefore improper before a jury. But Judge Hoffman, as he had done scores of times before, ruled against objections by the defense.

There was very little comment in the media about the testimony of these accredited newsmen. Among the few who did mark the events in the courtroom was columnist Murray Kempton. He tempered his customary cynicism in this fashion: "It may be argued that reporters do not deserve to be trusted as people; but that is something else from a condition where they cannot be trusted because one of them might be a cop."

Some reporters unfortunately seem to like playing cop. Consider the case of Ronald J. Lawrence, police-beat reporter for the *St. Louis Post-Dispatch*. In testimony on June 16, 1971, before the House Internal Security Committee, Lawrence said he had infiltrated the Young Socialist Alliance of St. Louis in September 1969 and had continued as an active member until August 1970. He was even elected treasurer; and his personal treasury was reimbursed "for his expenses" in the sum of 400 dollars to 500 dollars by the St. Louis Police Department.

Lawrence testified he believed the St. Louis YSA, whose strength he set at six to twelve, was dedicated to "overthrowing the government." He quoted a member as saying, "There is nothing wrong with assassination and destroying buildings if it accomplishes our aims." The alleged quotee, a truck driver, told the *St. Louis Journalism Review* (August 1971): "I never said anything remotely resembling that statement. Even if it were my philosophy I wouldn't be so trite." He said the group had three to five members and had disbanded when a couple of them moved away from St. Louis. Lawrence, he said, despite repeated requests, had never returned the group's financial records.

Lawrence told the House committee the *Post-Dispatch* had rejected his proposal of a news story about the YSA and "several

Communists," public-school teachers Lawrence regarded as a threat to their students. At least one school teacher, a YSA member, was fired early in 1971. She believes her dismissal was the result of Lawrence's making the YSA records available to her employer (Lawrence denied it).

The committee chairman, Richard H. Ichord (Democrat of Missouri), reprimanded the *Post-Dispatch* for rejecting Lawrence's story. The *Post-Dispatch* did carry a report of the committee hearings but did not include the incendiary remarks allegedly made by the YSA member. The alleged remarks were published by the *St. Louis Globe-Democrat*, a far more conservative newspaper.

Lawrence said he made regular reports to the St. Louis police intelligence unit, and Captain Ernest Halveland, the unit commander, insisted that Lawrence had a perfect right to work with the police. Historically, he said, reporters have cooperated with police in cases involving criminals. He couldn't recall exactly how the arrangement with Lawrence had come about but, he said, "we got a bargain." He conceded that none of Lawrence's fellow YSA members had broken any laws.

Within the *St. Louis Post-Dispatch* newsroom there was acute discomfort about Lawrence's extracurricular activities for the police. The management put pressure on him to stop being a paid police informer, but Lawrence countered that he made no profit from the information he turned in—in fact, he said, he spent a lot more than he recovered for expenses.

Charles Prendergast, metropolitan editor of the *Post-Dispatch*, feels that the roles of reporter and police informer are "mutually exclusive." "When he [Lawrence] took his first buck from the police department," Prendergast said, "it cast a shadow over the newspaper staff." The shadow is still there.

The business of reporters infiltrating organizations is not a new phenomenon. Many reporters have lived on the Bowery, joined the Ku Klux Klan, spent time in jail and inhabited mental institutions for a period of time in order to live the life of the story they were preparing. Defenders of the use of reporters-as-agents cite these examples. But what they overlook is the fact that the reporters in these cases are acting solely for their own publications or broadcast outlets—and not for the police or the government.

If the constituted authorities choose to—or are forced to—take action as a result of this published or broadcast material, that is something else again. A distinction must be made between reporters acting in the interest of making vital information public and reporters acting in the interest of established authority seeking to inhibit the right of free association, free assembly and free speech.

In November 1971 the Twentieth Century Fund, a foundation for research and public education, issued a report entitled *Press Freedoms Under Pressure*, prepared by a Task Force on Government and the Press comprising journalists of varying political views. The report expressed concern over the government's practice of compensating journalists for "services and expenses" in gathering information and commented specifically on the Salzberg-Gilman testimony at the Chicago conspiracy trial.

A query about the practice was put to the FBI by the task force, and a reply ("prepared by Director Hoover"), dated June 7, 1971, was received from John W. Hushen, FBI director of public information. It said:

> The FBI accepts from any person information which may be of value in the course of an FBI investigation. The FBI does not now, and never has, actively recruited journalists as informants. However, there is no policy against accepting information from a journalist or any news media representative if it is volunteered, which was the case with Mr. Louis Salzberg and Mr. Carl Gilman. Both of these individuals furnished information to the FBI on a voluntary basis. They were paid for their services and expenses.

The task force refused to accept the characterization that the reporters' information was "volunteered" as an act of citizenship and commented: "When journalists get paid for providing information to the FBI or any other law enforcement agency, the result is an infiltration—and sullying—of the profession. . . . The practice is damaging to press independence and is wrong."

Far more widespread and pernicious is the practice of government law-enforcement and intelligence agents posing as newsmen and photographers—a practice which the FBI, for example, insists it does not permit. The denial is dishonest, as events have proved.

In the spring of 1971, Representative William R. Anderson,

Democrat of Tennessee, called in reporters to discuss the conspiracy charges involved in the alleged plot to kidnap Presidential adviser Henry Kissinger and to bomb government installations—the so-called Berrigan case. Among those present was Jack Nelson, a correspondent of the *Los Angeles Times*. A familiar figure taking notes caught Nelson's attention, and he recalled him as an FBI agent. Nelson passed the information along to an aide of Representative Anderson, who confronted the notetaker. The man denied he was an agent, said he was a writer, but dashed out of the room when the aide asked for his identification. He was followed out of the building to his car, and a *Life* magazine check of the license plate later traced the car to the FBI.

Samuel J. Archibald, director of the Washington office of the University of Missouri's Freedom of Information Center, is scornful of official policy statements proscribing impersonations. "They're going to do it," he said, "and hope to hell they don't get caught."

And they do it again and again. At the "Counter-Inaugural" staged by radical dissenters in Washington in January 1969, when Richard Nixon took office as President, a *Washington Post* news aide (apprentice reporter-photographer) was on the fringes of the counter-inaugural crowd in the company of a *Post* police-beat reporter. The reporter identified a busy photographer, laden with press credentials, as an undercover agent of the Metropolitan Police Red Squad. The enterprising aide took a picture of the undercover agent, had it developed and presented it to the city editor, who promptly filed it in his desk. Six months later the photo was published by a Washington underground newspaper, with an identification noting that the same cop had been in Chicago during the time of the conspiracy trial.

Since Washington is headquarters for scores of governmental and military agencies, it has also, in typically bureaucratic fashion, a plethora of police-intelligence units gathering information for these agencies. Here are some examples of their activities:

A letter to Representative Cornelius Gallagher, Democrat of New Jersey, asserted that it is a common practice for members of the 116th Military Intelligence Group to pose as press people. As late as the spring of 1970, Gallagher reported, the 116th MIG unit used a TV video tape recorder to film major demonstrations in the capital. Sound equipment was mounted on a truck with the legend "Midwest News" inscribed on its panel.

At a news conference in Washington, a woman who identified herself as "Ditty Ayers, freelance writer," was exposed as Dixie Gildon, Metropolitan policewoman. She had been observed frequently at other news events (including a sit-in at the office of the then Health, Education, and Welfare Secretary Robert Finch). Her identification usually was a college or small-town newspaper.

In June 1968 reporters for the *Boston Globe* and the *Washington Post* at a draft-card-burning ceremony outside the Supreme Court spotted some bright new television cameras and tape recorders among the familiar worn equipment of the press corps. They identified the operators of the cameras and some "reporters" interviewing demonstrators as FBI agents.

Early in 1970 two men wearing red-stenciled badges reading "Press" were seen filming an antiwar demonstration in Washington. A telltale property sticker on their camera read "U.S. Capitol Police." When a legitimate reporter asked about the contradiction, the men conceded they were capitol police—but insisted they were members of the press, too.

Responding to a protest about this incident, Chief James Powell of the Capitol Police said that no member of his force "has been identified" as a participant "in what you termed to be a masquerade." Officials of the force, he said, had been instructed to make sure that such masquerades would not be attempted. "If we photograph any groups in the future," he declared, in what seemed to be a tacit admission of past performance, "we will do it as uniformed officers."

There is little reason to doubt that the masquerade goes on. A Metropolitan Police officer boasted that his force was able to contain demonstrations so efficiently because "we know what's going on." His officers assume the guise of telephone repairmen, narcotics addicts, bums and prostitutes, he said, so why not reporters? What was the harm in that?

Senator Alan Cranston, Democrat of California, a former newspaperman, had an answer. "I am convinced it does a great deal of harm," he said. "It harms newsmen and cameramen—the thousands of legitimate American reporters who base their jobs, and often their safety, on the thin edge of public trust. But most of all, it harms the American public—the millions of readers and viewers who will not get a complete and accurate story because news sources no longer believe they can level with newsmen."

That is precisely what is happening in many areas of the country, particularly among dissenting groups. Late in 1970, according to the *Chicago Journalism Review* (January 1971), Robert Gruenberg, a hardworking Washington correspondent of the *Chicago Daily News*, was given a hard time at a meeting of a black organization because he was suspected—unfairly—of being an FBI agent. And when an unmarked station wagon passed a group of demonstrators in the capital recently, the marchers shouted: "There goes WFBI!" The wagon, in fact, was carrying staff members of the legally licensed radio station WTOP. But the attitude was clear and thoroughly understandable.

One Knight Newspapers reporter, Saul Friedman, lamented over a personal problem. A politically astute man but conservative in dress and manner, he said: "I look like a cop, and the kids who don't know me won't talk to me because they think I am." And since long hair, mod clothes and moustaches have become the fashion among journalists and policemen both, the problem has become even further complicated.

Two unmistakably coplike individuals appeared in December 1970 at a peace rally on the campus of Northern Illinois University at De Kalb. They said they were from "Station WJJO-TV, the cable TV station in Lawrenceville." Suspicious local reporters wondered why a little TV station 250 miles distant would bother with a demonstration in De Kalb. So they checked and discovered that there was no TV station with the call letters WJJO anywhere except perhaps in the fortress mind of the FBI.

In October 1970, during a visit by Vice-President Agnew in Wichita, Kansas, press credentials were issued to at least four local cops who photographed a street theater group outside the Century II Auditorium who were miming the Vice-President's platform manner. One cop was exposed by local reporters.

In Detroit a city cop masqueraded as a photographer from the *Grand Rapids Press* to observe a General Motors stockholders meeting in May 1970. No one could understand why. He was exposed by a staff member from the *Press*.

Army intelligence agents obtained press credentials from the

New York City Police Department to watch Stokely Carmichael and H. Rap Brown. A Chicago police intelligence division agent posed as a newsman to gather information at a protest rally of black students. An Army agent assumed a reporter's guise in Richmond, Virginia, to keep an eye on the activities of the Southern Christian Leadership Conference.

In Puerto Rico complaints by reporters about the presence of disguised police agents at a demonstration led to an admission by the Commonwealth secretary that his department had been handing out press credentials to police for eight years. The event which triggered the protest took place ironically on July 4, 1971, in San Juan.

In downtown Los Angeles, in front of the Parker Center, headquarters of the Los Angeles Police Department, a young reporter watched a Chicano demonstration in the spring of 1971. He noticed two panel trucks, one marked "KMPC," a local radio station, the other bearing the legend "KH-TV." He asked a radio newsman emerging from the KMPC truck what KH-TV stood for. "Don't you know?" the newsman said. "Go ask them," pointing to the KH-TV truck. The young reporter put the same question to a man at the control board in the KH-TV van. The man looked at the reporter's press card pinned to his lapel, hesitated a moment, then said, "Police Department." He turned back to watch the crowd.

There are times when the masquerade is not even necessary, when newspapers of "easy journalistic virtue," as the *Guild Reporter* phrased it, offer to do the job for the police. One such was the *Sacramento Union*, a Copley chain newspaper, whose editors volunteered photographs of disorders and demonstrations to the FBI. And in Chicago there has for years been a comfortable liaison between the Chicago Police Red Squad and Ron Koziol, a reporter for the *Chicago Tribune*. Koziol relied heavily on Red Squad files in an effort to discredit the Walker Report—*Rights in Conflict*—about the disorders surrounding the 1968 Democratic National Convention in Chicago. The *Chicago Journalism Review* has described Koziol as "the Red Squad's conduit to the public."

In December 1970 a former Army Intelligence officer named John O'Brien disclosed that the Army had been spying on hundreds of civilians in Illinois. The story received page one display in every Chicago newspaper and was, of course, a major news story in most cities. The Chicago press stories left the reader with the impression that this was all news to the newspapers (the only exception was Morton Kondracke of the *Chicago Sun-Times*).

But O'Brien told the *Chicago Journalism Review* (April 1971) that the *Chicago Tribune*, for one, had detailed information for several years about the activities of the 113th Military Intelligence Group, based in Evanston. Instead of publishing the information, O'Brien said, the *Tribune* used the 113th MIG as a *source* of information. Further, the *Tribune* itself operated as an information source for Army Intelligence.

The central figure here once again was Ron Koziol, the reporter with easy access to the Chicago Police Red Squad. According to O'Brien, Koziol was a drinking companion of the 113th MIG group leader, Thomas Filkins (during the Chicago conspiracy trial Koziol called Filkins "daily"), and was on "first-name" terms with several other MIG officers.

O'Brien said Koziol had been "passed on to us as a confidant and sympathizer of the Chicago Red Squad" and that a number of official military reports had been compiled on the basis of information supplied by Koziol. Koziol conceded to the *Chicago Journalism Review* that he had known of the Army's spying activities long before they were disclosed, but had never written about them because "no one ever asked me to." Nor had he proposed a story for the *Tribune* because "the editors here make many of the assignments on our paper."

O'Brien's disclosures first broke in the Field papers in Chicago (the *Sun-Times* and the *Daily News*). Immediately thereafter a *Tribune* reporter named Charles Mount went to O'Brien's home and asked him why he had gone "to the competition." Annoyed by Mount's approach, O'Brien slammed the door on him and his photographer, but was astonished the next day to find in the *Tribune* a long "interview" with him under Mount's byline. It was clear to O'Brien that much of the information about him had come from the 113th MIG.

The Pentagon, of course, denied that its officers had been spying on civilians in Illinois and then pledged that it would discontinue the practice. The disclaimer and the promise came soon after Senator Sam J. Ervin, Jr., Democrat of North Carolina, announced that his Subcommittee on Constitutional Rights would hold hearings on the matter. The hearings, in February 1971, established beyond doubt that surveillance of citizens in Illinois had been widespread.

As the masquerade of the agents became more blatant, hitherto complacent or silent news personnel began publicly to denounce the practice. In Washington 28 *Washington Star* reporters declared in August 1970 that they would expose any undercover agent they found among the news corps on assignment. Their manifesto said:

> We pledge, and we urge colleagues to follow, that we will announce the presence of any police agent we recognize masquerading as a newsman or newswoman. If it is necessary to stop a news conference long enough to verify credentials, we will do so. In street situations we will try to identify the agent, get photos of him if possible and complain to the department.

Senator Cranston inserted the pledge in the *Congressional Record.* A copy went also to the *Washington Post,* where reporters met with their editors and wrote to Police Chief Jerry Wilson asking him to order the practice discontinued. Soon thereafter a police spokesman said it would henceforth be "against department policy for any of its members to represent himself in any way as a member of a news-gathering organization." The department said, however, that it would be perfectly all right for an agent to come to a news conference with cameras, pens and pencils just so long as he didn't identify himself as a reporter. He could, for example, say he was a telephone man. "We're not closing that option," said the spokesman.

In the Wichita incident, Sigma Delta Chi, the national society of professional journalists, protested the use of official press credentials by police during the Agnew visit. Its freedom-of-information committee demanded an apology to newsmen by President Nixon and Vice-President Agnew both and a pledge by the City Commission that "this kind of blatant misrepresentation will never happen again." Police Chief Merrell Kirkpatrick at first told reporters that he had been unaware of the practice, then said he had authorized the police to use false credentials. Asked to explain the discrepancy in his statements, he said: "I'm authorizing it right now. If you don't like it, sue."

This kind of arrogance is encouraged privately by the Nixon administration. Publicly, in response to the Sigma Delta Chi protest, Nixon's Communications Coordinator Herbert Klein "regretted" the Wichita incident, but said he regretted also that Sigma Delta Chi "chose, in effect, to accuse the President of 'deception' and 'willful violation of a public trust.' . . . To blow one incident so out of proportion, it seems to me, contributes to an erosion of confidence by the public in the integrity of its elected officials and our democratic institutions of government." Coming from the chief press agent for one of the most willfully deceitful chief executives in the nation's history, this statement is admirable for its unabashed hypocrisy.

Other politicians are more direct. When the Sacramento Newspaper Guild protested the Copley newspaper practice of volunteering help to the FBI, Governor Ronald Reagan told a convention of the California Newspaper Publishers Association that he approved of police using press ID cards to infiltrate "subversive organizations and capture terrorists." He urged the publishers to issue press cards to police agents for surveillance of dissenting assemblies where the presence of police would be unwelcome. Reagan received a standing ovation at the meeting.

For the most part, the police are far more circumspect than the politicians. The aftermath of the De Kalb masquerade is instructive. The Illinois News Broadcasters Association complained about the fraudulent TV newsmen in De Kalb to Director Mitchell Ware of the Illinois Bureau of Investigation. Both Ware and his superior, Herbert Brown of the State Department of Law Enforcement, agreed that the episode was deplorable and Brown issued orders forbidding agents to pose as news personnel.

But Ware, who had himself been a television street reporter, nonetheless defended the practice to Alan Crane, the chairman of the freedom-of-information committee of the Illinois news broadcasters. His only concern, he said, was law enforcement. Later he told the *Chicago Journalism Review*: "If the only way to successfully get evidence was to impersonate a newsman, I'd have my agents go ahead and do it—but there you've got a definite case you're working on."

At times newsmen themselves become potential "definite cases," as Ron Dorfman, editor of the enterprising *Chicago Journalism Review*, discovered to his chagrin. In February 1969 the *Review* published a detailed exposé of the activities of the Chicago Red Squad. Several months later Dorfman lunched with one of his former editors at *Chicago Today* and asked the editor why the Chicago newspapers had not picked up the story. It was all old stuff (although never published), said the editor. In fact, he said, his paper had access to the Red Squad files and made frequent use of them—even to the point of checking on the background of its own reporters. Dorfman reported:

" 'Why, I've seen your file,' he told me as I choked on my lasagna. He explained that he suspected a reporter the paper was thinking of hiring 'was on Saul Alinsky's payroll,' so he went over to check. The suspicion proved false, he added, but so long as he was there he decided to check my file for the same reason."

There was a sequel to the story: When Dorfman was summoned in March 1970 to testify before the Illinois Crime Investigating Commission in connection with a supposed investigation of the Weathermen, he was confronted with a five-page single-spaced summary of his political activities of several years' duration. One item was his sponsorship in 1961 of a leaflet denouncing the fanatic Major General Edwin Walker (who had been removed from his post with the United States armed forces in Europe for flagrant violation of the civil liberties of American soldiers) when Walker spoke at McCormick Place in Chicago.

John O'Brien, the agent who blew the whistle on the 113th MIG, has declared that the Army has clip files on virtually every reporter who has written about antiwar activities. Chief interest is in those reporters with access to antiwar groups and spokesmen for dissenting groups in general.

The Department of Defense and Presidents from Kennedy through Johnson and Nixon have persuaded themselves that American reporters in Southeast Asia who have insisted on reporting events as they have happened—and not as United States Military Assistance Command press officers say they happened—have been a primary cause of the failure of the American intervention in Vietnam, Laos and Cambodia. According to this reasoning, it is necessary to intimidate or at least to encompass the messenger of bad tidings. The first step is to engage in surveillance of the messengers and to determine their sources of news. In pursuit of this goal, the police and investigative arms of the United States government have been extended to infiltrate the ranks of the press in Southeast Asia.

Early in 1970 the Central Intelligence Agency proposed to the privately owned servicemen's newspaper, the *Overseas Weekly*, that the newspaper could help resolve its problems in obtaining distribution through the chain of post exchanges abroad. All the weekly had to do was to take on its Saigon news staff two CIA agents, both "highly qualified men." The *Overseas Weekly* let it be known that it had rejected the offer.

A few weeks later four men appeared at the desk of the United States Public Affairs Office in Saigon, presented a letter from the "American University Press" and asked for accreditation as correspondents. In routine fashion, the officer in charge asked them for their Vietnamese press credentials, a prerequisite for United States accreditation. Instead, the four—two Americans and two Vietnamese—presented badges identifying them as official United States government investigators.

The officer requested guidance from his superior and, on instructions, issued the accreditation. That was on January 8, 1970. Legitimately accredited correspondents detected a false flavor when the quartet appeared in their midst and soon determined that the American University Press men were fraudulent. They expressed a suspicion that the four had been assigned to spy on them to trace their news sources.

The Associated Press and the National Broadcasting Company broke the story. A check by the *New York Times* disclosed that American University Press, a New York firm, was a service organization producing catalogues and circulars for book publishers. A spokesman said: "We do not know these two men [the Americans, identified as Howard Hethcox and William T. Tucker] and we have never had any correspondents."

It is, of course, official government policy not to issue press credentials to anyone except a bona fide correspondent. "Somebody goofed," said a Pentagon official with embarrassed innocence. The United States Command reported that those responsible for issuing press credentials had been "admonished concerning the proper procedures to follow in accreditation." The credentials were picked up on January 27. In approved Pentagonese, another United States Command official said: "The policies which prohibit the issuance of accreditation to identified agents will remain in effect. Further steps have been taken with all personnel involved in accreditation to insure compliance with this policy."

It should be noted that the statement referred to *identified* agents. Presumably if they had gone *unidentified* there would have been no problem.

On February 6 the United States Command announced that "the person" responsible for the "goof" had been reprimanded and transferred to a new assignment. It refused to identify the culprit, maintaining that only "poor judgment rather than a deliberate disregard for policies had been involved." It reacted with indignation to a suggestion that the agents' mission had been related to the American press corps. The Associated Press, however, reacted differently. In a dispatch from Saigon published in the *New York Times* it said:

> Sources close to the Defense Department speculated that the investigation might have been ordered in the light of growing dissatisfaction in Washington and Saigon over the reporting by United States newsmen of "unfavorable" news, both on the military developments and on reports of censorship involving the armed forces news media in Vietnam. The sources said that the giving of unauthorized information to newsmen by the military might be regarded as a punishable offense under the Uniform Military Code of Justice and could lead to courts-martial of the offenders.

Thus, even though the mission failed because of exposure of the agents, the Defense Department nonetheless succeeded in warning potential sources publicly that they could be subject to court-martial if they gave information to correspondents. It was unlikely that the warning went unheeded—and the public's right to know was administered another goofball.

A more bizarre episode was uncovered through the persistent investigative reporting of a *Milwaukee Journal* reporter named Alex P. Dobish. His stories exposed further hypocrisy in the

Defense Department's "official policy" concerning the accreditation of bona fide correspondents. Four months after the military command in Saigon had reaffirmed its official policy, Dobish on May 21, 1970, began a news story in this manner:

> A correspondent killed in an accident near Saigon last week worked for a Butler [Wisconsin] based news service that has no paying clients and was organized by a former Army security man. The service is the Local News Service of Butler. Gary Zeller of Mequon [Wisconsin] . . . is a partner. Zeller admitted that the service has no clients but denied that it was a cover for infiltrating the American news corps in Vietnam. Reporters in Vietnam have complained recently that servicemen have received accreditation not to cover the war but to spy on American reporters, particularly their sources.

The dead man was Leon Ripley, sixty-four, a 38-year veteran of the Air Force. Following his death in a jeep crash, the United States Embassy listed his home town as Millerton, Pennsylvania. Dobish found no listing for him there, nor anyone who had ever heard of the Ripley family. The United States Military Command gave Ripley's address as the Butler Hotel in Butler, Wisconsin. The village president there had never heard of either Ripley or the news agency.

The inconsistencies led Dobish to undertake an inquiry which led to Zeller in Mequon. Zeller said he had left Army Security in 1968 but declined to describe his work; he told Dobish he had taken an oath not to talk about that for ten years after his discharge. Such oaths are commonplace in organizations such as the CIA and the National Security Agency.

Zeller said the news agency had two other partners—his brother Peter (who was in Thailand "on assignment") and a man named Arlie Marten. Neither had had any news experience, Zeller conceded. Marten, a Milwaukee die cutter, said the news agency sold to several clients but could recall the name of only one—the *Baraboo News Republic*. The editor of the *News Republic* said he had never used any Local News Service copy—in fact, he had never heard of the outfit. After that comment, Zeller confirmed the complete absence of clients. The "correspondents," he said, wrote mostly about servicemen, and the stories were sent to home-town newspapers. Ripley, who was being paid space rates, had sent in several stories, Zeller said, but since none had been published, he had never drawn any pay.

On May 25 Dobish learned that three correspondents for the Local News Service—including the dead Leon Ripley—were on the payroll of the Military Service Company of Santa Cruz, California, a firm selling supplies to officers and noncommissioned officers' clubs around the world. One of the three, Floyd Eggert, the firm's sales manager in Saigon, turned in his press card to the United States Command after the *Journal* had begun publishing Dobish's articles. He would have lost it anyway, an Army spokesman said, explaining helpfully that Eggert wanted the card mainly to receive post-exchange and military transportation privileges available to correspondents. It was undertaking an inquiry of its own, the Army said.

The third "correspondent" was a man named Frank Noble. Subsequently Dobish learned that Peter Zeller, the man in Thailand, was a commercial pilot and that he also was employed by the Military Service Company. Both Noble and Peter Zeller had moved on to Thailand from Vietnam.

The manager of the military supply firm said he did not know why the men on his payroll had been accredited as correspondents, nor did he know they had even claimed to be newsmen. "If a man works for me," he said, "I don't ask what he does with his spare time. We didn't ask them."

There was an interesting sidelight to the story. In September 1969 United States Senate investigators discovered gross irregularities in the operation of noncommissioned officers' clubs ranging from kickbacks for supplies to black-market money operations. "We weren't involved in that," said the Santa Cruz supply company manager, but soon after the revelations three of the four phony correspondents were taken off the payroll.

The *Milwaukee Journal* was not satisfied with any explanation of the Local News Service, either by the owner of the service or by the Army. Noting the growing suspicion that the organization was acting as a cover to "keep tabs" on reporters and their news sources in Vietnam, an editorial published on May 31, 1970, said:

At any rate, the fact that salesmen and whoever else they may be can get credentials as correspondents easily does not say much for the pertinent military regulations or the thoroughness of those in Vietnam carrying them out. It helps explain how the many cases of graft, corruption and cut corners occur in the area.

That may be. But still missing was an explanation by the Army of the fraudulent news agency. There is no record of a report of its investigation.

From all these incidents there emerges a pattern of methodical use of press privilege to militate against the traditional freedom of the press in gathering and disseminating information. Federal, military, state, county and city agents have invaded the news field in a pervasive manner which limits the effectiveness of the media (by casting doubt upon the legitimacy of all news-gathering personnel) and limits the freedom of dissenting movements (by creating fear and suspicion within their ranks).

Governmental and police agencies automatically deny that the practice is in operation; then, when it is exposed, they issue statements declaring that the practice is against the policy of the agencies. Weathering sporadic squalls engendered by indignant news media people (and some publishers and managers of broadcast facilities), they resume the practice in a more refined manner to avoid detection.

In the last few years, as the protests against war and racism have taken hold in the country, the masquerade has taken on correspondingly greater proportions—but so also have the protests against the masquerade, from civil liberties groups, the Newspaper Guild, broadcasters' associations, professional journalism societies and, most effectively, from individual news gatherers.

The masquerade is facilitated by the fact that in most major cities—New York, Los Angeles, Baltimore and Chicago, for example—press cards are issued at the discretion of the police commissioner alone. In Washington—an unusual area because it is such a major center of news sources and events—more than 2,000 newsmen and women carry press credentials which are approved by a committee of police and newspeople.

As has been amply documented, this caution has not eliminated the practice of infiltration (because of the proliferation of news agencies and the vast federal and military bureaucracy), but it probably has restricted it to an extent. A similar joint operation, with the participation of a more representative group of news personnel than the more nearly élite Washington press corps, could be applied with greater effectiveness in smaller cities with less complicated problems than Washington. Unfortunately, there has not been much progress toward this procedure because the media people have not been sufficiently alerted to the pernicious results of infiltration; and their employers have for the most part been complacent or even voluntary adjuncts.

Journalists and organizations of journalists have always been wary of acting in concert—even in defense of their own interests. The unwritten rules of "objectivity" have supported this posture. Employers have traditionally emphasized (in their own interest) the role of the reporter as one of disinterested observation ostensibly to maintain a balance in the gathering and presentation of the news. This psychological attitude has been largely adopted by the reporters themselves, partly in the mistaken assumption that the unwritten code of objectivity was valid, and partly because it helped to maintain the news corps as a rather special privileged group a rung above the ordinary citizen. Even in the founding days of the union of nonmechanical newspaper personnel, the American Newspaper Guild (its name was changed in 1971 to The Newspaper Guild in deference to a large Canadian membership) adopted the word "guild" in its title rather than "union." This was done to assuage the sensitivities of editorial members who shrank from associating with clerks, advertising solicitors and secretaries.

The entry into journalism by young men and women who were intimately involved in campus and street protests in the decade of the 1960s has broken down much of the traditional reserve concerning a common effort to work out mutual problems. More than their elders they interpret the privileges for the press embodied in the First Amendment as they were actually designed by the men who constructed the First Amendment—as a guarantee that the press would at all times be able to function as the protector of the public interest against attempts by predatory government to erode the public interest.

This attitude of necessity requires the maintenance of an adversary role by the media vis-à-vis government—an attitude which has unfortunately been dissipated by many publishers, editors and media people who have come to regard themselves as the partners of government because of an assumed identity of interests.

One of the most significant developments militating for a restoration of the adversary role—in some cases to establish it for the first time—has been the rise of journalism reviews in the last three years, beginning with the *Chicago Journalism Review* in the aftermath of the Democratic National Convention in Chicago in 1968 (see Chapter V). At that time police clubs landed on the heads of journalists as well as those of dissenting demonstrators and casual bystanders, and the journalists were moved to action when they sought and failed to move their employers to protest this blatant violation of their rights and their bodies.

Since then, reviews have been established by journalists in 15 cities of the United States, from New York to Honolulu. They have turned the spotlight on their own publications and broadcast facilities—their partisanship, corrupt practices, collusion with dominant interests in the various cities and high-handed internal practices. And they have concentrated with zest on the inner workings of the police and investigative agencies, both local and federal. Much of the information contained in this chapter is based on material which appeared first—and, sadly, exclusively— in the journalism reviews.

There is perhaps only one way to resolve the problem of agent infiltration of the media, and even that cannot guarantee a complete solution because of the authority of established power in the United States of the 1970s. It would entail a concerted effort by every existing organization in the news-gathering field to protest the practice of infiltration and demand its abolition. It would require the utilization of the combined power of the associations of publishers, editors and broadcast executives, the organizations of newsmen and women and photographers, the professional journalism societies and the faculties and student bodies of the journalism schools.

In collaboration with civil liberties groups and associations of concerned lawyers, such a force could go a long way toward transforming the parchment of the First Amendment into an applied, living doctrine, not only in the matter of infiltration but in many other pertinent areas of government-media conflict.

But even if this unlikely union could be effected, a prior—and difficult—mission would have to be undertaken. That is the education of the entire journalistic fraternity—from publisher and network official down to fledgling reporter—to an awareness that its dominant interest in the preservation of a democratic society lies not with a repressive, tight-minded governmental apparatus, but with an informed and enlightened public.

CHAPTER IV

THE SIEGE
OF PENTAGONIA

The people of this nation, in whose name and by whose ultimate consent all high government officials serve, have both the need and the right to be thoroughly informed on decisions.

THOMAS JEFFERSON did not say that. Robert S. McNamara did, in the preface to a collection of his speeches delivered during his tenure as Secretary of Defense under President Kennedy and President Johnson, and published in 1968 after he had left the Johnson administration to become director of the World Bank.

In 1971 Arthur Krock, the former chief of the Washington bureau of the *New York Times,* titled his most recent book *The Consent of the Governed, and Other Deceits.* It is possible that Krock had read McNamara's collected speeches—an assignment of unusually cruel punishment—but he hardly needed to do so in arriving at his title: at age eighty-five, he had known 12 American Presidents and countless Cabinet officials.

A less cynical man who has known fewer Presidents but more people (as distinguished from government officials) phrased it less elegantly but more pungently just before publication of the Pentagon Papers by the *New York Times* had been aborted by federal court order. He was Jimmy Breslin, reporter and student of politics-in-the-raw, in the unaccustomed role of Class Day orator at Harvard College on June 16, 1971.

"I was just thinking on the way up here," said Breslin, "that the Berrigans are in jail and the Bundys are in the street." Since the brothers Bundy, McGeorge and William P., were so closely identified with Harvard and the Kennedy and Johnson administrations, that comment in Harvard Yard had a piercing point. Breslin continued:

> This week we all found out that [soldiers have] died to keep alive the lies of some people who thought they were important. This is a very great institution here. But with these sustained reprisals hanging in the air, I just think that you might think you have something to overcome, coming out of here too.

There are many Americans with something to overcome—and to learn—in the aftermath of the Pentagon Papers, not only in the universities and the federal government, but also in the communications establishment, with which this chapter is concerned. Few events in recent years have been so revealing of the inner relations between the government and the communications industry. Nothing has borne so directly on the public's right to know, a concept which for more than 25 Cold War years has been far more violated than honored. Few developments have cast a colder light on the credibility of the highest elected and appointed officials and, in reflection and by omission, on the communications industry itself.

For the owners and operators of the newspapers, the managers of the radio-television networks and the men and women who work in the news industry, the summer of 1971 was a crisis point. Since November 1969, Vice-President Agnew had been blanketing the lecture circuit with his assaults on press and television news commentators; the Justice Department had been seeking through grand jury subpenas to intimidate reporters by forcing disclosure of their news sources; the White House news coordinator, Herbert Klein, had been attempting to circumvent a not entirely compliant Washington press corps to deal directly with flattered news executives throughout the country; the President himself through a series of selective briefings had been anointing his favorite newspapers and columnists and marking others for outer darkness, or at least for a purgatorial interim.

This was the atmosphere in which the Pentagon Papers were published, first by the *New York Times* on June 13, 1971, then in relay by the *Washington Post*, the *Boston Globe*, the *St.*

Louis Post-Dispatch and several other newspapers. The times and events would seem to have called for the most searching kind of self-examination, not only of the factors behind the publication of the Pentagon Papers, but of the whole question of the government-media relationship and the responsibility of the communications industry to the public. The immediate core issue derived from the Nixon administration's concerted attack on the media; in a larger context it was related to the origins of the Cold War at the close of World War II and the role of the communications industry in relation to Cold War policy making in Washington. In this context an examination of the communications media during—and before—the time span of the Pentagon Papers is in order.

A key question in the examination is this: How much of the information contained in the Pentagon documents was available to the media, and, if much of it was, why was it not made public?

The opportunity rarely arises from a left viewpoint to quote with approval a comment by Joseph Alsop. However, on June 23, 1971, Alsop wrote:

> The orgy of public hypocrisy, touched off by the . . . Pentagon documents, is something that has to be seen to be believed. . . . In reality, any senator who did his homework and any reasonably realistic and hardworking reporter could easily discover what was actually going on, in the period covered by the *Times* quotations.

However accurate this appraisal, there remains the question of what the hardworking reporters (presumably including Alsop) did with their discoveries, if and when they made them. Nonetheless, there was confirmation of Alsop's view from another correspondent who has generally expressed approval of the United States intervention in Southeast Asia. On June 17, 1971, Keyes Beech, a veteran of the Indochina theater, wrote in the *Chicago Daily News:*

> The *New York Times* report . . . held few surprises for the correspondents who have covered this war from the start. In general, the Pentagon account confirms what some of us knew, half-knew, or suspected without being able to document. Some of us had and wrote the

story piecemeal. While we could see what was happening here, we could not know what was happening in Washington.

What *was* happening in Washington, as far as the news corps was concerned, was recorded in the *Columbia Journalism Review* (Winter 1970–71) by Jules Witcover, Washington correspondent of the *Los Angeles Times*. Months before the Pentagon documents were made public, Witcover wrote in his article titled "Where Washington Reporting Failed":

> While the press corps in those years diligently reported what the government said about Vietnam, and questioned the inconsistencies as they arose, too few sought out opposing viewpoints and expertise until too late, when events and the prominence of the Vietnam dissent could no longer be ignored. In coverage of the war, the press corps' job narrowed down to three basic tasks—reporting what the government said, finding out whether it was true, and assessing whether the policy enunciated worked. The group did a highly professional job on the first task. But it fell down on the second and third, and there is strong evidence the reason is too many reporters sought the answers in all three categories from the same basic source—the government.

There was a fourth task not cited by Witcover which may be the most pertinent of all. Beyond the question of whether the policy *worked,* the basic question, unasked, was *whether it was wise, whether it was in the public interest.* The reason for the correspondents' confining approach, Witcover ruefully conceded later and Keyes Beech confirmed in his book *Not Without the Americans* (Doubleday, 1971), was that the news corps, both in Indochina and in Washington, was still enthralled by the Cold War and its central philosophy—the theory of the international Communist conspiracy.

The pervasiveness of this philosophy within the media, even in the earliest stages of the Indochina question, was delineated by Susan Welch of the political science faculty of the University of Nebraska in a thorough survey of four major American newspapers from 1950 to 1956.[1] The newspapers were the *New York*

---

[1] In a paper prepared for delivery at the sixty-sixth annual meeting of the American Political Science Association in Los Angeles in September 1970; and in an article in the *Nation,* October 11, 1971, part of an essay to be included in *Communications in International Politics,* edited by Richard I. Merritt (University of Illinois Press).

Times, Washington Post, San Francisco Chronicle and *Chicago Tribune.* Following are some of Miss Welch's conclusions:

It was in the 1950s, not the 1960s, that this distant and undeclared war became established in the minds of both the public and public officials as a showdown between the forces of Communism and anti-Communism, vital to the "free world"; that Ho Chi Minh was identified as a tool of a larger Communist movement, and that victory in Indochina was seen as vital to the preservation of all Asia and beyond. What the press did to help establish these views is important. . . . The press echoed the administration in its definition of the Indochinese situation. In only one instance were the basic assumptions underlying United States policy questioned. The terms of the debate hardened at a very early stage in policy making, and remained constant throughout. The assumptions of the administration were reiterated and emphasized in news stories and editorials alike.

Much of the information gathered by the press . . . was administration-sponsored, directly or indirectly. . . . Support for the position of the administration (both before and after the Republican takeover) as expressed in editorials was high for all but the *Chicago Tribune* . . . . [It] was reflected by the rhetoric with which the Indochina war [between the Vietminh and the French] was discussed. News stories also reinforced the preconceptions of the administration largely because most of the stories dealt with quotes and comments of those involved in the decision making.

The conservative *Chicago Tribune* alone questioned the basic assumptions of administration policy, largely because of the *Tribune's* isolationist position. Fighting Communists at home was a worthy pursuit, it felt, but sending American men and money abroad, particularly to bail out the colonial French, was patently absurd. But the liberal press—the *Times,* the *Post* and the *Chronicle*—reacted with "preestablished programs of action —helping to defend a free—or almost free—people against Communist aggression." From 55 to 85 percent of the "hard news" items about Indochina were of this variety. When the news source was independent of the administration and indicated that neither French nor American policy was working, the indications were discounted in the newsrooms and the editorial sanctums. The timidity of the press as to the "ideological implications" involved in Indochina was presented dispassionately and clearly by Miss Welch:

> There might have been a certain degree of risk in proclaiming too loudly Ho Chi Minh's nationalistic appeal without immediate disclaimers of his status as a puppet of Moscow, or Peking. The period 1950–56 involved an internal climate not designed to encourage those who did not see Communism in this prescribed pattern. The whole early Cold War era also tended to mold feelings about Communism into black and white patterns, with little place in the accepted pattern for unusual combinations of nationalism and Communism. The Korean struggle only reinforced already held preconceptions about the aggressive and Moscow-Peking-directed nature of Communism.

The overt excesses of the McCarthy period subsided in the decade that followed, but the institutionalized Cold War philosophy maintained the "molded feelings" to keep public opposition to governmental policy at a minimum. The media went along. In his *Columbia Journalism Review* article cited earlier, Jules Witcover raised a significant point anticipating the furor over the Pentagon documents and the reasons for it. He said: "One can speculate how the course of the war might have been affected had more members of the Washington news community relied less on their government and more on its responsible critics in appraising the veracity and effectiveness of government policy."

In June 1971 public reaction to the publication of the documents was based not so much on an understanding of the issues involved in the American presence in Indochina as on a realization that the public had been lied to for years. The reaction could not be based on an understanding of the issues, because the issues had rarely been presented in a manner that would enable the public to form opinions or make judgments about the events that shaped the issues. Therefore, in the news stories and editorials about the documents, far more stress was placed on the circumstances involved in obtaining and publishing the documents, and on freedom of the press, than on the *contents* of the documents. The core issue thus was never fully discussed.

There was a defensive echo of Witcover's comment in a retrospective editorial in the *New York Times,* appropriately on July 4, 1971. It said:

> Even if these secret decisions, now being revealed in the Pentagon Papers, had been generally understood by the public at the time, we are not at all sure that in the climate of those days, the results would have been any different. Given the fear of Communist penetration and aggression throughout the '50s and most of the '60s, it is quite likely that the American public would have supported the basic rationale of escalation even if the respective administrations had been as forthcoming as democratic procedures demanded.

The *Times* may be sound in this conclusion, but the uneasy question implied is neither asked nor answered directly. Did not the vast majority of the United States media—including the *New York Times*—advance the myth of the international Communist conspiracy and help engender the atmosphere of fear? They did not dispute Joe McCarthy's ends—only his methods. They worried far more about damage to American prestige abroad—that is, the credibility of American policy—than damage to Americans and American principles of freedom at home. They did not report on the open and systematic violations by the United States of the Geneva agreements of 1954 (though they did publish the government's denials) or the reasons for the rise of the National Liberation Front of South Vietnam. Nor did they demand withdrawal of American support for a brutal and corrupt administration in Saigon—until the situation became so untenable that even the Washington end was forced to take action. The case history of the media and Ngo Dinh Diem, whose life and death figure so prominently in the Pentagon documents, is instructive.

For the American public the myth of Ngo Dinh Diem seems to have been fashioned in equal measure by Cardinal Spellman, Michigan State University (acting on behalf of the Central Intelligence Agency) and a group of publicists led by Joseph H. Buttinger, an Austrian anti-Communist who had won the favor of Colonel Edward M. Lansdale, the CIA chief in Vietnam in the 1950s. Thus, when Diem came to the United States in 1957 as the President of the Republic of South Vietnam, the communications media were prepared to do somersaults for him on the welcoming red carpet—and did.

The *New York Times* declared that "by establishing democratic forms, President Diem had carved a deep niche in official esteem in Washington." A New York City banquet was presided over by Henry Luce of *Time*, and *Life* applauded his "great accomplishment" in abrogating the 1956 elections, ordered under the Geneva agreements, to decide the future of Vietnam. The *Reporter* magazine and the *New Leader* (which had provided two of its editors for the executive committee of the American Friends of Vietnam, along with Max Lerner and Arthur Schlesinger, Jr.) were effusive in their praise. In 1960 he was still "doughty little Diem" to *Time*, and *Newsweek*'s Ernest K. Lindley described him as "one of Asia's ablest leaders."

Thus it went through the period of blatant repression by Diem of all political opposition and the consequent rise of the National Liberation Front of South Vietnam. These developments went almost entirely unreported in the American press, except for a few left-wing weeklies. Wilfred Burchett, as a correspondent of the *National Guardian* and a contributor to newspapers abroad, set up a home base in Cambodia and traveled extensively throughout Southeast Asia. He was a frequent visitor to North Vietnam (long before any other Western correspondents were there) and was permitted into areas of South Vietnam controlled by the Liberation Front. His cabled and airmailed dispatches appeared regularly in the *National Guardian,* whose editors regularly had extra proofs run off and hand-delivered to the daily newspapers in New York and the wire services. They were ignored.

Occasionally a Burchett report which had been published in the *Asahi Shimbun* of Tokyo (circulation five million) was relayed back to the United States, where it appeared in abbreviated fashion in a few newspapers. Later, when the war was admittedly going badly for the United States forces and when it became apparent that Burchett had access to authoritative information in both North and South Vietnam, the Associated Press requested articles from him which appeared with an italic headnote describing him as a "Communist journalist" and warning that his dispatches should be read with that in mind. Burchett protested to the Associated Press and the description was modified to "a journalist close to Communist leaders." In the United States press the description did not disappear until the late 1960s. Yet while Burchett escaped from his headnote, the American public was still a prisoner of the prejudices of newspaper editors and publishers.

By 1962 it was clear to the *New York Times,* at least, that something was going terribly wrong in Vietnam, and it sent one of its ablest reporters, Homer Bigart, to Vietnam (it was he who coined the slogan "Sink or Swim with Ngo Dinh Diem"). Bigart became involved in what became known as the "second war" in Vietnam—the war of the correspondents against the combined United States-Vietnamese authority in Saigon. In fact, it was not a war at all, but a serious conflict between some correspondents[2] and almost all official functionaries as to how to carry out American policy most efficiently—in brief, how to win the war in the shortest possible time. This is not to deny that there were first-rate examples of honest and courageous reporting both in the field and in Saigon. But what was painfully apparent was the contradiction between the reporting of the best of the correspondents and the conclusions they drew from their own reportage, about both United States policy and the aspirations of the Vietnamese people.

By insisting on presenting to the American public the facts about the Diem government, the "Young Turks" in Vietnam (as they were called) hastened a review of Washington's *tactics,* but not its *policy.* That policy for Indochina has remained unaltered from President Kennedy's decision in 1961 to commit forces in depth to Vietnam until this day. The group of remarkably able and dedicated newspapermen assigned to Saigon in the years 1962–63 strove mightily to make the American public aware that

---

[2] At the height of the controversy about Diem, only the Associated Press, the United Press International and the *New York Times* had full-time correspondents in South Vietnam. When a major story broke, a stream of correspondents poured in from Hong Kong, Tokyo and Bangkok. Neil Sheehan was then correspondent for UPI, Malcolm Browne for AP and Charles Mohr was Southeast Asia bureau chief for *Time.* With David Halberstam, who succeeded Homer Bigart for the *New York Times,* they comprised the group of journalistic rebels whose dispatches were contradicted by junketeering correspondents such as Joseph Alsop and Marguerite Higgins of the *New York Herald Tribune,* sent out to Vietnam for that purpose. By July 1966 there were 360 accredited correspondents in South Vietnam, about a third of them actual reporters, the rest technicians, interpreters—and CIA agents.

the "Miracle of Diem" was a costly myth and that a change was needed. Their goal, however, was not an end to United States intervention, but reform of that intervention to attain an American victory.

This was reflected in the writings of Halberstam, Browne and Sheehan after their tours of duty in Vietnam. In 1967 Browne had moved from acceptance of the "credible" American presence in Vietnam (expressed in 1966) to an anguished conclusion that "Asia and America seem doomed to play out the tragic drama to the end."[3] In 1965 David Halberstam said the United States could not agree to a neutral Vietnam which would create a "vacuum" for Communist "subversion." Withdrawal would encourage the "enemies of the West" to attempt "insurgencies like the ones in Vietnam" throughout the world.[4] In 1966 Sheehan conceded that "the military junta in Vietnam would not last a week without American bayonets to protect it." But, he said, there was no alternative to the American strategy to "continue to prosecute the war" and to develop a "killing machine" to be turned on the enemy "in the hope that over the years enough killing will be done to force the enemy's collapse through exhaustion and despair."[5]

There is no doubt that Sheehan and Browne (both now on the staff of the New York Times, as is Charles Mohr) have come a far way from their despairing and limited views of the middle 1960s. So has Halberstam, and it was ironic in its way that Sheehan became so intimately involved in the publication of the Pentagon documents and that he and Halberstam were called to appear before a federal grand jury in Boston in the fishing expedition following the disclosure by Dr. Daniel Ellsberg that he had given the documents to the New York Times. Perhaps "purposeful" would be a better description than "ironic." For the vindictive arm of government is long, and the malice of government officials seeking to cover their tracks (as so many of the civilian strategists of Vietnam policy have been seeking to do) is pervasive. Sheehan

---

[3] In a perceptive review of Roger Hilsman's To Move a Nation (New York: Doubleday, 1967), in The Nation, June 5, 1967.
[4] In The Making of a Quagmire (New York: Random House, 1965).
[5] In an article entitled "Not a Dove, But No Longer a Hawk," in the New York Times Magazine, October 9, 1966.

and Halberstam, after all, committed the cardinal sin: they refused as reporters to "get on the team," and that, at any stage of governmental operations, is an unforgivable act.

Perhaps a clue to the limitations of even the best of the reporters in Vietnam in the 1960s—in addition to their lack of historical perspective and knowledge of the area they were covering—may be found in an examination of journalism's unwritten and adjustable rules of objectivity. According to these rules, the only reliable sources of information about Indochina were untainted "free world" centers, and most central of all was the government of the United States. Sources of information outside the government were suspect, and radical sources almost entirely rejected. The most distinguished Asian scholars had not quite recovered their acceptability lost during the McCarthy years[6], and besides, they almost universally disapproved of the American intervention. Why go to *them* for background when abstracts of State Department white papers abounded?

Correspondents of left-wing American journals and respected European correspondents such as Jean Lacouture and the commentators of *Le Monde* were rarely quoted. The radicals, of course, wanted the Vietnamese to "win," and the French, once they were out, wanted the Americans to "lose," because France, too, had lost.

When Harrison Salisbury of the *New York Times,* in a startling series of dispatches from North Vietnam at the turn of 1967, discredited Washington's denials of bombings near Hanoi and confirmed the Burchett reports that had been appearing regularly in the *National Guardian,* he was charged by Chalmers Roberts of the *Washington Post* with using a subversive typewriter in the service of Ho Chi Minh. The campaign of venom against him by his own colleagues was almost unprecedented. (The *Times* itself, in its devotion to balance and objectivity in the news, featured on page one an article by Hanson Baldwin, its military affairs analyst,

---

[6] Between 1945 and 1950 specialists connected with the Institute of Pacific Relations, a prime McCarthy target, reviewed 22 of 30 books about China for the *New York Times* and 30 of 35 books for the *New York Herald Tribune.* From 1952 to 1955, the years of McCarthyite prevalence, not one of these authorities was engaged to review a single book by either the *Times* or the *Herald Tribune.* These figures are from Roger Hilsman's *To Move a Nation.*

taking sharp issue with the findings of Salisbury on the scene in North Vietnam.) Salisbury was deprived of a Pulitzer prize for his series when the Pulitzer board blatantly overruled the committee of editors who had selected Salisbury for the award.

There was an echo of all this at the Paris talks on Vietnam in June 1971. Madame Nguyen Thi Binh, the representative of the Provisional Revolutionary Government of South Vietnam (which the *New York Times* still calls the Vietcong), said that the Pentagon documents "confirm a truth that we have often expressed at this table, to wit, that the American administration . . . conceived plans for unleashing war and spreading it stage by stage."

The North Vietnamese delegate at the same session produced a white paper—published on July 10, 1965, in English among other languages, and broadcast to the world over Radio Hanoi— entitled "Twenty Years of American Aggression and Intervention in Vietnam." It was a document of remarkable accuracy, as the Pentagon Papers demonstrate. Included was a description of the infamous Plan No. 6, drawn up by Walt W. Rostow, then chairman of the State Department's Planning Council, calling for increasing commitments of United States ground forces and air power.

In December 1965 Nguyen Huu Tho, chairman of the National Liberation Front, said in a statement (confirmed by the Pentagon documents) that the United States was operating under a "McNamara Plan" aimed at "pacifying the South within the two years of 1964–65 and representing a new and greater effort to improve the critical situation of the puppet government and forces, and to concentrate their forces on pacifying the main areas under the Front's control." Such statements, said Erwin Knoll,[7] "received scant attention in the American media. They were merely 'Communist propaganda,' and our government, which knew better, hardly bothered to issue rebuttals."

The July 1965 white paper was available to the American press immediately after it was published. It was the subject at the time of both a leading news article and an editorial in the *National Guardian*. No American newspaper of general circulation used it.

---

[7] In the *Progressive*, August 1971. Knoll is Washington editor of the *Progressive* and co-author with William McGaffin of *Anything but the Truth* (New York: G. P. Putnam's, 1968), about the credibility gap in Washington.

But Vietnamese were not the only pariahs for the American media. Even certified non-Communist Americans foolhardy enough to be skeptical of or oppose administration policy or pronouncements were ignored or discredited. Consider the story of the Gulf of Tonkin incident in August 1964.

I. F. Stone in his weekly newsletter,[8] almost alone among the Washington press corps, presented evidence immediately after the event indicating that the alleged attack by North Vietnamese gunboats against the United States fleet was a fraud. His reports were ignored by his colleagues, who, years later, would review his books (based largely on his earlier published material) and honor him as the conscience of the Washington press corps. But the postmortem flattery smacked of confession-booth relief and even caste condescension. This tenacious little bulldog, as they liked to call him, was eminently qualified to be the mascot of the White House Correspondents Association, but never a member. Not that Stone had ever wanted in.

On August 5, 1964, Secretary McNamara held a news conference—maps, pointers, and field-grade flunkeys at his elbow—to explain in his computerized fashion what had happened in the Gulf of Tonkin. There was not one probing question from the reporters, although it might have seemed inconceivable to at least some of them that two little North Vietnamese gunboats would seek out and attack the mighty American fleet, knowing full well what the reprisal would be.

The New York Times, after Tonkin, saw in the alleged attack "an ominous perspective . . . the beginning of a mad adventure by the North Vietnamese Communists." The mad adventures, however, were on the other side—a fact which became clear in the American escalation of the war immediately thereafter. And the calculated fraud was exposed further in statements by members of the crews of the United States vessels involved in the incident, long before the Pentagon Papers were published.

Dissenting legislators (there were few enough of them then) fared little better than Stone. On August 10, 1964, Senator Ernest

[8] Stone ceased publication of his newsletter with the issue of December 14, 1971, to become a contributing editor of the New York Review of Books. The Weekly is available on microfilm from University Microfilms, a subsidiary of Xerox.

Gruening of Alaska, who, with Senator Wayne Morse of Oregon, five days earlier had cast the only dissenting votes against the Tonkin Gulf resolution, delivered the first speech on the Senate floor advocating withdrawal of American troops from Vietnam. The speech was a reasoned and factual presentation of the circumstances of American involvement. The next morning Gruening sought out newspaper accounts of his speech. There was not a line about it in either the *New York Times* or the *Washington Post*. Had he been able to repeat the exercise with most if not all other newspapers in the country that day, the search would have been equally futile.

A significant indicator of the communications media's attitude during the 1950s and 1960s was provided in the *New York Times* editorial of July 4, 1971. "We do not think," it said, "that the respective officials involved made recommendations or took decisions that they did not conscientiously believe to be in the public interest. As an early opponent of the escalation of American military force in Vietnam, this newspaper has never attacked the motives of those leaders."

The key words here are "escalation" and "motives." The *Times* did not oppose *intervention* in Indochina, as we have seen. On the contrary, it endorsed it with exhortation to victory. ("Thomas Jefferson would have no quarrel" with Ngo Dinh Diem's definition of democracy, it said as far back as 1957.) The *Times* did begin to oppose escalation when it became apparent that there could be no military victory in Indochina. Similarly, it never questioned the *motives* of the succeeding administrations, because it subscribed wholeheartedly to the policies being motivated.

Speculation is a doubtful practice at best. But we should include the period before 1960, for which a reasonable speculation might be as follows: If the communications media had presented in responsible fashion the history of Indochina and the aspirations of its peoples; if they had opened their facilities to the opponents of developing Cold War policy to encourage a public debate based on realities and not on myth—if it had done these things, would the government, confronted with such an informed public, have dared to embark on a venture which has cost millions of Indochinese lives, thousands of American lives, incredible destruction of the life-giving land of Indochina and incalculable damage to the spiritual fabric of American life?

This leads to a central question about the publication of the Pentagon documents bearing directly upon the responsibility of the communications industry and the public's right to know. The revelations concerned events taking place before 1968. In response to the government's charge that publication was damaging to the security interests of the country, the *Times* responded editorially on June 16, the day after publication had been suspended:

> It is in the interest of the people of this country to be informed. . . . A fundamental responsibility of the press in this democracy is to publish information that helps the people of the United States to understand the processes of their own government, especially when these processes have been clouded over in a veil of public dissimulation and even deception. . . . Once this material fell into our hands, it was not only in the interest of the American people to publish it but, even more emphatically, it would have been an abnegation of responsibility not to have published it.
>
> Obviously the *Times* would not have made this decision if there had been any reason to believe that publication would have endangered the life of a single American soldier or in any way threatened the security of our country or the peace of the world. The documents in question belong to history. . . . Their publication could not conceivably damage American security interests, much less the lives of Americans or Indochinese.

Five days later, when the *Washington Post* began publication, the *Times* emphasized again that the documents "in no way affect current plans, operations, or policy; and there seems no longer any justification for these papers . . . to bear the kind of classification that keeps them from general public access." The next day, June 22, the *Boston Globe* began its publication of parts of the documents not yet published. Its editorial likewise assured its readers that "the nation's security" was not involved in publication.

The implication here was that neither the *Times* nor the *Globe* nor perhaps any other newspaper would publish classified material relating to current or future events, no matter how salutary to the national interest public knowledge of that material might be. The conclusion was that the *Times*, in any case, had not altered its policy in regard to such information since the Bay of Pigs fiasco in 1961.

It will be recalled that in April 1961 *Times* correspondent Tad Szulc came into possession of information in Florida that a United States financed and supported invasion of Cuba was imminent. The *Times*, at the request of the White House and largely on the advice of James Reston, then Washington bureau chief, withheld publication of key facts of the story on the ground that it was in the national interest to do so.

Again, in October 1962, the *New York Times* and the *Washington Post* had firm knowledge during the so-called missile crisis of President Kennedy's plans for a military blockade of Cuba and for intercepting any foreign-flag ship attempting to reach the island republic. The newspapers withheld publication at the request of President Kennedy. The crisis was resolved by a Soviet agreement to remove missiles emplaced on Cuban territory in return for an American pledge that there would be no repetition of the 1961 invasion attempt.

In the 1961 incident, United States involvement in the aborted invasion of a sovereign state was in clear violation of international law. In the 1962 incident, the Soviet Union was clearly within its rights in placing missiles in Cuba, at the invitation of the Cuban government and under Cuban control, however distasteful it may have been to the government of the United States. The bristling reaction to the missiles (to this day there has been no precise description of their potential) was outrageous in view of the fact that hundreds of American missiles had been placed close to the borders of the Soviet Union.

Beyond this, Drew Pearson reported on October 26, 1962, that the missile crisis had been engendered in Washington by the Kennedy administration to shore up its political prospects in the November 1962 elections against Republican charges that it was being soft on communism "ninety miles from our shores." And Max Frankel in the *New York Times* of October 23, 1962, indicated that one compelling reason for the need for secrecy about Washington's plans was fear that the Soviet Union might take the matter to the United Nations and undercut the effect of Kennedy's ultimatum—an ultimatum which could have led to war between the United States and the Soviet Union. As late as 1966 the *Times* was still justifying its suppression of the missile crisis story.[9]

There is a connection between the Cuban events and those of June 1971. The *Boston Globe* sent Crocker Snow, assistant managing editor, to New York during the first week of the publication of the documents to find out how and why the *Times*'s decision to publish was reached, and how the staff felt about it. Snow determined that there was a "curious relationship" between the June 1971 decision and the one taken years earlier at the time of the Bay of Pigs. He recalled Kennedy's hindsight comment to *Times* executive editor Turner Catledge: "If you had printed more about the [Bay of Pigs] operation, you would have saved us from a colossal mistake."

Had this "embarrassing memory" played a part in the decision to publish the Pentagon documents? Snow asked. Very little, said the editors. One told Snow: "This is a very, very different thing. These are basically historical documents, and the Cuban stories were about pending missions. I can say honestly that if this secret material now had been about ongoing missions, then we wouldn't have used it."

The mind conjures the image of an ashen editorial writer, sitting at a charred typewriter, painfully recording that, in retrospect, the decision to drop an atomic bomb on Peking, in retaliation for the defeat of the American Ping-Pong team by the Chinese at the Sands Hotel in Las Vegas, was poorly conceived. The *Times*, the editorial would say, had information that a contingency plan for the preemptive retaliatory protective-reaction strike was in existence, but withheld the information because it concerned ongoing policy, and disclosure might endanger the life of even one American airman.

While this fantasy may seem absurd to some, the reality was less absurd to thousands of Indochinese whose charred remains continued to pile up in a noncontingent pattern as a result of ongoing United States policy whose underlying principles were

[9] In a speech by Clifton Daniel, then the *Times*'s managing editor, on June 1, 1966, to the World Press Institute at Macalester College in St. Paul, Minnesota, and printed the next day in full in the *Times*.

still accepted by an overwhelming majority of the communications media. Who then will blow the whistle on this policy in the genuine national interest?

The Pentagon Papers demonstrated that the government not only refuses to give information but also lies and distorts the facts. Is it not, therefore, the responsibility of newspapers and television networks to make the record public when they are persuaded that a planned government action could bring the nation up to or over the brink of an illegal, immoral and disastrous war? This is not to argue that the media in a wartime situation should have published in advance, say, the date of the invasion of Normandy in World War II. There are, of course, situations when security must be maintained. The publication by the *Chicago Tribune* in World War II of the information that the United States had broken the Japanese naval code was reprehensible.

But Cuba is another matter. We were not at war with Cuba. We simply wanted to smash its revolution, and the media were in general accord with this policy. And Indochina is another matter. War has never been declared there, and a majority of Americans have finally concluded that the United States must extricate itself. If the government persists in thwarting the public will, do not the media have a responsibility to intervene in behalf of the public? If they do not, who will?

"Who elected the *New York Times* to get into the game? some people ask," James Reston wrote on June 20, 1971, "and the answer is nobody but the men who wrote the First Amendment to the Constitution." A fair answer, and one Reston might have given to himself when he advised his publisher not to publish the facts about the Bay of Pigs invasion (Reston still refers to the CIA's Cubans as "freedom fighters") and the missile crisis. But the answer implies something more than responsibility in hindsight.

"The political game as it is now played in Washington is like a football game without boundaries, rules or officials," Reston declared in the same article. "All the men in the press box can do is report the shambles." Poorly stated. The men who drew up and fought for the First Amendment privileges and protections for the press did so precisely because they sought to prevent the shambles from occurring. In Reston's metaphor, they wanted the press to guard the stadium gates like watchdogs to prevent the crooked managers, the fixed players and the blood-money gamblers from taking over.

The *Times* was a toothless watchdog when Coach Eisenhower's Washington All-Stars were playing Russian roulette in their U-2 spy planes over the Soviet Union in 1960, and before. Several *Times* editors later conceded that the *Times* knew all about this dangerous game, but published nothing about it. Premier Krushchev made his famous U-2 accusation just before a scheduled summit conference with President Eisenhower in Paris in May 1960—a conference called to advance the "spirit of Camp David" supposedly established during Khrushchev's visit to the United States the year before.

The sainted Eisenhower, the nearest miss to General Washington the nation has ever had, lied about the U-2s, and the *Times* soberly published his lies—even though it knew the facts. The press in general decreed that Khrushchev did not want to talk peace anyway. Then Khrushchev produced the photographs of the U-2 wreckage and mug shots of pilot Gary Powers. The Paris conference broke up before it had begun, and an Eisenhower trip to the Soviet Union was canceled. The game was called on account of international darkness, and the nation slid back into Reston's Cold War shambles. *That* is the most dangerous game of all, and the *Times* was an accomplice before and after the fact because it did not genuinely subscribe to the public's right to know.

In January 1972 an incident occurred which seemingly put to test the question whether the most prestigious newspapers of the country would alter their policy of not publishing secret documents about ongoing or future policy. The episode acquired the name "the Anderson Papers," after Jack Anderson, the Washington-based muckraker whose column appears in 700 newspapers. On January 3 Anderson wrote that he had come into possession of secret summaries of White House meetings of December 3, 4 and 6 disclosing a firmer anti-India attitude by the United States government than had been made public during and following the India-Pakistan dispute over East Pakistan. The creation of the state of Bangladesh followed the Indian invasion of East Pakistan.

Much of the information in the Anderson columns pictured White House adviser Henry A. Kissinger as the President's chief spokesman in the matter. Kissinger insisted that Anderson had "wrenched" the information "out of context." Anderson, to prove his contention, thereupon released the full text of memoranda of the White House meetings, and they were published on January 5 by the *Washington Post* and the *New York Post*. The *New York Times* asked Anderson for the documents and published them in full on January 6. The *Washington Post* described Anderson's actions as "an undoubted contribution to the public's right to know."

While the documents undoubtedly did shed light on the insular arrogance with which policy decisions are reached, they added little to the public's knowledge of United States attitudes toward India and Pakistan—attitudes whose bias against India was clearly evident in United States actions and comments at the United Nations, and in statements by the White House and the State Department. Further, in any comparison with the Pentagon Papers, it should be noted that the documents were turned over to Anderson *from within the government*—and there is considerable reason to believe that the leak was motivated not so much by concern for the public's right to know as by jealousy and dissension among warring factions within the administration. It was common knowledge in Washington that both the State Department and the Defense Department had long resented Kissinger's "running the government from the White House basement," and the Anderson coup had all the earmarks of a palace intrigue to "get" Kissinger.

While Anderson may be credited with nobler motives in making the information public, an examination of the administration's public statements on India and the secret documents revealed differences only in degree and intensity. Comparisons with the Pentagon documents fall noticeably short. Neither in content nor in significance do the two sets of documents compare. Furthermore, by the time the documents were published, Bangladesh was a *fait accompli*. In the last analysis, the Anderson papers did not test the willingness of the press to publish major documents about current or future policy.

The leadership of the *Times* nationally was demonstrated by the chain reaction following its publication of the first of the

Pentagon Papers. In rapid order the documents began to appear in the *Washington Post, Boston Globe, Chicago Sun-Times,* the Knight newspapers, *Los Angeles Times, St. Louis Post-Dispatch, Newsday* of Long Island and the *Christian Science Monitor.* Granted by then it was too sensational a story to suppress, there was much more involved. It was evident that those newspapers generally regarded as the most responsible understood they had a common and compelling necessity to support one another in the face of an unprecedented government attempt at "prior restraint"—that is, action taken to prevent the publication of a news story or transcripts of documents.

This was the problem that confronted the editors (and the legal department, which sometimes overrules or supplants the editors) at the *Times* in the three months during which they had possession of the documents and weighed their decision to publish or not to publish. The atmosphere at the *Times* and in the surrounding mid-Manhattan area could have been appropriate for an elaborate spy melodrama. Men and women were spirited out of the *Times* building in West 43rd Street to set up secret headquarters at the Hotel Hilton, their privacy protected by *Times* company guards (eventually the *Times* had nine rooms on two floors of the hotel). Special secret composing rooms were established with only trusted typesetters admitted. Questions as to the whereabouts of missing Washington bureau men were met with "Don't ask."

In Washington there were similar scenes at the *Post,* of briefer duration but perhaps of even greater intensity. There an all-night battle between the "business side" and the "editorial side" at the home of executive editor Benjamin Bradlee ended with a victory by the editorial side to publish.

First reactions in the newspaper world were marked by indolence and ineptitude and, in many areas, caution. The Times News Service, with 300 clients, alerted its subscribers on the afternoon of June 12 (Saturday) that it would move a major story at 6:00 P.M. The *Louisville Courier-Journal* gave prominent place to the story, but the *Chicago Tribune* ignored it. UPI did not send a story out until Sunday afternoon, and AP waited until Monday afternoon (both services are permitted to pick up stories from member newspapers immediately). Neither *Time* nor *News-*

week remade their pages on Saturday night, although there was time.

The television networks handled the story even more casually. ABC put the *Times* story aside to read at a future time. At CBS, during the *Face the Nation* program on Sunday with Secretary of Defense Melvin Laird (who had been briefed by Attorney General Mitchell as to his possible replies), neither the CBS correspondent nor the *New York Times* man on the program asked a single question concerning the documents. Only NBC realized the significance of the story and devoted almost half of the time of its Sunday evening news to it.

In general, however, the performance of the television networks was limited in the weeks that followed. While they covered the legal battles and the Ellsberg involvement fully, they paid scant attention to the content of the documents, and it was not until the end of December 1971 that any network devoted any appreciable time to the papers themselves. That was the two-hour program *Vietnam Hindsight,* produced by NBC and devoted mainly to the origins of American involvement and the events leading to the assassination of Ngo Dinh Diem on November 2, 1963.

But a high degree of excitement was engendered in the last two weeks of June, particularly about the question of freedom of the press and the interpretation of the First Amendment. And the excitement was warranted. Never before in the history of the country had the issue of "prior restraint" been raised in terms of legal action and pursued through the courts by the government—not even during the two-year period in which the Alien and Sedition Acts were in force from 1798 to 1800. Even these acts invoked postpublication penalties, and they expired before the Supreme Court was able to rule on the constitutional issues.

A proper question to be asked at this juncture is: If the Congress is forbidden by the First Amendment from enacting legislation in the area of freedom of the press, by what right did the executive branch intervene to ask the judiciary to act, and by what right did the courts accede to the executive's requests? There was a sharp exchange on this point during the Supreme Court hearing on June 26, 1971, between Justice Douglas, an unyielding advocate of absolute interpretation of First Amendment freedoms, and, surprisingly, the attorney representing the *Times,* Alexander M. Bickel of Yale Law School.

Bickel argued that the courts might have the power to restrain the press if Congress passed a law specifically authorizing it to do so. Justice Douglas looked up sharply from his notetaking and said: "The First Amendment says that Congress shall make no law abridging the freedom of the press. Are you saying that Congress can make some laws abridging freedom of the press? [That] is a very strange argument for the *Times* to make that all this can be done if Congress passes a law." Bickel wisely made no response.

It was indeed a strange argument on behalf of a newspaper petitioning to lift the judicial restraining order against continuing publication of the Pentagon documents. It was even more strange in view of the position taken by four justices against accepting *certiorari* (review) on the ground that, because of the First Amendment's clear language, the court had no jurisdiction in the case.

A head-on test of this principle might have occurred if the *Times* had ignored the initial injunction in the Federal District Court in New York and continued publication of the documents. But the *Times,* as a newspaper which abides by the "rule of law," was not willing to make the challenge; nor, it seems, was any other newspaper. However one might have hoped for such a challenge, it was not logical to expect it from newspapers which have consistently rebuked demonstrators for "going outside the law."

There was another alternative for the *Times:* it could have published the entire set of documents in one issue of the paper and thus rendered moot the issue of prior restraint—at least in the Pentagon Papers case. But newspapers, however much they may protest that they are a public service, are profit-making enterprises. The *Times's* circulation had been declining at a fairly steady rate through 1971. Here was a chance to recoup some losses through a series of articles spread over a period of time with tremendous impact. It would hardly be speculative to suggest that hard heads in the counting house prevailed over softer ones in the editorial department.

What was the long-range meaning of the Supreme Court's decision to permit the *Times* to continue publication? Perhaps the soundest answer came from one of the nation's leading authorities on constitutional law, Thomas I. Emerson of Yale Law School. He wrote:[10]

> The result was certainly favorable to a free press. Put the other way, a contrary result would have been a disaster. It would have made the press subject to a very considerable extent of advance restriction. It would have changed the whole relationship between the press and government. The outcome was a sound outcome. On the other hand, the legal theory that the court adopted is, I think, cause for concern.
>
> Only three justices came out strongly against a system of prior restraint—Black, Douglas and Brennan, and Brennan would make some narrow exceptions. Black and Douglas apparently permitted none. Justice Marshall probably would go along with them, but actually he based his opinion on a different ground—that Congress had denied the power to the President, and the Court therefore did not get into the question. But if you assume there were four who would vigorously apply the doctrine of no previous restraint, nevertheless there were five whose opinions seriously undermine the doctrine against prior restraint. Certainly the three dissenters would have made exceptions, but also Justices White and Stewart announced that any anticipated publication which raised an immediate danger to national security would be grounds for an injunction, and the dissenting justices would have gone at least that far.

There were two major problems, as Emerson saw the decision: (1) the specified exception—that advance restraint of a newspaper was proper if the government proved a grave and immediate breach of national security—is a wide-open exception which would probably allow the government to obtain an injunction in most cases where the question of national security was raised; (2) if the courts ultimately interpret the concept of "grave and immediate breach of national security" rather narrowly, the very application of the rule would constitute a system of prior restraint because it would hold up publication while the courts investigated whether there was indeed a breach of security.

Emerson found the media to be in a vulnerable position. The rapid changes in the Supreme Court, tilting the balance dis-

---

[10] In *The Columbia Journalism Review* (September/October 1971), an issue devoted almost entirely to the media and the Pentagon documents.

tinctly toward the restrictive Nixon-Mitchell view of civil liberties, made the position of the media even more vulnerable. On this point, Emerson had some advice for the media in seeking allies to protect its freedom:

> I would say that one of the main things that the media can do is to educate the public to the significance of the whole system of free expression. . . . The *New York Times* case has opened up the possibility of making people aware of what the role of the press is; that its role isn't simply to take handouts given by the government; it's for the people.
>
> The major problem with the system of freedom of the press today is the inability of many points of view to find an outlet. That is a very serious problem. I think that it is important for the media to be aware of that, to anticipate it, to try to take account of it. In other words, just as I think the government ought to subsidize an opposition to itself, in a sense monopolistic elements in the communications industry should subsidize some opposition to themselves. I think it would be a much healthier and ultimately more successful system.

It was unlikely that either the government or the communications industry would give serious heed to Emerson's Jeffersonian counsel. In the more than two years during which the Nixon administration had sought to pressure the communications industry to cast off even its tepid adversary role vis-à-vis government, the industry to a large extent played the artful dodger, yielding a bit here, making a tentative thrust there, but generally avoiding a direct confrontation with the government. The publication of the Pentagon Papers altered the situation, but subsequent events have not demonstrated that the communications industry has absorbed the obvious lesson of the Pentagon Papers—that the only proper role of the media is not as partner to government, but as spokesman and forum for an enlightened and informed public opinion which it should help to create.

In the first days after the documents were published, there was a heartening closing of ranks to resist the abrogation of the First Amendment—for that is what it had come down to. The directors of NBC and CBS, themselves under governmental siege, voiced their support of the newspapers. ABC, concentrating on a "happy news" approach in accord with the Agnew syndrome, was silent.

The American Society of Newspaper Editors joined the fight, as did the Associated Press Managing Editors Association, the Newspaper Guild and *Editor & Publisher*, the generally stodgy journal of the newspaper industry. The *Boston Globe* recalled the dark days of the witch-hunting, black-listing 1950s with a warning that it could happen again. Its political editor, Robert Healy, wrote: "After all, the issue is not simply the right [of newspapers] to publish these documents, but the right of the people to read them."

The classic arrogant response to this position was given by General Maxwell Taylor, who had served in the deceit élite of both the Kennedy and Johnson administrations, and therefore was a person of prominence in the Pentagon documents. On the question of "the people's right to know," he said:

> I don't believe in this as a general principle. You have to talk about cases. What is a citizen going to do after reading these documents that he wouldn't have done otherwise? A citizen should know the things he needs to know to be a good citizen and discharge his functions, but not to get into secrets that damage his government and indirectly damage himself.

The disclosures, he said, were laying the foundations for "bad history." That meant, in plain English, that it would make the central figures in the drama—Taylor among them—look bad. And that, at all costs, particularly at the cost of truth, had to be avoided. Opposed to the Taylor view, Tom Wicker wrote in the *New York Times* on June 16, 1971.

> No statute exists that says that government officials must be protected from the exposure of their follies or misdeeds. Indeed, the great lesson of the Pentagon record is that the ability to operate in secret breeds contempt for that very public in whose name and interest officials claim to act.

That is a great lesson indeed, but it applies to the newspapers which refused to publish information in their possession during the years of the Pentagon Papers as well as to government officials who sought to keep secret their policy-making actions. For the communications media it ought to have meant a continuing effort to tear the shroud of secrecy and misinformation from every area of governmental policy making, and particularly about the seemingly endless war in Indochina. But after a period of vigorous self-congratulation, the media lost interest altogether in the contents of the Pentagon documents, especially as to the light they might cast on current policy and actions, and resorted to their customary way of doing things.

Body counts and kill ratios still dominated the news stories from Indochina, and "Hanoi" was credited with all "enemy" military actions in Cambodia, Laos and South Vietnam. Missing from the media—and from the American consciousness—was any recognition of the role of National Liberation Front of South Vietnam, the Cambodian National Liberation Front and the Pathet Lao, the liberation movement of Laos, each of which is in control of the major portion of its respective country, and each of which in fact is opposing the forces of the United States and their mercenary troops—not "Hanoi."

When the bombings of North Vietnam were resumed in force late in 1971, and administration spokesmen, in language which could have been taken verbatim from the Pentagon documents, sought to justify the bombings, the media reported the explanations without contest in the traditionally objective fashion. An enterprising newspaper could have laid the official statements side by side with similar statements from the Pentagon documents, and the point would have been sharply underscored. But such enterprise was not countenanced, if it ever was proposed.

Even more striking was the treatment in the media, and particularly the *New York Times,* of the man whose initiative, enterprise and single-minded purpose enabled the publication of the Pentagon documents. On August 5, 1971, Daniel Ellsberg was ordered by a United States District Court judge in Boston to be removed to California to face charges of illegal possession of secret government documents. The *Times,* one felt, would regard itself as personally involved—with due regard for the need to protect its own legal position—and deem this news worthy of page one display. It decided, however, to place the story (ten inches of type) on page six of its August 6 issue.

An Appeals Court held up the extradition order on August 6, and the *Times* on August 7 moved the story up to page four (13 inches). Ellsberg was not in court in Portland, Maine, where the action took place, but held a news conference in Boston and made some statements which could provide a motive for his relegation to the *Times's* inside pages. He said he was disappointed that the newspapers were not printing more of the Pentagon documents. "The *New York Times* and the *Washington Post* have most of the papers," he said, "but the public doesn't have them. I have to say this means many newspapers in this country which have access to large sections of the Pentagon study are now in the business of withholding it from the public, just as the Defense Department was for so long in that business."

That was a strong enough statement to elicit comment from the *Times* or the *Washington Post*, but none was forthcoming. In fact, Ellsberg dropped out of the *Times* for the rest of the week, and its *News of the Week in Review*, on Sunday, August 8, did not consider his situation of sufficient interest for an item in the review, let alone for editorial comment.

Coverage of the Ellsberg case did improve in the *Times* after the second indictments by a grand jury in Los Angeles in December 1971, but an examination of the *Times's* editorials from June through December 1971 yielded only one comment about the Ellsberg case. That was an editorial critical of the government's use of wiretapping in pursuing persons in the academic community who may have sympathized with or assisted Ellsberg's efforts to make the Pentagon documents public.

The *Boston Globe* was prematurely accurate in describing the climate surrounding the Pentagon Papers' publication as similar to that of the 1950s, "when intellectuals, Hollywood writers, professors and labor leaders were being summoned before a congressional committee and then being judged in contempt because they refused to answer questions about their alleged Communist beliefs." Substitute the words "grand jury" for "congressional committee" and "alleged Ellsberg connections" for "Communist beliefs" and one has a fair picture of the atmosphere on the East Coast and the West Coast in the summer of 1972.

Even the most vigorous efforts—if they were indeed to be made—by the media to ensure a fair trial for Ellsberg and the others who were indicted, or may still be, could not absolve the media of their responsibility in the situation. That could be achieved only by an acknowledgment that the wrong persons were being placed on trial and that the government's efforts were a diversion to delude the public once again as to the real nature of the American crisis.

In the *New York Times* of June 13, 1971—the day the first of the documents appeared—James Reston described as persons of "unquestioned personal moral character" Secretary of Defense McNamara, Secretary of State Dean Rusk, Walt W. Rostow and the Bundy brothers. It is a strange characterization of men engaged for years in the process of deliberately deceiving the American public in order to continue killing both Indochinese and Americans to prove the correctness of their policy.

As of the middle of 1972, all of these moral men were still active in public life. McNamara—with a second five-year term—was presiding over the billions in the World Bank; Rusk was teaching history to unsuspecting young people at a Southern university; McGeorge Bundy was distributing Ford Foundation largesse as chairman of the board; brother William had been confirmed (by David Rockefeller) as editor of *Foreign Affairs*, a journal which seeks to present American foreign policy in its most benevolent light; Rostow was heavily engaged at the University of Texas in Austin, presenting to history as a benign democrat one of the grossest men ever to achieve the Presidency.

All the high-minded editorials about the inviolability of the First Amendment and the "vitality of the American form of government " (*New York Times* editorial, July 4, 1971) notwith-standing, the communications industry will have abdicated its responsibility completely unless it seeks an answer to the com-pelling question: How could these things be? If the industry does not stand united in an adversary role to government—the only proper stance for a free press in a democracy—there will be ever greater incursions on its freedoms and the freedoms of others. Ultimately the public may be left without a major defense of its interests against predatory government.

And a Berrigan will still be in jail.

Part Two

TURMOIL BELOW

CHAPTER V

THE STING
OF THE GADFLY

THE communications industry has always been hostile to criticism from outside the industry and almost entirely self-indulgent within. Until the 1960s, serious criticism, with some remarkable exceptions, was rare. The exceptions were blockbusters, but closed ranks within the industry managed to confine the damage to a few falling sticks of type.

Among the exceptions were Will Irwin's book *The Shame of American Newspapers* (1910) and Upton Sinclair's *The Brass Check* (1920), a bitter indictment of the press and particularly the Associated Press. There were George Seldes's books of the 1930s and 1940s, with bugle-call titles such as *You Can't Print That!*, *Can These Things Be!*, and *Let the People Know;* Harold Ickes's *The House of Lords* (1939), and George Marion's *Stop the Press!* (1953), which, more than its predecessors, placed the newspaper industry within the context of the system of American monopoly capital.There were, of course, many other books about the press, but they were for the most part only tangentially critical and defensive of prevalent practices. In these books the major villain was government.

The exclamation marks in the titles of several books may have stemmed from the authors' exasperation in their attempts to find publishers. *The Brass Check* was "published by the author" at Pasadena, California. George Marion's publisher was Fairplay in New York. That, of course, was George Marion himself. In 1953, the year of Senator Joe McCarthy's maximum influence, the only fair play a radical author could get was what he gave himself. Seldes, as a foreign correspondent of high standing, was published by the big houses (at least in the earlier days), but reviews of his books were harsh or nonexistent. His books may still be found, for a dollar or two, in secondhand bookshops, and they will prove historical eye-openers for a younger generation of readers.

Seldes's newsletter *In Fact*, published from 1940 to 1950, was a constant gadfly, placing in sharp focus (as Ralph Nader did for a later generation) the unsavory, unhealthy and unsafe practices of the tobacco, automotive and drug industries, for example, and the tenderly solicitous attitudes toward these industries by the press monopolies. In the field of foreign affairs particularly, *I. F. Stone's Weekly*, launched in 1952, was a brilliant successor to *In Fact*.

There must be a special place also for the late A. J. Liebling and his evilly cheerful essays in the *New Yorker* magazine during the 1940s and 1950s under the title "The Wayward Press," subsequently published in book form. They were a penetrating indictment of the press and its coverage of important news events, written with devastating wit and humor.

Seldes, Marion, Liebling and Stone were vigorous proponents of a union of working newspapermen and women, and all four were early members of the Newspaper Guild, founded in 1933. There were sound economic reasons for a union of editorial and commercial employees in those depression days. Payroll cuts and "payless paydays" were common, as were troglodyte publishers such as Lucius T. Russell, publisher of the *Newark Ledger*. Russell one day picked up a piece of chalk, drew a line through the middle of the *Ledger* newsroom, and said: "Everyone on *that* side of the line is fired." They were—and a few days later were rehired at lower pay.

No thoughtful editorial staff member rejected the economic reasons for establishing the Guild (although a minority balked at rubbing elbows in meeting halls with ordinary clerks). But some hoped for something broader than traditional unionism, especially those who had become disillusioned with their practical experiences of freedom of the press, as opposed to the theoretical concept of the First Amendment.

These experiences had persuaded many reporters and desk edi-

tors that the Newspaper Guild had a responsibility far beyond the
question of wages, hours and working conditions. Reporters knew
that many of their stories were distorted after leaving their typewriters. Wire-service copy was often marred by half-truths and
omissions. Some publishers and editors favored certain politicians
and advertisers in the news columns or, as on the Hearst Newspapers, had a "Shit List" to guarantee that the listees never
received a sanitary mention.

What was the responsibility of a newspaperman or woman?
The press, after all, was supposed to be the watchdog of the public
interest, and newspapers could not be published without the
acquiescence and cooperation of the working press. Such reflection, however, was not encouraged within the Guild. The officers
emphasized that the Guild was not an association of professional
journalists: it was an industrial union of editorial workers, clerks,
stenographers, maintenance men and advertising solicitors. It
would not be fair to those not directly concerned with gathering
and editing the news to involve them in questions about the content of newspapers. That was not the function of a union. Besides,
the question of ownership was clear: what appeared in a newspaper was the responsibility of the owner.

This fraternal repression of editorial dissent, superimposed upon
increasing disillusionment, had an ironic result. The Guild units
of the most reactionary publications (Hearst's *Journal-American*
in New York and Time Inc., for example) counted in their ranks
the highest percentage of radicals (the term then was "reds") in
the newspaper industry. Premature "underground" publications,
mostly mimeographed, began to appear. The one at the *New York
Times* was titled *New Times*. Some on the news staffs joined the
Communist party as an expression of their political and journalistic discontent. Others became increasingly frequent patrons of
a nearby barroom that was a virtual appendage of each newspaper.
There were mighty lions in those liquid lairs. How many publishers and editors were cruelly dissected in a splendid alcoholic
haze!

Other critics from outside the newspapers sought to inspect the
performance, content and responsibility of the press. The most
pertinent and comprehensive survey of the modern press was

presented in 1947 as the Hutchins Commission Report, officially, *A Free and Responsible Press: A General Report on Mass Communications: Newspapers, Radio, Motion Pictures, Magazines, and Books.* The report was published by the University of Chicago, of which Robert Maynard Hutchins then was chancellor. The commission, with Hutchins as director, was made up of university experts, lawyers and industrialists, none identified with the political left and none involved with the commercial media.

The commission concluded that, while the press had developed enormously as an instrument of mass communication, the proportion of people who could express their ideas and opinions through the press had decreased. Those in control had not provided a service adequate to the needs of society and had even engaged in practices which society condemned.

"One of the most effective ways of improving the press," the report said, "is blocked by the press itself: By a kind of unwritten law, the press ignores the errors and misrepresentations, the lies and scandals of which its members are guilty." Its most innovative and controversial suggestion for improving press performance and responsibility was the establishment of an independent agency to appraise and report annually on the performance of the press. It would be free of government control and would have no power except moral suasion "to educate the people as to the aspirations which they ought to have for the press" and which the press ought to have for the people.

Twenty-five years after the Hutchins report was published, no agency to evaluate and watch over the communications media (television was not a force in 1947) had been established. In the early 1960s local press councils, a mini-version of the Hutchins recommendation, comprising citizens from all areas of public life, were proposed. The procedure was for a local council to meet with the newspaper publisher and editor or television station operator to exchange views toward making the various media more responsive to the needs of the community. It was not until 1967, however, when the Lowell Mellett Foundation helped to finance experimental projects, that the idea was tested. Councils were set up in small cities in California, Oregon and Illinois. They reported mixed results. The main benefit was affording the community the means to confront the industry with its needs and grievances; but practical results depended upon the receptivity and cooperation of the media operators, and this was only spasmodically forthcoming. Some councils were disbanded after the Mellett funds ran out; others were continued with local funding.

The press council idea had much to commend it, and the reluctant cooperation of the great majority of media proprietors in the tested areas indicated that they feared not so much an encroachment on freedom of the press as a watchful eye on their license to do what they wished without concern for a public accounting. Further, as the complexion of the cities changed through the 1960s increasingly to brown and black, an equitable press council would have had to reflect this shifting color line. The communications industry, however, was not willing to put into effect the high-sounding principles about racial equality espoused on the editorial pages.

But the industry had a continuing, uneasy awareness of being watched, particularly after the Agnew explosions of 1969–70. Public-opinion polls projected a growing mistrust by the public of the media, and in 1969 the governing board of the American Society of Newspaper Editors held its annual meeting in London as a manifest of their concern about self-policing the communications industry. They engaged in a comprehensive study of the British Press Council, created in 1953 as a nationwide entity and credited—despite some severe criticism of its operations—with improving the standards of the British press.

The ASNE group was reluctant, however, to recommend establishment of an American counterpart, citing the infinitely greater size of the United States, differences in the judicial systems, concept of ethics and public attitudes. The board went so far as to propose an ASNE Grievance Committee "to receive complaints in substance about the performance of daily newspapers." But the complaints would be restricted to those by one newspaper organization against another.

Interestingly, at a session of the Association for Education in Journalism in August 1970, a proposal for an American press council similar to Great Britain's was made by Norman Isaacs, who had been president of the ASNE at the time of the London meeting.

Despite prevailing opposition, he said, "we may have the beginnings of such an institution within four or five years."

There were some within the industry, however, whose frustration would not tolerate the slower cadence of Isaacs's forecast. They began even before his prediction to form internal "press councils" without the participation of the owners of the media. In individual cities and geographically concentrated regions, they joined together to examine the performance of the media in their city or area, and their own role as participating performers. They were for the most part reporters, rewrite men and women, and broadcast technicians, young and fairly new to the industry. But they frequently enjoyed the sympathy and cooperation of their more experienced colleagues who shared their exasperation at not being able to achieve full and free expression in gathering, writing and publishing news and commentary.

There was a striking example of this disaffection in Chicago in the weeks following the Democratic National Convention in August 1968. The cause was the unconscionable police brutality against war protesters, young radical dissidents and even uninvolved onlookers in the streets of the city. Reporters and photographers, particularly from the Chicago media, were also clubbed and mauled by the police, and when they repaired to the anticipated safety of their own newsrooms, they suffered perhaps greater injuries to their morale. There, as one reporter said, "our own editors told us that we didn't see what we really saw under those blue helmets." On-the-scene reports were ignored, copy was altered, news pictures were discarded and the editors made it clear that their allegiance was not to their beaten staff, but to the man who had given orders for the beatings—Chicago's Mayor Richard J. Daley.

Out of this editorial outrage arose a movement for redress of grievances, not only against the mayor and the police, but against their own bosses, editors as well as publishers. That's how the *Chicago Journalism Review* was born.

The first issue was published in October 1968 under the auspices of a new organization, the Association of Working Press. And though the spark, of course, was the aftermath of the convention, resentments in other areas were deep and of long standing. In the prologue to its first issue, the editors of *CJR* wrote:

When the cameras and the conventioneers went home, the local media returned to the fold. Many of us, reporters in Chicago, could only watch what happened in silent frustration. Mayor Daley was permitted to take over the media. [His] contempt for the media was no longer veiled. . . . Daley openly insulted newsmen, charged they were dupes, and assailed the integrity of the Chicago media. And as he threw verbal excrement in the faces of Chicago journalists, we took it like slaves.

But the slaves finally revolted, and the Association of Working Press opened its doors to reporters, photographers, rewrite men and women, news editors and broadcasters in the Chicago area. Its principal objectives were:

1. Ensure the rights of reporters and photographers to cover important events without interference from the police department or any other governmental agency.

2. Increase the representation of Negroes and other minority groups of the Chicago news media to a level proportionate to their representation in the population of the city.

3. Improve professional standards of fairness and accuracy in the media, and publicly condemn obvious breaches of journalistic ethics.

4. Contribute to the continuing education of the press corps through seminars, lectures and publications.

There were no bylines in the first six-page issue of *CJR*. Its editors feared reprisals from the newspapers, but there were none, and bylines appeared. The three dominant names in the early issues were Henry de Zutter, education reporter of the *Chicago Daily News;* Christopher Chandler, urban affairs specialist of *Chicago's American* (later transformed into *Chicago Today,* an evening newspaper owned by the *Chicago Tribune*); and Ron Dorfman, also of *Chicago Today,* who resigned to work full-time with *CJR.* De Zutter and Chandler later left to publish a new Chicago magazine. Dorfman remained, and his innovative mind and spirit have made a distinct imprint on *CJR.*

The *Chicago Journalism Review* in 1972 was a neat, professionally prepared magazine, with articles by some of the best-known names in Chicago journalism. Its coverage was wide-ranging: exposés about suppression of news of police brutality, and about kindly treatment of corporate industry in the business pages of the press; slipshod reporting about *Rights in Conflict*, the Walker report on violence in Chicago, and blind spots in the report itself; and surveys of the coverage of racial news and employment of minority people in the Chicago media. Two of the more notable articles were a detailed description of the workings of the Chicago Police Red Squad, and a documented recapitulation (an entire issue) of the police murder of black militant Fred Hampton on December 4, 1969, proving beyond doubt that the murder had been unprovoked and showing further how the *Chicago Tribune* had striven to present a false picture of the murder and its aftermath.

In the first months of *CJR*, Chicago's newspapers maintained an uncomfortable silence about it, but their editors gave their views freely to interviewers—a mixture of hostility, sufferance and either feigned or resigned acceptance. Clayton Kirkpatrick, editor of the *Chicago Tribune* (which late in 1971 received an unaccustomed accolade from *CJR* for its new liveliness and efforts toward fairness), said at first that he was reluctant to concede that *CJR* was necessary "for reporters as a way to bring their criticism to editors' attention." Later, however, he declared it to be a "useful publication [which] stimulates an interest in professional qualities." Neither he nor his colleagues on the other Chicago dailies would concede that *CJR* had moved them to change their ways. There was a patronizing quality to the editors' comments, and an understandable distaste for having their internal wash spread out for inspection on the banks of the Chicago River. To cover their embarrassment, they criticized *CJR* for becoming "too involved in the inner workings of the press" (Maxwell McCrohan, managing editor of *Chicago Today*) or for "picayune carping" (Daryle Feldmeir of the *Chicago Daily News*). All agreed with Feldmeir that a reporter "ought to air gripes and bitches" within his own organization.

But that, as Ron Dorfman noted, was precisely why *CJR* had been founded—because the staffs got nowhere with their internal bitching, and *CJR* "focused previously diffused hostilities of working stiffs for management into more rational channels."

In mid-1972 the *Chicago Journalism Review*'s circulation was about 8,000, with a readership spread from Hawaii to Afghanistan (and one in Fiji, according to Dorfman), but with about 75 percent in the Chicago area. Dorfman said the general reaction among media managements was "irritation and annoyance; but some changes have been made." He cited these examples:

> The Field Newspapers [*Daily News* and *Sun-Times*] reinstituted coverage of the Criminal Courts Building after we criticized them for not having any; United Press International sent a senior editor to do a takeout on Cairo [deep-going racial unrest in that Illinois city] after we criticized their stringer's coverage (the senior editor did not do much better); coverage of street gangs by all media improved considerably after we published lists of sources with phone numbers; the Field papers adopted a policy against gratuities after we published a story noting Christmas-gift hauls by City Hall reporters.

Dorfman felt also that *CJR* had helped to make the media somewhat more responsive to public needs. He attributed this in part to what A. J. Liebling called the "country club syndrome." Many *CJR* readers, said Dorfman, were influential persons with whom the "news brass socialize; and when they have to explain themselves at cocktail parties (the country clubs, remember, have been infected with radical chic), it is terribly embarrassing." As for the working press itself, Dorfman said:

> They can't be apathetic if the criticism is on the mark. The first copies of *CJR* to arrive in an office are eagerly scrambled for and read thoroughly (for example, the issue with the report about sportswriters on the take from the racetracks). . . . The local press corps has responded with determination to improve media performance. Nearly 200 journalists have contributed articles and art work to *CJR*.

Chicago is an unusual city for journalism: it still has four daily newspapers, although they are under two ownerships—The Chicago Tribune Company and the Field Enterprises. No other city can make that claim—not even New York (three), Philadelphia (three) or Los Angeles (two). The decline in the number of big-city newspapers has been caused by three factors: the growth of television as a news source; the movement of people (mainly white and middle class) out of the inner cities, leading to the rise of prosperous and sophisticated suburban dailies; and handsome profits accruing from the sale of newspapers to the powerful conglomerates such as Newhouse, Thomson, Perry and Copley. The trend toward unimaginative and cautious chain journalism has disturbed and frustrated young journalists coming into the industry and has led in turn to a proliferation of journalism reviews. By mid-1972 there were reviews in 12 cities: Honolulu, Long Beach, (covering Southern California), Atlanta (an experimental supplement to the *Columbia Journalism Review*), Denver, Holyoke (Massachusetts—covering the Connecticut Valley), St. Louis, Cleveland, Philadelphia, Providence, Chicago, Milwaukee and finally, after several abortive attempts, New York City. There were others, such as the *Central Standard Times* of Wichita, dealing frequently with the press but falling primarily into the category of "alternative" publications. The reviews were concerned with more than newspapers: since radio and television news had become the primary source of information in most areas of the country, the reviews concentrated also on broadcast journalism.

Some media people began to regard the new phenomenon as a "journalism review movement," but there was actually little collaboration among the publications. Their common bond was that all were produced by working media staffs, seeking in constructive fashion to bring about improvements and reforms in the established media. Some were one-man operations (*Point of View* in Cleveland); some were financed in part by foundation funds; and at least one (*Review of Southern California Journalism*) was published under the auspices of a professional journalism organization, Sigma Delta Chi. Most had a small magazine ($8\frac{1}{2} \times 11$) or newsletter format, but four (St. Louis, Connecticut Valley, Providence and New York) were tabloid size, ranging from eight to 20 pages. Most were published biweekly, monthly or quarterly. A few appeared only when money became available. Only one (Cleveland's *Point of View*) could truly be considered radical in the political sense, although the *Chicago Journalism Review* on occasion has fitted the description. The single word characterizing the general outlook of all the reviews was "muckraking."

One other common characteristic of the reviews was the uncommon manner in which they received the silent treatment (in print or on the air) from the media in their areas. But if they were not acknowledged by the target newspapers, their rise was carefully charted in the established trade and professional publications of journalism, such as the *Columbia Journalism Review*, *Quill* (Sigma Delta Chi), *Editor & Publisher*, the *ASNE Bulletin*, and in the press sections of *Time* and *Newsweek*. Many articles about the reviews showed grudging admiration but criticized them for being unprofessional and unattractive. To a degree the criticism was warranted, and it emphasized the narrow training in the schools of journalism and in the media also.

What the young journalists lack in production skills, however, is compensated for by their sharp barbs aimed at the basic fault of the media—unwillingness to come to grips with the gigantic problems of the cities and their minority peoples, and to dig out the root causes of these problems. The reasons for the reluctance had become clear to the young journalists: the interweaving interests—financial and social—between the owners of the media and the dominant industrial and political figures. Now almost for the first time this interlocking directorate was being exposed on the local level by working media people in a position to know where the bodies were hidden, and why they were not being permitted to drag them out for public autopsy.

A case in point was the exposure by the *Philadelphia Journalism Review* of a crass instance of censorship by *Philadelphia* magazine. The editor of *Philadelphia* had refused to publish an assigned article about Police Commissioner Frank Rizzo, a candidate in the mayoralty election, in which he was the victor. The article was unflattering. Following the election, the editor of *Philadelphia* accepted an important post in the Rizzo administration.

Unlike the *Chicago Journalism Review*, some of the newer reviews were months in the planning stage. One was the *St. Louis Journalism Review* in a city with two newspapers—the reactionary *Globe-Democrat* and the prestigious *Post-Dispatch*, still owned by the Pulitzer family, but exhibiting a faint but steady erosion of its courageously independent positions on state and national affairs. Founded in October 1970, two years later the St. Louis review had an editorial board of 20, a circulation of 4,000 and a financially stable sponsor, FOCUS/Midwest Publishing

Company, publishers of the magazine *FOCUS/Midwest*. *FOCUS/ Midwest*, according to editor Charles L. Klotzer, was a "deficit operation," but had "branched out" into computer typesetting. This paid for all deficits while keeping both *FOCUS/Midwest* and the *St. Louis Journalism Review* afloat.

The St. Louis review from the outset has taken a careful look at St. Louis media performance in major news events—election coverage, racial issues in a city with an almost 50 percent black population, the Pentagon Papers and the Attica prison massacre. Klotzer said that there had been "no public recognition of the review's existence except for one mention in the last paragraph of a *Post-Dispatch* article covering a speech I made about the review to the local Sigma Delta Chi chapter. Of course, privately there is a considerable amount of discussion." Response at the managerial level on the *Post-Dispatch* has been noticeable in the sense that the managers knew that someone finally was looking over their shoulder. That kind of peering, however, produced only overt hostility at the *Globe-Democrat*. Staff response at both papers has ranged from "enthusiastic approval" to "dim awareness," according to Klotzer.

The *St. Louis Journalism Review* managed to focus on the local media situation without parochialism. For example, when it examined how the St. Louis media covered the Pentagon Papers crisis, the local coverage was related to the national coverage. Again, a first-rate survey of black and minority hiring in the St. Louis media was set against the national average.

More localized, perhaps, because of its geographic separation from the mainland, the *Hawaii Journalism Review* sought without measurable success to open traditionally closed doors in what its editors call the "plantation's government and business preserves." After a year of publication, its circulation was a select 800 among legislators, councilmen, journalists and university people.

"Hawaii is hard to ruffle," said Bob Jones of the editorial board. "Editors sometimes take issue with our observations [for example, that the dining-out column of the *Honolulu Advertiser* was palpably advertising space without being so labeled], or erroneously feel that we have not done an adequate reporting job. We do not necessarily run all points of view in a single issue (we list ourselves in the mast as a journal of opinion and observation), but we do run rebuttals in the following issue. We try to stay out of petty newsroom administrative beefs and concentrate on specific stories and malpractices in journalism." The impact of the Hawaii review, Jones felt, had been minimal. "Many of the matters we have tackled still exist," he said. "Economics wins out over criticism."

In Denver *The Unsatisfied Man* took its name from a comment by Frederick G. Bonfils, founder of the *Denver Post:* "There is no hope for the satisfied man." It was launched, with some foundation help, by the Colorado Media Project, comprising more than 60 reporters, editors and broadcasters. Low-keyed and with a sense of humor, it is doing a thorough job of constructive criticism of Colorado's media, including coverage of the "atomic beat," Washington reporting by the Colorado media, payola in the city rooms and pressure tactics by television stations to obtain license renewals from the Federal Communications Commission. In July 1971 *Cervi's Rocky Mountain Journal* published an unsigned critique of *The Unsatisfied Man* describing it as "little more than the creation of a new syndrome: narcissistic-schizophrenic with overtones of paranoia." The editors of *TUM* reprinted the article in full in the August issue and tentatively identified the author. In unnarcissistic fashion, it opened its pages also to other reporters who seemed eager to defend the managements of the Denver media for which they work—an obvious demonstration of the need for a journalism review in Denver.

The *Philadelphia Journalism Review* was organized by six members of the editorial staff of the *Philadelphia Inquirer,* but its sponsorship rapidly expanded to staff members of the *Bulletin,* the *News,* the wire services and broadcasting. Its contents expanded similarly from a confining complaint sheet to a thoroughly professional forum for questions of concern to media staffs —advocacy *vs.* objectivity in the news, efforts to obtain a greater voice in policy-making decisions and the problems of white journalists covering racial news. In early 1972 it was distributing about 3,000 copies in the Philadelphia-Camden region.

In Long Beach the *Review of Southern California Journalism,* a quarterly, reflected in its early issues its academic origins—the California State College chapter of Sigma Delta Chi. It seemed somewhat distant from the world of commercial journalism, but in successive issues it moved eagerly into that world with articles by media people, interspersed with pertinent comment from teachers and students of journalism. An example of this positive mixture was the Fall 1971 issue with an article by Steve Roberts, *New York Times* correspondent in Los Angeles, titled "Why Journalists Are Tools of the Establishment" (the journalists got off too lightly); a review of an excellent (but ignored) book critical of the media, *Don't Blame the People,* by Robert Cirino, and a survey of how the press treated the Pentagon Papers, both in Southern California and nationally.

In New England there were two journalism reviews—*Thorn,* published by the Connecticut Valley Media Review, covering Western Massachusetts and Vermont, and the *Journalists' Newsletter* of Providence. Both were being published on an irregular basis and showed scars of financial stress. But they were earnest, searching and forthright in their comments about the media and, somewhat self-consciously, their own role as journalists. They seemed content to confine their criticism to their own locales, and since both regions were heavily populated and had a high concentration of universities, there was much ground to cover. Their targets were well selected, but their fire was, at least in the early issues, scattershot.

New York City is the publishing center of the nation, the headquarters of the broadcast networks and the home base for much of the radical movement. Yet it proved more difficult to organize and launch a persevering journalism review in New York than elsewhere in the country. One major reason may be the attitude of élitist professionalism afflicting a large part of the media staffs. This attitude stems in part from conditioning in the journalism schools, where New York is projected as the "Big Apple," the zenith of media achievement. And once New York is achieved, new conditioning is administered to develop the fantasy that a New York newspaper or broadcast journalist is a cut above out-of-town journalists, as they are designated.

However miserable the New York journalist—bored, censored, frustrated by trivial assignments—he must maintain the Potemkin Village facade to the public view. In these circumstances, involvement in a journalism review that would reveal the media as something less than a public trust would tarnish the illusion. It would also prove an obstacle to continued acceptance in the élite milieu of the media, where a staff writer can briefly rub ecstatic elbows with an editor or publisher at the most desirable bars. Vanity, avarice and envy are the holy trinity of most media people on the make in New York. And even if the Big Apple has demonstrable worm holes, the credo of the trinity makes a bite mandatory.

In 1970 at least two ventures into critical journalism were undertaken in New York for brief periods. They were a publication with the Jell-O-like title *Pac-O-Lies*, published by a group of radical journalists under the aegis of the New York Media Project; and *Inside Media*, published by Media Mobilization, a not so radical but equally disenchanted group based to a large extent in the broadcast media. *Pac-O-Lies* survived for four issues, much of its content sharp and revelatory, in the soundest muckraking tradition, but suffering, as the radical movement was, from some overblown rhetoric and a lack of clear direction. Its language was alternately belligerent and defensive. It vacillated between what should have been its major function—exposition of the sins of the media—and its predilection to espousal of radical-movement ideas.

Inside Media approached its task with more sobriety and with more insight. Its first (and unfortunately its last) issue had excellent material on the subpena campaign against the media by Attorney General Mitchell, the issues involved in WPIX-TV's battle to obtain a license renewal from the FCC, police agents infiltrating the media and the women's struggle for equality at the newsmagazines.

A third publication of 1970 was the *AP Review*, published by employees of the Associated Press, a short-lived goldmine of source material for the sins of commission and omission in the giant wire service. The first issue had, among other things, an intra-organizational exchange showing how an article by Peter Arnett, Pulitzer prize reporter for the AP in Vietnam, had been censored. Published also in *AP Review* was a memo from New York headquarters with instructions to reporters in the field to ignore situations which might show the United States fighting forces in a poor light. The article was widely (and almost exclusively) reported in the radical press. The *AP Review* never published a second issue.

It was not until the fall of 1971 that New York finally acquired a journalism review giving evidence of permanence. It was founded by Richard Pollak, a former editor of the press section of *Newsweek,* and William Woodward, a reporter for the *New York Post,* who resigned to undertake the publication. It was called (*More*), the notation that reporters and rewrite men and women place at the bottom of each page of copy to indicate there is more to come.

(*More*) was the result of several months of discussion with people highly placed in the media—some of the meetings were held in the bastion of the enemy, the private dining rooms of the Harvard Club in Manhattan. It was clear from the start that the publishers of (*More*) had made a careful study of other journalism reviews and applied their conclusions to the psychology and makeup of the media and their staffs in the Big Apple. "This is where the targets are," said Pollak. "We want to scrutinize the New York press in the same tough-minded way that the press ought to be covering the rest of the world."

An editorial in the pilot issue (June 1971) asked for a "commonsense understanding by publishers that journalists ought to be free to write about their profession without jeopardizing their jobs." For their part, the editors of (*More*) established an "ironclad policy" never to commission or publish articles by journalists about their own organizations. The pilot issue seemed more interested in big-name bylines than tough-minded scrutiny (two Pulitzer prizewinners and a former White House press secretary, none of them reaching much below the surface in their commentary), but the names and the national range of coverage won for (*More*) a spate of publicity that paved the way for a successful launching in September 1971.

The shakedown voyages of the first months seem to have proved the vessel seaworthy. While prominent names persisted (nothing wrong with that if the content matches the reputation), there was added to the publication an imaginative probing in vulnerable areas of the industry. The result was a series of excellent investigative articles about how the media operate—woefully deficient hiring policies for blacks and Puerto Ricans at the *New York Post;* dull and deficient coverage of business news at the *New York Times;* and the beginnings of a steady look at the television empire in New York.

By early 1972 (*More*) had 5,000 paid subscriptions nationwide, and was selling 5,000 more on newsstands in New York, Washington, D.C., Boston and Berkeley. As it began to find its targets, there was a concomitant decline in publicity and a rise in protests from the targets and their friends. (*More*) took advertising— a departure for journalism reviews and inevitably a test of its willingness to withstand the temptations of financial success as against editorial integrity.

In the summer of 1972 new reviews were established in the San Francisco Bay area, Baltimore and Minneapolis-St. Paul.

Thus from Hawaii to California to Denver to Providence the spunky watchdog patrol was keeping an eye on the larger watchdog and the way Big Brother was watching the world. Management was publicly resigned and privately hostile, hoping that the barking at its ankles would cease and the barkers vanish. Staff reaction was mixed—some delighted that the reviews were in business, others wary and still others angry at the interlopers for disturbing cozy arrangements under which certain news-staff favorites identified with management in return for the illusion of power and influence.

There were sporadic stories about the reviews in the press and in the magazines (broadcast journalism was almost completely silent), but few attempts to analyze the phenomenon of their appearance. One effort appeared in September 1971, in the consciously bland Communications section of the *Saturday Review* (since discarded by the new owners). The author was Norman Hill, a freelance writer and public-relations man whose views about the reviews were neither bland nor bright. He compared them unfavorably with the "comparatively quiet school-sponsored reviews that stubbornly adhere to an almost quaint dedication to objectivity, accurate language, and education for the profession."

Hill complained that the reviews regarded the media as "targets" rather than "news sources," an odd complaint since the reviews were concentrating on media inaccuracies and could hardly be expected to use media material as a news source. For individual reviews, Hill had harsh judgments:

Chicago Journalism Review: "A strident, controversial compendium of political sniping, gutter language, rasping hostility toward 'the boss,' seamy exposés, and, occasionally, incisive reports."

Review of Southern California Journalism: "A parochial and naïve melange of sophomoric efforts by teachers and students garnished with pornographic photographs (to demonstrate press freedom), insignificant campus issues, and top-of-the-head juvenalia."

Philadelphia Journalism Review: "Simply rotten."

The only kind word was for Denver's *The Unsatisfied Man,* but even there Hill sensed a "drying up of editorial ideas." On the whole, he found many signs that "the local journalism review is just a passing fad, a safety valve for one college generation afflicted with extraordinary irritability and impatience, and an ideological vogue."

Hill's report suffered from a curious type of distemper, a rare form found only among the watchers of the watchdog's watchers. It is a disease aggravated by addiction to strong and colorful adjectives which can become pernicious. Hill's view in short was myopic and prejudiced, unscholarly and ill informed.

The journalism reviews are not an unnatural phenomenon: they mark the rise of an intelligent and searching generation of journalists who know that something is terribly wrong in their profession. Seeking to set standards and ideals which were not encouraged by the media managers, they are attempting to find answers themselves and are reaching out for public support. Far from rejecting as "quaint" the principles of objectivity (they would call it fairness), accuracy and education, they are trying in all three areas to improve the publications for which they work: to make objectivity mean the most probing kind of journalism, not a device to maintain the status quo; to persuade both their colleagues and the public that the only natural role of the communications media is an adversary one to government and established power.

In all fairness, it is still too early to assess accurately the quality and the promise of most of the journalism reviews, except perhaps of a four-year veteran such as the *Chicago Journalism*

Review. The most hopeful fact about them is that they existed—lively, pertinent, irreverent, making mistakes and sometimes giving vent to a personal spleen, but on the whole positive and constructive. For their minor transgressions they are denounced from the loftiest pulpits of journalism by preachers whose righteousness shrouds hypocrisies monumental enough to curl the whiskers of Horace Greeley.

There is, unfortunately, no journalism-review "movement." Journalists are still too individualistic for that. Nor is there a coherent political or social strain among the editors and publishers of the reviews: the failure of the radical movement to develop a cohesive philosophy of its own has left its negative mark on the new generation of journalists. Ambivalence is apparent in some of the publications, as it is in the discontented newsrooms. It has never been easy for an American journalist to abjure even the superficial camaraderie of a professional setting—as the media workshops tend to be—and take a dissenting stand apart from his fellows.

It may be that the reviews will not become permanent because some of their organizers actually regard them as temporary—and this in itself sets limits to their effectiveness. With few exceptions, the reviews are reformist, not radical. All of those involved see with varying degrees of clarity the faults and evils of the media; but for most of them the task, as they see it, is to force changes within the media to make them more honest and serviceable, and therefore less degrading, places to work. To be sure, they probably see themselves as rebels, but rebels within the cause—the cause being the establishment of journalism itself. And, like many rebels of the past, they are subject to the blandishments of the establishment, which could turn them—sometimes without their realizing it—into effective tools of the establishment, with sufficient freedom of speech and movement to give them the illusion of independence. At that point, some might declare the battle won and the need for the gadfly no longer valid.

There are some exceptions. One is Roldo Bartimole, editor and publisher of Cleveland's journalism review—*Point of View.* As the founder of the oldest of the modern journalism reviews—preceding even the *Chicago Journalism Review*—Bartimole's story is instructive. It will be discussed in the following chapter.

CHAPTER VI

ONE MAN

THE Cleveland journalism review, *Point of View*, was started in June 1968 as a one-man operation by Roldo Bartimole. It is still (1972) being published as a one-man operation and is perhaps the sharpest critique of the media—and the city it serves—being published anywhere. This, then, is the anatomy of a David armed with only a verbal slingshot pitted against the industrial Goliath of northern Ohio.

Bartimole, now in his middle thirties, came to Cleveland from Bridgeport, Connecticut, where his father was an Italian butcher, by way of Boston, where he went to Northeastern University on a GI Bill study grant. While in Boston, he worked for a small community daily and got his first taste of investigatory journalism writing a series on slum housing. It was his introduction to a world of which he was only dimly aware.

In Cleveland he worked for the *Plain Dealer*, the only morning daily, a member of the S. I. Newhouse chain, with a circulation of 400,000. He had little respect for the *Plain Dealer* and shifted over to the Cleveland bureau of the *Wall Street Journal* (for which he still retains some respect). He resigned from the *Journal* in the spring of 1968 to begin *Point of View*. He sent out the first issue in June with a broadsheet appeal for readers in which he wrote:

> If you believe as I do, that Cleveland's newspapers are beyond reha-
> bilitation . . . that they are, if anything, a means of advertising canned
> salmon and bras—hardly of much social utility since any idiot knows

you go to a supermarket for one and a department store for the other
. . . that another, more radical perspective is needed to give a view
that newspapers and television wouldn't if they could, then *Point of
View* may be of some value.

Bartimole obviously believed he had something of value to
say, so he set up shop in the basement of his home, went to work
on a borrowed electric typewriter and became the scourge of
Cleveland's press, TV and radio, public officials, and business and
financial powers. In his one-man crusade his method of work and
his outlook resemble I. F. Stone's. His forthright opinions are supported by diligent research, study of official reports (sometimes
confidential and leaked to him) and attendance at meetings. His
facts go unchallenged, but not his person: a utility company,
smarting under a *Point of View* attack, set about to investigate
his background, rather in the same fashion that General Motors
looked into Ralph Nader's. Bartimole liked that—it proved he was
getting through. His admiration for Nader is clear. He says:

> Most newspapers allow for no creativity. Pick up any paper on a
> Monday morning and you see how many people were killed in auto
> crashes. To me there isn't even any story there. There would have been
> a story if some newspapers had done what Ralph Nader did with the
> auto companies—what should be a journalist's job.

"It's impossible to cover anything 'objectively,'" Bartimole
says. "The press uses this as a crutch and ends up telling one side
of the story. What newspapers call 'community responsibility'
means 'hide everything from the public that might bother them.'"
His approach is to hide nothing. He published the salaries, hold-
ings and directorships of Cleveland's corporation leaders, went
after the police and even devoted an issue to the City Club
Forum, Cleveland's "citadel of free speech," castigating it for in-
viting only "safe speakers." That got him an invitation to speak.
A constant target is the United Appeal drive, which he regards as
"extortion to get the poor people to pay the cost of charity."

Point of View's subscription list was 900 at the turn of 1972,
but its readership was much larger. In this era of facsimile (*Point
of View*'s size is 7 × 10), one law firm Xeroxes 40 copies regularly,
and the *Plain Dealer* library has a standing order for ten Xeroxes.

Circulation is mostly in the Cleveland area, but it reaches into other Ohio cities, and 100 copies go out of state. Most Cleveland area readers are sympathetic liberals, with a surprising number of antiestablishment conservatives, lawyers, politicians, businessmen and community organizers.

An issue about a specific event—for example, the Glenville shootout between police and black militants in which seven blacks and three police were killed—gets much wider distribution. The Cleveland newspapers and radio and television stations had, without adequate inquiry, described the incident as an "ambush" by blacks of the police. *Point of View* presented contrary evidence. With the help of special groups, 15,000 copies were produced and distributed and were used in meetings organized in the city and the suburbs to counter what was being published and broadcast. Eventually, and probably as a direct result of the questions raised in *Point of View*, the American Civil Liberties Union was given a half-hour television show to challenge the official version.

With few exceptions, the Cleveland media have sought to ignore *Point of View*. A suburban newspaper published a profile of Bartimole, and the *Cleveland Press* (Scripps-Howard evening paper, circulation about 400,000) carried a feature story on Thanksgiving Day 1970. Bartimole's name was misspelled in the headline.

He has been an occasional guest on a radio talk show and was invited to do paid commercial television commentaries on WKYC-TV, owned by the National Broadcasting Company, but was fired between the first taping and the first scheduled broadcast. Word had got to NBC who Bartimole was. The station's editors were embarrassed. "Be kind to the editorial department," they said to Bartimole. "We had nothing to do with that." Bartimole's response: "What a weird but apparently true statement for an editor to make about an editorial decision."

From May to October 1971 Bartimole wrote a column about the media for the *Call & Post*, Cleveland's black weekly (circulation 30,000). The column scheduled for the issue of October 2 urged wage earners not to contribute to the United Torch campaign, which Bartimole had denounced as a tax dodge for the rich that failed utterly to solve the problems of the poor. William

O. Walker, the *Call & Post* publisher, vetoed the column on the ground that the newspaper intended to support the Torch campaign. Bartimole, by way of compromise, proposed that Walker agree to publish the column and repudiate it editorially, if he so wished, in the same issue. Walker rejected the proposal, and Bartimole stopped writing for him.

Up to that point there had been no censorship of the column, although other entries had been equally harsh. Bartimole knew that there had been attempts "downtown" to persuade Walker to drop the column, but the publisher had stood his ground. Of his departure from the *Call & Post* Bartimole said:

> Although I enjoyed writing the column and felt it an important opportunity to reach many thousands of people I would not otherwise communicate with, I also felt the principle of free expression could not be sacrificed. I regret losing a vehicle that has proven to be an effective means of reaching the black community.

The question involved in Bartimole's decision was a difficult one. Should a crusader with an outlet like the *Call & Post* give it up on the basis of one episode? Would it not have been wiser to accede to the publisher in this case in order to continue the crusade on other matters? Perhaps. But any yielding to censorship sets a precedent for the future. The responsibility, in the last analysis, rested not with Bartimole, who was defending the right of free expression, but with the publisher, who was denying it, even on the mistaken assumption that he was acting on behalf of poor black people who might share in the proceeds of the United Torch funds. If Bartimole had yielded to pragmatism, it would have been a denial of his basic principle of freedom of expression.

Bartimole, however, maintained another outlet for his criticism of the media—a column with the unwieldy title "Mediaocrity," published in the Cleveland underground paper *Great Swamp Erie da da Boom*. He also had a *Point of View* commentary of the air each week for Cleveland's WNCR, an FM rock-music station directed toward young people.

It is the published *Point of View*, however, which draws most of the howls from Cleveland's business and social élite and among those whom Bartimole calls their handmaidens in the media. The ERCA story is a cameo of how Bartimole operates.

ERCA stands for Educational and Research Council of America. Bartimole has described it as a "tool of industry and foundation élites pouring racist and ring-wing propaganda into public-school textbooks under the guise of a legitimate education research organization." The *Encyclopaedia Britannica* has validated Bartimole's characterization of ERCA as racist by refusing to publish its social studies textbooks as offensive to minorities.

In the fall of 1969 the *Plain Dealer* published a seven-part series on ERCA which won for it the 1969 Cleveland Press Club award for investigative reporting. But something was missing: the eighth and final part of the series was not published in the *Plain Dealer*. The final installment, as one of the reporters explained in a note to his city editor, concerned "the interlocking directorships between ERCA and the [Cleveland] foundations, which have put about $3 million into the council. There are eight or nine cases of trustees holding dual positions—a rather clear-cut case of self-dealing."

Editor and publisher Tom Vail returned the note with key sentences underlined and the comment: "What's wrong with that?" Yet despite Vail's dismissal of any possible impropriety, the article was not published. That is, not in the *Plain Dealer*. It was published in full in *Point of View*, with the reporter's note and Vail's comment, and one from Bartimole reading:

> This suppressed story panicked Tom Vail and his editors. For it shows how the élites finance their little conspiracy with tax-free foundation funds. ERCA corporate conspirators read like a Cleveland Who's Who. When it became apparent that the élites were perpetrators, Vail chose again Freedom to Repress. . . . Vail is too dangerous to be allowed to decide what Clevelanders will or will not read.

This exposé was followed a few days later in *Point of View* by a devastating eight-page survey of television news broadcasts in Cleveland which opened in this fashion:

> TV JOURNALISM—AIR-WAVE POLLUTION. The state of journalism in Cleveland is at such a low level that one can best describe

the reporting here as the production of poor fiction. Nowhere is the World of Make Believe more evident than on the television screen at news time.

The survey listed the owners and operators of the stations (Storer and Kaiser for the other two main television outlets) and their audience size and news sources; detailed the interlocking network of newspaper-television control of news outlets in northern Ohio; and laid out a pattern of denial of access to welfare, peace and minority organizations.

The number of leaks to *Point of View* from within newspaper staffs and television units is an indicator of the dissatisfaction among the working press of Cleveland. Those leaks permitted Bartimole to reveal the suppression of the ERCA story, as well as the ghoulish practice at the *Plain Dealer* and *Press* of calling families of war dead to solicit "In Memoriam" ads for special Memorial Day sections. The *Press* supplement, Bartimole noted, "informed readers that the war in Southeast Asia had claimed the lives of 548 men from the Cleveland area and they have left 108 widows and 74 children. It ought to be good for future business."

The Memorial Day 1970 supplement in the *Press* ran to 20 tabloid pages, supplemented by bulk mini-ads from funeral homes, beauty salons, restaurants, car dealers and a few politicians, apparently in search of graveyard votes. And for that cash-filled future based on Southeast Asian prospects, there was a house advertisement: "Keeping alive the memory of departed loved ones is the greatest tribute that can be paid them. This can be tastefully and effectively accomplished by placing an 'In Memoriam' notice on anniversaries and special days in the *Cleveland Press* . . . Call Miss Bond . . ."

Mainly, however, *Point of View* keeps watch on the living—and it is impartial with its brickbats. It suggests that seemingly civic-minded speeches by the city's "élite" condemning prejudice against blacks by ethnic groups are not really a call for racial harmony, but rather an attempt to pit one group against another. It has also published detailed stories about backstairs shenanigans to buttress its contention that the business interests of Cleveland were quite pleased with the administration of Mayor Carl B.

Stokes. Stokes himself was roasted for his unwillingness to depart from traditional politics to effect basic changes in the life of the black and poor neighborhoods.

Does Bartimole feel his efforts have had much leverage in changing Cleveland's news media? His response is mildly heartening:

> Possibly only on specific stories. For example, "exposé" articles on a black community organization which receives federal funds recently in the *Plain Dealer* were not given the usual big front-page play, as has been the practice. *PoV* has been directly critical of similar past "exposés." Also, I think that in some respects specific reporters, because of articles appearing in *PoV*, have been able to "sell" their editors on stories because they *might* appear in *PoV*. I would hope also that reporters are having some leverage upon editors because of the type of material printed in *PoV*. For example, continuing criticism of certain leaders, particularly private businessmen, has made them appear a little less sanctified and therefore open to criticism because of *PoV*.

On the other hand, reproduction in *Point of View* of copy edited out of *Plain Dealer* stories and of editors' private memos spread suspicion in the newsrooms, even a kind of paranoia, and increased the hostility of those who already felt unkindly toward Bartimole. Reporters sympathetic to *Point of View* became subject to managerial pressures, and unoffending personnel were blamed for what the management termed "security leaks." Here the old clubhouse rules went into effect: a newsroom takes on the guise of a governmental agency and the standard of "loyalty to the team" is raised above the cluttered desks. Meanwhile, at lunch the editors share confidential information with the vice-president of the bank and the chairman of the board of the steel company.

At times, however, the vice-president and the chairman of the board do speak *their* piece to the editors, because of something that has appeared in *Point of View*—and if it is not their ox that is being gored. How come Bartimole printed this stuff about so-and-so, they will ask, when it didn't appear in your paper? The media respond to this kind of pressure with far greater alacrity than to pressure from lesser mortals. The *Press* has even credited *Point of View* with having been the first to publish certain stories, and

Point of View items have been used with credit by gossip and tele-vision columnists. More frequently, both the *Press* and the *Plain Dealer* will follow up *Point of View* items without reference to where the information first appeared. A few examples:

> Cleveland business leaders last summer "bought peace" . . . by paying some black activists about $40,000 in a 10-week period to do what they had decided to do already—keep it cool . . . Ralph Besse headed it up.
> —*Point of View*, June 26, 1968

> . . . last summer when $41,000 reportedly was raised in the business community for a Peace in Cleveland project. . . . Ralph Besse, Illumi-nating Company board chairman, headed the fund raising, according to reports. Today he said he had no comment on it.
> —*Cleveland Press*, July 26, 1968

> Consider the funding of a public relations man for Mayor Carl B. Stokes. Now it wouldn't be proper for a foundation to give funds to a private business. So the Greater Cleveland Associated Foundation, in renewing a grant that ends up subsidizing Bill Silverman as image maker for Stokes, actually makes the grant, more than $70,000 this year, to Government Research Institute, another big business tool.
> —*Point of View*, May 6, 1969

> City Council President James V. Stanton has asked for a federal inves-tigation into the tax-exempt status of the Greater Cleveland Associ-ated Foundation in light of the foundation's recent $72,000 grant that eventually will find its way into the hands of William A. Silverman, a close adviser of Mayor Carl B. Stokes.
> —*Cleveland Plain Dealer*, May 24, 1969

Bartimole had no great pretensions when he started *Point of View* in June 1968, and he acquired none—an attitude which may be a clue to his effectiveness. For all his idealistic zeal, he remains a realist about the future. He says:

> I think it will remain a persevering task to keep on questioning the media, and to raise issues not even mentioned yet in the media. I would expect no great changes in the news media because I don't

believe major societal changes evolve quickly and without someone having prepared the way. I would hope at best to have been part of "preparing the way" for changes that will have to take place in the mass media if it is to be at all relevant in solving problems.

Those who think of themselves as critics of the media, he said somewhat ruefully, are their best friends. But "it's better, at least right now, that they see us as the enemy, and we see them as the enemy."

Bartimole says he does not want *Point of View* to become too successful or too well-known, "because that would force me to think about matters that are not as important as the issues being raised." His greatest hope is that people will use *Point of View* as a resource for programs to change conditions that have come under *Point of View's* fire.

He seems to want to maintain a certain mystique about *Point of View* which may fit in with his desire for a measure of detachment, as befits an independent crusader. This was evident in his refusal to moderate his views of censorship, in terms black or white, when he dropped his column at the *Call & Post*. He said: "I even feel it a bit of a loss when I become real to a reader by meeting him or her. There's a feeling I get from people that they think *PoV* appears somehow mysteriously since it appears to have no financial backing and no organization backing or producing it."

Rumors vary about Bartimole's financial sources. The most persistent, he said, is Cyrus Eaton, but

that's untrue, as all the others are. Eaton isn't and never has been a subscriber, and probably has never read it. *PoV* is a one-man operation. It has been able to survive financially because all, except the actual printing, is done by me, with a little help from Sue, my wife. This includes the mailing every two weeks, even to the hand-folding and typing of the mail stickers (every fourth issue), thereby avoiding overhead costs. Even the typewriter (an electric by necessity) is borrowed.

Bartimole is chary of advice for young people, particularly those in journalism. But he has one basic piece of guidance to which he completely subscribes himself. "I hate to sound corny," he says, "but if you're going to be honest about your commitments, you should—if you can—leave a daily life that goes against you, maybe for a couple of years, maybe for a lifetime."

Thus his advice is not to drop out but to stay in and fight—on your own terms. The Weathermen, he told an interviewer for the *Cleveland Press* in 1970, are not going to solve the problems by bombings, "but I don't blame them as much as I blame those who frustrate the solutions. My point is that nobody you elect is going to solve problems because they are going to be boxed into the system, whether they are liberals or conservatives."

He notes that "knowledgeable Americans" talk about solving problems of other countries by breaking up big landholdings and spreading the land more equitably among the people. And in developing countries, land is the major source of wealth. But, he adds:

> In this country, capital is the major source of wealth. Yet, you don't hear these people say let's spread it around so we don't have these terrible contrasts between wealth and poverty. Poverty programs and job training programs are going to be just window-dressing until there is more distribution of the wealth in this country.

So Roldo Bartimole keeps hammering away at the élite of Cleveland, seeking to demonstrate to all who will read and hear, in that sprawling city of cosmic contrasts, the validity of his theories. His weapon is the word ("I am continually surprised by the impact of the printed word") and his main target is the venders of the millions of words daily in the commercial press and the broadcast industry of Cleveland.

His opinion of the *Cleveland Press* is low ("What's that carved on the facade of the *Press* building about 'Giving the people light' . . . ?"), but his contempt for the *Plain Dealer* is monumental. With amusement and exasperation he offered a clipping from the *Plain Dealer* of December 21, 1971, reporting the retirement of William M. Ware, executive editor of the newspaper, after 38 years with the *Plain Dealer*. In a speech at a farewell luncheon Ware concluded that American newspapers today were doing the most responsible job of journalism that has ever been done in this country. "And yet," he said, "we have more criticism and less credibility than in many generations."

Ware had an answer for this apparent contradiction: "I think this is because we are doing such a good job in a complex situation." Of course, said Ware with omniscience, newsmen "don't pretend to be omniscient or perfect. We have the same percentage of human error and venality as any other business . . . but while we may not always be right, our aim is right." There was one exception to this, he said, taking direct aim: Cleveland's "underground" press, which he described as "irresponsible and subversive, contributing nothing to the city."

Bartimole was pleased. "I take it as a compliment," he said, "that even upon retirement these thoughts are foremost in his mind. I believe he is talking about *Point of View* and the 'Mediaocrity' column, although, as usual, not mentioning my name." He paused, then said: "I think at this point the only possible way my name might appear in the *Plain Dealer* would be an obituary— my own, of course."

CHAPTER VII

THE NATIVES
GROW RESTLESS

THE proliferation of journalism reviews is a significant development in the American communications industry. Yet it is only the most overt expression of a growing unrest which carries the hope of major changes in the practice of journalism. Perhaps the most controversial development is the movement among editorial staffs to obtain a greater voice in determining the content, personnel and general policies of the publications for which they work.

This movement came late in an industry which has declared itself the most democratic in the world. Until the late 1960s few voices had challenged the monarchical control of publishers and broadcast managers over the gathering and publication of news. Even the Newspaper Guild sought to dampen the new movement, insisting, as it had since its inception in 1933, that the management and content of newspapers were beyond its jurisdiction. The unions in the broadcast field reacted in similar fashion.

The new movement had precedents, however, in Europe. The most notable example was at the Paris daily newspaper *Le Monde*, perhaps the most prestigious in Europe. There a plan for shared management had been devised in 1944, immediately after the liberation of Paris. In 1951 the founding director of *Le Monde*, Hubert Beuve-Méry, was forced out in a dispute with the owners of the paper, but the editorial staff, speaking through the newly formed Society of Journalists, refused to work without him. Beuve-Méry withdrew his resignation and participated in drawing up a new agreement. Under the plan, the staff by 1968 had a 40 percent share in the control of *Le Monde*. That included policy-making and managerial decisions—not day-to-day but in overall planning—and the right to block the sale of the paper. Since any major changes in the paper's structure (for example, the naming of a new managing director, who had to be a journalist) required a 75 percent majority, the staff, through the Society of Journalists, had a virtual veto.

Tradition-bound American publishers might be impressed with the results of the *Le Monde* experiment described in a book by Jean Schwoebel, *Le Monde's* chief diplomatic editor and one of the pioneers of the plan. The book, entitled *Press, Power, and Money*, has unfortunately not been translated from the French for United States publication. Under control of its editorial staff, *Le Monde* achieved first rank in influence in France, a new plant and a profit in 1969 of 3.5 million dollars on a gross income of 20 million dollars. A key to its editorial quality was its insistence on retaining a 3–2 ratio of news to advertising, exactly the reverse of prevailing practice in the United States.

Even at the time of the great French newspaper slump of 1971–72, when other newspapers were losing revenue and laying off employees, *Le Monde* managed to break even and retain its circulation at 500,000 (it had doubled its circulation in less than ten years). These statistics were even more striking in view of the decline in the number of Paris daily newspapers from 32 in 1945 to 11 in 1972.

During a visit to the United States in 1970, Schwoebel declared that in a capitalist country influence could be exerted only through a share of the ownership—the rest was without value. Thirty-two societies had been established in France, he said, all striving to emulate the *Le Monde* pattern, but they were meeting stiff resistance from the owners. Formed into a federation, the societies were seeking to achieve their aims through political pressure.

The federation did not operate as the Newspaper Guild, Schwoebel said. It was founded as a commercial group but later changed into a "civil" one. Profit sharing was not part of the societies' demands: "We want part of the ownership not for the profits—that is for the investors—but only for the juridical rights the property gives. As soon as we leave the paper, we no longer have rights." The federation had an assembly and a council of administration and declared its goal to be the unity of journalists in a common conception. "To unite journalists is very difficult," Schwoebel said. "You succeed only if you pick very solid, very reasonable arguments. And in my view we have united on very sensible, responsible problems."

The *Le Monde* experiment was contagious and attracted attention among frustrated and dissatisfied journalists in Germany, Italy, England and Spain. The feudal power of the owners of the press was a common factor in each of the countries, as well as elsewhere in France. And in France particularly, the student uprising of 1968 helped to give courage to the journalists of France, who walked out in a series of strikes that shook the press structure and the government-operated radio-television network.

There was a revealing and amusing confrontation in 1968 between the striking staff of the picture paper *Paris-Match* and the publisher, textile millionaire Jean Prouvost (who owned also the conservative daily *Figaro* and the powerful Radio Luxembourg). During the confrontation the following dialogue took place:

PROUVOST: I do own this magazine, don't I?
STAFF: Yes.
PROUVOST: It's my money, isn't it?
STAFF: Yes.
PROUVOST: Well, then, I'm the boss, am I not?
STAFF: Yes.
PROUVOST: Then in that case I decide what I please.
STAFF: [in chorus]: NO!

In 1969 a strike was called at *Figaro* when Prouvost refused to sign a new contract with the editorial staff. Prouvost's own partner associated himself with the staff, and the strike ended with a compromise settlement under which the editorial association of the staff retained its prerogatives under the old contract. A walkout at the weekly *L'Express* the same year forced its management to draw up a set of reforms recognizing the "right of employees to participate in the decision-making process." Again the issue was not financial control. "The time is now past," said a *Figaro* editor, "when a newspaper owner can buy a paper in the same way that a nineteenth-century entrepreneur bought a boat with a consignment of slaves." Another journalist said: "It's not the money. We want to raise the standards of the French press. We want to give it a new morality."

The prevalence of morality was not notable in the profit-hungry West German publishing industry. At a glance, it seemed to rest on pliant pillars: the bare breast and the bare bottom. In some cities, particularly Hamburg, newsstands took on the appearance of a mountain of flesh. Chief among the flesh peddlers was Heinrich Bauer, publisher, among others, of the mass-circulation *Quick*, which *Newsweek* once modestly described as "titillating." When the staff of Hamburg-based *Der Stern*, generally described as West Germany's *Life*, learned that a co-owner of *Stern* was about to sell his shares to Bauer for 42.5 million dollars, they rebelled.

Within hours of the report of the owner's intention, a resolution was adopted by 140 editors, reporters and photographers threatening to strike unless the deal was called off. It was. The would-be seller was forced to turn his shares over to his current partners, who then signed an agreement with the staff giving the editors and writers broad new authority similar to that at *Le Monde*. The character of the agreement was expressed in the preamble:

> *Stern* is a politically engaged magazine, but independent of political parties, economic interest groups and other lobbies, which intends to inform and entertain its readers. The editorial staff of *Stern* pledges themselves to an open democratic society and to progressive liberal principles.

Neither at conservative *Figaro* nor at liberal *Stern* was the action sparked by political radicals on the staffs. It is doubtful whether there *were* any radicals at *Figaro;* and in typically Germanic fashion, at *Stern* the greatest number of votes for the new editorial council went to the "father"—editor-in-chief Heinrich Nannen. In a sense, therefore, the European events took on added significance precisely because nonradical personnel reacted so swiftly and with such unity to the growing power of the press barons and their unwillingness to acknowledge, as *Stern*'s Nan-

nen expressed it, that "owning a newspaper is different from owning a spaghetti factory."

Except for the *New York Times* and the *Washington Post*, and
the press sections of *Time* and *Newsweek*, the newspapers of the
United States have given scant coverage to the events in France
and Germany. Among those who did comment, however, was
Robert U. Brown, editor and publisher of *Editor & Publisher*, the
weekly trade journal of the newspaper industry. Brown participated in the twenty-second congress of the Federation of International Newspaper Editors (FIEJ) in Istanbul in May 1969, and
reported his conclusions in *Editor & Publisher* (June 4, 1969):

> The trend in Europe is toward the unrestricted right of the editor
> to run his news and editorial department the way he wants to without
> consideration or responsibility toward the publisher or the owner. It
> amounts to some sort of "divine right." There seems to be very little
> discussion or acknowledgment of the right of the owner or publisher
> who hired the editor and put him into that exalted position in the first
> place. Once hired, the current thinking of European editors is that no
> one, least of all the publisher, has any right to question his editing
> decisions.

It was obvious from the events as they actually were happening,
and the nature of the agreements at *Le Monde* and *Stern*, for
example, that Brown was overstating the European situation.
But it was also clear that his comment had been made out of concern that the days of journalistic slave ships and spaghetti-print-
ing factories might be coming to an end in the United States, too.

While *Figaro* and *Stern* were boiling over in May 1969, and
Brown was stewing in Istanbul, the Magazine Publishers Association of America convened to mark its fiftieth anniversary
at Williamsburg, Virginia. Among the invited speakers was Jean-
Louis Servan-Schreiber, brother of Jean-Jacques and associated
with him at the weekly *L'Express* and at *L'Expansion*, an industrial publication. His topic was: "Will Publishers Lose Control
of Their Publications to Editors?" As though in response to
Brown's uneasy vision of the future, he described the strife in the
French press as a situation "which might very well in the near
future emerge in different countries of the world. [They] may be
the beginning of a permanent problem in our profession, just as

the Berkeley riots of 1967 started . . . the worldwide student unrest." The demand of the editorial staffs in France, he said, was that "information should become a public service protected from the power of money and capital." That sounded dangerously close to an accurate interpretation of the First Amendment. He went on:

It is true that publications are bought and sold as other goods and that people do not like the feeling of being traded. It is also true that not all publishers feel strong enough to ignore the influence of powerful advertisers on the editorial content. Although there have been instances of journalists publishing without capital, we have yet to imagine how capital alone can publish without journalists. For all these moral and professional reasons, while the journalistic associations are in fact questioning capitalist rule, we cannot afford to disregard them altogether.

A year later Jean Schwoebel was asked, when he also was in the United States, whether the *Le Monde* experiment might take root in an "élite or quality" newspaper in the United States. Possibly at the *New York Times* or the *Washington Post* or the *Christian Science Monitor*, Schwoebel replied, but "I know perfectly well that conditions are different in America." The United States was highly advanced in efficiency and energy, he said, but its people were slow to realize that "the real cause of chaos in the future involves a dimension beyond efficiency." Then, as Servan-Schreiber had done, he placed great stress on the question of economic control:

Your journalists are dependent on a society which still believes much in profitability—which is necessary. I think the view of profits, of commerce, in American society in a certain measure represents progress; in another way, not. I believe sincerely that it is much more difficult for American journalists than for us because in such a society as yours it is not regarded as a scandal that economic processes control the press. In European societies it *is* looked upon as a scandal. In my view such control is completely anti-American.

In ten years I am sure that this philosophy will have taken root in America. I say that not only journalists have a right, but clerks or workers have a right to press for their rights. But journalists are different. We are defenders of the truth. Now progress is a question of dialogue. We are at the end of a certain kind of journalism—of magisterial journalism—and of a certain kind of journalist—the magisterial journalist. And we must accept this dialogue.

Schwoebel was sound in his contention that things were different in the United States—and American journalists have helped to broaden that difference. This theory of the exceptionalism of American journalism was rooted in two strongly held beliefs: (1) that the owner of a media enterprise was entitled to all the income he could derive from it; (2) that journalists in the United States, even in the commercially competitive setting of the media, were individualistic professionals. And superimposed upon these beliefs has been the traditionally sacrosanct ideal of objectivity, projected by publishers (and accepted by most media staffs) as the only proper framework for the theory and practice of American journalism.

Under this principle of objectivity, American journalists have maintained a posture apart from and a degree above the general public. And while they have held to their positions, their publishers and the operators of the broadcast media have pirouetted through the commercial world in pursuit of maximum profits. The process is in fact a classical capitalist ballet in which both bosses and employees are far more concerned with success, image and status than with performance in the public interest.

On the surface, such an arrangement would seem to be comfortable and enduring for the participants. But, like much of life in the United States, it is tending to come apart at the seams. A deep unhappiness has become apparent among media staffs, ranging from the mighty empires on Madison Avenue to small-town newspapers. It has affected executives, reporters, news broadcasters, columnists and copy readers. The malaise takes many forms: frustration about assignments; anger at censorship and prejudicial editing of copy; contempt for managerial timidity; and resentment at lack of progress on the job. Yet this malaise has been kept under control by periodic elevation of privilege and paycheck. The publishers and their country-club companions in industry and government have seen to the former, and the unions in the industry—not without periodic hassles—to the latter.

In this atmosphere two counter pressures are being applied to media staffs: the determination of the owners to maintain the status quo, utilizing to this end the ideal of objectivity as against "advocacy" journalism; and the ever-increasing number of dissenters in American society demanding fundamental changes in a system of which the media are an integral part. The catalysts that brought this simmering situation to a boil were the dramatic events of the 1960s, on the one hand, and, on the other, a new generation of journalists who had been involved in these events on university campuses, in street demonstrations against war and poverty, and in the unprecedented protests against racism.

These young journalists came into the newsrooms directly from the front lines, as it were, without cynicism and eager to be of useful service in a communications network whose potential for the common good was unmatched in history. They felt they could persuade the communications industry to present, for all the world to see, the true condition of man as a prelude to action to change this condition. The image of the journalist they wished to destroy was, for example, the one in *Medium Cool*, the popular and realistic film about Chicago in the 1960s. In this film a television reporter-cameraman stands in front of a television set watching Martin Luther King, Jr., make an impassioned speech, and says: "Jesus, I really love to shoot film!"

When the young journalists presented themselves for service, however, they almost invariably encountered the stone-wall traditions. Don't get too close to a story, they were told, or you'll lose your objectivity and get emotional about it. The good reporter is objective, unemotional, detached. Don't let anybody tell you the best place to watch a football game is out there on the field. Don't fool yourself: the best place is from the bench. The end result of most of this advice was the kind of news story that skillfully presented the facts in objective fashion, eschewed interpretive analysis and, above all, preserved the reporter in armor-plated neutrality.

There was one flaw, however. The story in reality was lopsided. The source of the objective facts about the situation was too often police officials or government press officers. Rarely was the other side represented in detail, whether it was a suspect in an episode of violence, a foreign adversary in a complicated negotiation or the target of an investigatory agency. The attitude of the press toward Senator Joe McCarthy in the flowering Cold War years[1] was a classic example of objectivity run amok in favor of the predator. The media, under the cover of objective reporting, was largely instrumental in building McCarthy into the formidable figure he became. The reporters who were assigned to cover McCarthy (they were known as the "goon squad") knew Mc-Carthy was a liar and a charlatan, and that his charges were almost entirely baseless. Yet they insisted that the strictures of objectivity required them to report the senator's charges without comment—unless they were rebutted by the person under attack or by a political opponent of McCarthy who might then be quoted.

This, of course, was nonsense. If the reporters (and their editors) had proof that McCarthy's allegations were false—and a minimum of digging would have documented their findings—it was their responsibility to publish the documented refutation. The victims themselves were generally unavailable for comment or fearful of making a statement because an indictment on a charge of perjury was a likely result in the poisoned atmosphere of the time. A responsible press would have exerted every effort to help the victim set the record straight. But "objectivity" forbade this. The basic reasons for media reluctance, however, went deeper than this convenient catchphrase. They were prejudice and fear on the part of editors and, unfortunately, many of the reporters. The crippling myth of the "international Communist conspiracy" had taken hold in the ranks of the press, as well as in the general public.

The young journalists coming into the media, however, were not willing to accept the guidance of their weary elders, and they charted their own course. Significantly, their first moves coincided with the high point in the public protest against the war in Southeast Asia in 1969. In October of that year a moratorium was declared by the peace movement; all workers were asked to remain away from the job or to request time off to join demonstrations.

At the *New York Times* in mid-October representatives of 308

---

[1] There are detailed chapters about the press and McCarthy in a book by this author, *The Press and the Cold War* (New York: Bobbs-Merrill, 1970).

employees (many of them from the commercial departments) asked for and were denied the use of the newspaper's auditorium for discussions on Moratorium Day. They were told by Sidney Gruson, assistant to the publisher, that "it is a principle of this company that its facilities should not be used for what could be construed as political purposes." Instead, more than 150 *Times* employees on Moratorium Day held a silent vigil outside the building in West 43rd Street, and then joined a nearby rally sponsored by representatives of the book-publishing industry.

At Time, Inc., 462 employees of *Time, Life, Fortune* and *Sports Illustrated* sought the use of the Time-Life auditorium. Permission was given, and 500 attended antiwar discussions—among them publisher Henry Luce III. A spokesman explained that Luce "was just there to see what was going on. He wasn't wearing a button or an armband or anything." The employees signed a petition calling for an "immediate and unilateral withdrawal" from Vietnam, collected 1,400 signatures from passersby at the Time-Life building, and then joined the publishing industry rally. At *Newsweek* 200 employees remained off the job on Moratorium Day.

At the *Wall Street Journal* several employees raised the question of participating in Moratorium Day and were told by management that it was completely against the policy of Dow Jones (publishers of the *Journal*) to do anything "which might in the public eye cast the slightest doubt about the impartiality of its news coverage." Therefore, Dow Jones as an organization would not participate in any way. Employees wishing to take part, however, could get time off, "to be made up at a later date."

The *Times*'s Gruson told Stanford Sesser of the *Wall Street Journal* that he might be old-fashioned, "but I feel very strongly about purity of news columns. Pure objectivity may not exist, but you have to strive for it anyway." In Raleigh, North Carolina, Sesser found another Gruson who disagreed—his daughter, Kerry. As a student at Radcliffe, where she had been campus correspondent for the *Times*, Kerry Gruson had worn the red armband of student demonstrators while attending press conferences. She told Sesser: "Objectivity is a myth. . . . There comes a time when you have to take a stand. After that you try to be fair." The

Times's decision denying the meeting hall was wrong, she said: "The war has waked people up and started them thinking. To say that newspapermen aren't allowed to think because they're newspapermen is completely ridiculous."

One month later 500,000 persons took part in the greatest antiwar demonstration in the nation's history, in Washington, D.C. Yet the three major television networks decided not to cover the events live. Since there was no coverage, the issue of objectivity as such could not be raised. But the decision, by negation, mocked the whole concept of objectivity. The failure to cover was an incalculably greater barrier to objective truth than a crowd of reporters with red armbands.

The ferment within the industry by 1970 had increased to the point where groups of editorial personnel on several newspapers were meeting to discuss their functions and responsibilities, and the responsibility of their publications to the public. The basic issue was how they could make their collective weight felt with management about questions of policy, personnel and content. Almost immediately the phrase "reporter power" was coined. As with most such rhetorical slogans, however, it was out of proportion to the amount of activity involved—but it was to the point. Stories began to appear in journalism reviews about the reporters' associations in France and Germany, and grave warnings were posted in media trade journals about threats to the system of free enterprise and a free press.

Managements in some cities took heed of the stirrings below and responded positively to requests for discussion. The response was in part an effort to avoid an even more serious confrontation which almost surely would have resulted from a refusal to talk things out. The media managements were aware also of the angry mood in the antiwar movement, with which many reporters sympathized, particularly after the United States–South Vietnam invasion of Cambodia and the killings of students by troops and police at Kent State University in Ohio and Jackson State in Mississippi.

In February 1970 the Association of Tribune Journalists was created by *Minneapolis Tribune* reporters, not as a collective-bargaining group (the Newspaper Guild was the representative of editorial and commercial employees), but as an organization which would "bring its best thoughts into a dialogue with management." The group was formed, an organizer said, because the staff felt like privates in an army in which the editors acted like officers. "We were to do what we were told and like it," he said, "and no one gave a damn if we thought our orders were sane or insane."

At the Gannett newspapers in Rochester, New York, a rotating system was set up providing for staff members to sit in with the editorial board. A Journalists Committee in Providence held several meetings with management about specific staff and policy complaints. While in some areas (Buffalo, for example, where Guild monitors sat in on a staff-management meeting discussing editorial practices), the Newspaper Guild watched the proceedings warily, in others it added its weight to the extra-Guild demands. When two assistant city editorships became vacant at the *Minneapolis Tribune*, the local Guild adopted a resolution requesting that reporters, photographers and copydesk editors be permitted to "advise and consent to management's nominations." Management insisted that it would not give up its prerogatives (it had not been asked to), but agreed to consider staff nominations for the two jobs. In Denver a new contract in 1970 established an ethics committee and a human-rights committee to discuss minority hiring and certain editorial practices which the staff found to be demeaning. Granted these were small steps: they were notable because they had never been taken before.

The pattern, for the most part, in the internal media ferment was not radical but reformist. The dissenters had no desire to take power. The situation at the *New York Times* was typical. *Le Monde*'s Jean Schwoebel had met with a group of dissidents there who were seeking to alter the paper's stodgy image (they had been dubbed "The Cabal"). He found them much more inclined to confine themselves to their own problems than to lead a national revolt—something which the staff of the *Times,* because of the paper's prestige, could well do. Later, in a conversation with Ron Dorfman, editor of the *Chicago Journalism Review,* one *Times* cabalist, J. Anthony Lukas, remarked with some aston-

ishment about Schwoebel's views: "He's talking about *ownership!*"
That obviously was not in the minds of the *Times's* dissenters,
nor the prevailing view among the 60 activists at the *New York
Post* who had been meeting with publisher Dorothy Schiff.

The *Post*, with the largest evening circulation in the United
States, has a complete monopoly in the New York evening field.
It is a fat, penny-pinching, cramped newspaper, short on cultural
standards and long on syndicated opinions and analysis. Despite
its liberal pretensions, it has frequently been accused of discrimination against black and Puerto Rican staff members and of hypocritical hiring practices in this area. It is, in short, a disgracefully
inadequate newspaper in the cultural capital of the nation, and
many of its staff members have long been aware of a concomitant
cultural lag in the newsroom. In this unhappy setting, staff members joined to confront the reluctant publisher, Mrs. Dorothy
Schiff, and her chief editors with demands for improved editorial
and personnel practices.

At one point Mrs. Schiff defended the *Post's* firing of a young
black woman who had been tried out as a reporter. She strayed
so far from the facts that she snapped the patience of one of the
Post's most loyal reporters—Ted Poston, a 35-year veteran, able
writer and devoted management counselor. Poston's qualifications
should have led to an editor's chair years before, but he had a
handicap: he was black.

In February 1970 Poston sent a memorandum to Mrs. Schiff
detailing the perennially shoddy practices of the *Post* regarding
minority staff members. The memo, published in the October
1971 issue of *(More)*, the New York journalism review, concluded:
"I think that it will be criminal for the *New York Post* to dissipate
the unquestioned loyalty it has developed over the years from
liberals and minority group communities by refusing to face and
correct a situation which some of your executives won't even
admit exists."

Poston received an icy reply from Mrs. Schiff, who shortly
thereafter was defending the *Post* before the New York State
Human Rights Commission in a case growing out of the firing
of another young black reporter. The commission found valid the
charge that the *Post* maintained a policy of employing no more

than three black and Puerto Rican editorial employees at one time (out of a staff of 63), and ruled that the reporter, William Artis, had been fired "in contravention of the human rights laws."

At about the same time, a *Post* woman reporter was fired for refusing an assignment to interview the wife of a big league baseball pitcher. She felt that the assignment was degrading both to the wife of the pitcher and to herself; that the only reason the woman was being interviewed was because she was the pitcher's wife. The staff rose in defense of the dismissed reporter and threatened to close down the paper. The reporter was rehired.

At less liberal papers the reaction of publishers and editors has been more liberal. The Associated Press Managing Editors Association, comprising editors of papers with an Associated Press franchise, in 1971 commissioned a report on "Activism and Advocacy" under the direction of Ed Miller, executive editor of the Call-Chronicle Newspapers of Allentown, Pennsylvania. Miller visited four newspapers in Buffalo, Portland (Maine), Denver and Milwaukee, seeking "to document what was happening rather than make judgments." When he got into the newsrooms, Miller found that his range of investigation went far beyond his alliterative subject. It covered such subjects as off-the-job activities by reporters, advocacy reporting, ethics, newsroom revolts, journalism reviews and—affecting all these other questions—the matter of credibility. Miller approached his task with a refreshing openmindedness, even though it was clear that he was more at ease in discussion with his counterparts than with dissenting staff. His findings are instructive because they deal with four newspapers generally regarded as responsible, and in four different sectors of the United States. Following are highlights of his report.

Buffalo Evening News: The editorial staff Professional Standards Group raised seven issues with management: training procedures, minority hiring, stylebook, dignity and professionalism (later termed "civility"), investigative reporting, resistance to writing promotional stories and reporter's conscience. The group felt that the *Evening News* was more often a booster for the "landed gentry" of the community than a critic and investigator, and that it ignored the needs of the city's ghetto residents. The "real enemy," one said, was "the system of doing things in a certain way for 40 or 50 years." Miller himself said:

Staffers, particularly young reporters, are feeling hemmed in. They see their profession as a means for social change but are frustrated when their managers do not march to the same drummer. To some degree it's a problem of youth; but waiting for young enthusiasm to mellow would be a sad solution. Some may see it as a modern labor-management battle, but even that old standby is not purely the case. Buffalo's Professional Standards Group found as much resistance among the ranks of the Guild as it did from management.

Managing Editor Elwood M. Wardlow of the *Evening News* judged the Standards Group's efforts as neither a success nor a failure. Some of their suggestions had been adopted, he said, and management *was* listening better. There had been no recrimination against those who stated the case most forcefully. City Editor Bud Wacker summed up: "The conditions which caused [the movement] are still present." Miller added: "That is not a self-indictment, but rather a candid and honest appraisal of one newspaper that recognizes a problem which will not go away."

Denver Post: The resistance in Denver took the form of a journalism review, *The Unsatisfied Man,* and managerial reaction was sharp. The *Post*'s managing editor, John Rogers, commented: "Too much of the time the effectiveness of whatever valid criticism might appear is eroded by their purely personal criticism. . . . There's too much invective rather than investigation. Too much subjective carping. This, unfortunately, is abetted by too frequent examples of bad reporting and faulty conclusions." He couldn't recall a single instance of change at the *Post* as a result of the review's criticism.

A parallel development at the *Post* was the creation of the Ethics Committee as an adjunct to the Newspaper Guild, seeking to set higher standards in staff conduct—refusal of gifts, for example, or cutting down on junkets designed to inspire news stories which in reality were free advertising. "We got resistance from management," said a committee member, "and ridicule from the staff," many of whom regarded the committee as "nosey do-gooders." But the committee persevered and worked out with management a memorandum on staff ethics which was likely to become a continuing agreement.

An assistant managing editor, asked about the *Post*'s hiring of "activists," said: "The premise of management is to hire these young Turks to strike a balance on the staff. They're given every opportunity to move up the ladder." He said he would not be "turned off" by an applicant who wanted to work on a newspaper to change the world, but he wouldn't "want a whole staff that way." Managing Editor Rogers felt there was good rapport between management and staff, and an "open-door" policy was helping to maintain staff stability. One staff member was candid about his colleagues: "One of the problems around here is that people would bitch about stories not being done, but virtually all of the time if they had gone to the desk the chances are that they would have been done. There is a helluva lot of laziness."

Portland Press-Herald and *Express:* Executive Editor Ernest Chard said: "Applicants come in with a greater sense of mission than they used to. There seems to be a rejection of establishment pursuits as the young crowd looks to newspapers as a way of projecting social service. They wish to be in the swing of things, an influence on shaping society, and they think newspapers provide a medium to do this."

As in the other cities he visited, Miller said, the attitude of the younger reporters in Portland was: "Let's set the pace, not follow it." Too often, they said, newspapers failed to deal with a problem, such as the environment, until it was forced upon them. In Portland the reporters were asking for an opportunity to research community problems in depth to determine causes and solutions rather than simply recite the manifestations of the problems. "You must give reporters with proven competence the opportunity to have a voice," said Editor Chard. He cited the case of a city hall reporter who wrote an opinion column once a week. The politicians were critical, and some executives felt it would undermine the reporter's credibility with his sources. But no one could demonstrate that the reporter was unfair in his news coverage, and the column continued.

Miller found that "the particular stumbling block of larger organizations, communications up and down the chain of command," did not appear to be a serious problem in Portland.

Smaller size was one factor, he felt, but a more important one was that "the paper's primary asset in dealing with the problems of advocacy and activism seems to be internal flexibility. There appear to be enough safety valves to prevent explosion."

Milwaukee Journal: This newspaper, one of the most outspoken critics of Senator Joe McCarthy (it sought in its pages to counter as quickly as possible his demonstrable distortion and lying), takes a tough line toward outside activities by its staff. "We have a clear-cut policy," said Managing Editor Joe Shoquist. "Anybody in the news and editorial operation should be as uninvolved and as passive as possible. We forbid practices which might reflect unfavorably on the newspaper or its credibility." Some don'ts: no political action—either running for office or working in politics; no participation in demonstrations; no publicity jobs—not even for churches. How did Shoquist feel about activist applicants for jobs? He responded:

> We want to avoid prejudiced reporting, but I worry more about the inhibiting effect we have on idealistic reporters than the dangers of editorializing in the news columns. I expect young reporters to be fired with enthusiasm. We want a strong social conscience, but they soon discover they will have to do it through the system. An activist's alternatives are underground newspapers or other minor publications which have no influence in the scheme of things. But the activist soon learns that he can make the greatest impact by working on a respected newspaper which is believed.
>
> A reporter or editor is required to make some sacrifices in his civil rights. That's really a small price to pay for the compensations, for we're in a position to do so much for our world and our society, we must not undercut our effectiveness. We must keep the slate as clean as possible. Having a clear-cut policy helps us stay on this course.

The *Journal* sends its editors to meetings of community groups, such as county government officials, educators and lawyers. Once a month it sponsors dinners to give the community an opportunity for an exchange with the editors. The stress is on credibility. Shoquist elaborated:

> We want an objective *attitude*, not just a recitation of the facts. Analysis, interpretation, and even some opinionating may be neces-

sary if we are to inform people. Just repeating words or actions may not be truthful reporting. We have people capable, knowledgeable, and mature enough to analyze and interpret. We do identify this material doggedly, so the reader knows precisely what's being presented. But the need for presenting this is there.

Many staff reporters agreed with this managerial approach, although there was disagreement as to how much voice staff members had in decision making at the top. An editorial-page feature called "In My Opinion" is used occasionally by staff members as an outlet. A column titled "Accent in the News" permits another outlet six days a week for observations, comments and sidelights. And on Sunday there is a column called "Write On" reserved for any black member of the staff, not just reporters (there are eight black reporters in the "professional ranks" at the *Journal* out of a total of 160).

Although management at the *Milwaukee Journal* seemed to take credit for an enlightened attitude within the newsroom, however hard-nosed it was about outside activities, it is clear that a staff group called Journal 14 (after a Milwaukee draft-resistance group) was in some measure responsible for the enlightenment. These were reporters and copyeditors seriously concerned with basic questions of news philosophy, standards, traditional methods and the scope of coverage. They were for the most part the more experienced members of the staff, unlike their resisting counterparts at other newspapers. They were aware that the growing complexity of society demanded a more careful look at race questions, life-styles and poor people than could be provided by the "tape-recorder" style of journalism. In this spirit they prepared and signed a report to management which led to meetings with the editors and effected some reforms. "There was a general change in attitudes," one member said, adding:

"There's lots of talent around here seriously concerned about improving the product. Our motive was to create a better paper. The quality of reporters is a key." He referred to the "nonsystem" in effect at the *Journal* which he described as a failure of communications between reporters who were experts in their specialized fields and their editors, whose only advantage was their authority. None of this, Miller concluded, was "out of step with management thinking and practice at the *Milwaukee Journal.*"

Miller listed three central concerns derived from his survey and what he thought should be done about them: consistency (the same policy regarding ethics, activism and advocacy should be applied to publisher and reporter alike); flexibility (the title of editor does not guarantee that its holder is the repository of greater wisdom than that of the reporter); and communications (the communications industry ought to learn the art of communication within its own newsrooms). Miller concluded:

These factors in turn have an impact on the way a staff member views the organization. You cannot speak of activism without first assessing a paper's standards and practices. If a reporter is told that he cannot demonstrate for a cause but the publisher is allowed to sit on the various news-making boards on the community, is that properly dealing with the conditions of activism? If a reporter is told that he cannot inject his opinions into his news columns, yet he believes the paper bends its stories in favor of major advertisers or community projects, how does an editor effectively discuss advocacy journalism?

In other words, the condition is not limited to a handful of young, motivated reporters on urban newspapers. These are merely the most visible and vocal symptoms. Editors must remember that young activists are looking not only outward to the changing community but inward to the organization. Thus, if a newspaper is to deal with tensions of activism and advocacy journalism, it must first determine if its own actions and principles of operation are not in some ways contributing to those tensions. Perhaps we've been looking outside to society for the causes of activism and advocacy journalism when we should have been looking inside the organization as well.

These are thoughtful words from a man on the managerial side of the newsroom who took seriously his assignment from the Associated Press Managing Editors Association and contributed a valuable report both for his colleagues in the association and for media people in general.

For certain groups within the media Miller's words have special meaning—groups which for generations have felt particularly the prejudices and strictures of the system in which they lived and the communications media to which they aspired. Seemingly diverse, they have much in common. They are the black people and the women and the young men forced into the Army by a draft or by an economic system which deprives them of the right to a civilian livelihood with dignity.

How they fared under the traditional system of journalism and how they rose to assert their rights will be described in three following chapters. But first let us take a longer look at another sector of the media, the broadcasting industry.

CHAPTER VIII

TV: EYEBALL
TO EYEBALL

Diversity: "There never were in the world two opinions alike," Montaigne wrote, "no more than two hairs or two grains; the most universal quality is diversity."[1]

MONTAIGNE did not anticipate the radio-television industry which operates 24 hours a day to prove him wrong. For diversity the broadcasters have substituted distortion: a counterfeit presentation of a nation, a picture so removed from reality that it will take years to repair the damage to the misinformed American mind. This is a harsh charge, but substantiated time and again by the men and women who work in the industry—a communications network of 800 television stations and 6,500 radio stations supposedly operating under regulations of the Federal Communications Act of 1934 that their programming be "in the public interest, convenience, and necessity."

More than 95 percent of American homes have television sets, considerably more than have indoor plumbing, and 25 percent of these homes have more than one set. The average home has its set turned on more than six hours a day—a third of the waking day. Between the prime time hours of 8:00 to 11:00 P.M., more than 75 million people are watching television, nine-tenths of them tuned to one of the three major networks. How have the networks fulfilled the enormous responsibility in the public inter-

---

[1] *Of the Resemblance of Children to Their Fathers,* Book I, Ch. 37.

143

est attendant upon such a vast audience? A devastating evaluation[2] was made by David W. Rintels, a television writer and
chairman of the Committee on Censorship of the Writers Guild
of America, West:

> [On] the question of whether current television programming and
> censorship practices and the inevitable resulting product are in the
> public interest as the law requires, we [the television writers] be-
> lieve emphatically that they are not. And while we are the first
> victims of these practices, the ultimate victims are the American
> people.
>
> With such enormous influence comes enormous power, and with
> such power should come—must come, in the public interest—re-
> sponsibility. We agree wholeheartedly with industry spokesmen who
> say that television has a responsibility to entertain. But we also be-
> lieve that television has a responsibility not to present one narrow
> view as the whole truth. A responsibility not to shy away from
> reality, from issues, from controversy, from substance, from public
> discussion of all matters in the public interest. Yet it is our contention
> that in prime time entertainment television, which most of the people
> watch most of the time, and which has by far the largest impact of
> all television, these responsibilities are being shirked, willfully and
> totally.

Rintels said two basic issues concerned the writers: first, the
right of the men and women who write for television to deal in
ideas, truths and realities free from the repressive censorship and
program practices under which they do in fact write; second, the
right of the American people to be exposed to something more
than an endless cycle of programs that mislead them and distort
the realities of what is happening today. The gravity of these
issues was underscored by statistics cited by Rintels from a poll of
the Writers Guild. Of those who responded:

> Eighty-six (86) percent have found, from *personal* experience, that
> censorship exists in television. Many state, further, that they have

---

[2] In testimony in the winter of 1972 before the Senate Subcommittee on Constitutional Rights, headed by Senator Sam J. Ervin, Jr., which was conducting hearings
on freedom of the press. The testimony was published, only slightly shortened, in
two installments in the *New York Times* of March 5 and 12, 1972.

never written a script, no matter how innocent, that has not been censored.

Eighty-one (81) percent believe that television is presenting a distorted picture of what is happening in this country today—politically, economically, and racially.

Only eight (8) percent believe that current television programming is "in the public interest."

Rintels documented his statements (and the results of the poll) with some case histories "from thousands of examples." Here are some instances of censorship: a young black woman having a friendly drink with a white attorney (in *The Young Lawyers*) written out of the script by ABC; a film on venereal disease, developed with scrupulous good taste, written for *Dr. Kildare,* rejected as "offending"; story themes dealing with the question of amnesty for draft evaders and homosexuals in government (treated sympathetically) refused by NBC, as was a third script—about the Pentagon's storage of nerve gas near an urban area—reportedly because the subject would be offensive to sponsors who had dealings with the Pentagon. (NBC's parent is the Radio Corporation of America [RCA], one of the country's biggest defense contractors.)

"Writers by the dozens," said Rintels, "report that they have written characters who are black and have seen them changed to white; they have proposed shows about South African apartheid, Vietnam, old folks, mental disease, politics, business, labor, students and minorities; and they have been chased out of the studios." Rintels once proposed a story about a young GI killed in action as a result of his conflict between bravery and fear. Great idea, said the producer, who sent it to the network. The network also approved, but asked for two revisions: change the locale to Spain and make the GI a bullfighter.

Perhaps the most flagrant example was ABC's eight-year-old program *The FBI,* which, under the imprimatur of Director J. Edgar Hoover, once claimed that the programs were based on real FBI cases, then altered that to "inspired" by FBI cases. Most of the scripts actually came out of the minds of television writers. On *The FBI,* Rintels reported, there has never been a program about any aspect of the violation of the civil rights of a minority.

No FBI agent has ever bugged a house or tapped a phone or paid a hired informer, nor is any writer allowed to suggest that these practices take place. No program dealing with violations of anti-trust laws is permitted. Further, all actors, writers and directors are screened by the FBI in Washington, and only those "politically acceptable" are hired to work on the show. Rintels concluded:

> By now the message should be clear. The American people are being force-fed a dishonest picture of the work of a government agency and any writer who attempts to portray the real world, suggesting that white-collar or business crime exists or that crimes against people's rights are as much a source of national concern as crimes against their persons, is simply not allowed to do so.

What should also be clear is that this system of operation is not forced upon the industry, but accepted, and even abetted by most of its managers as being entirely in the "public interest." And while the examples cited by Rintels fall into the "entertainment" category, they deal with matters of great concern, particularly when "entertainment" impinges on public affairs. Nor is there any doubt that censorship operates also in the area of broadcast news, and this is doubly pernicious because the majority of Americans today get their news almost exclusively from television and radio, particularly all-news radio in major urban centers broadcasting 24 hours a day.

A distinction should be made here between live unedited news (such as President Nixon's visit to China), which is unmatchable for its immediacy and impact, and carefully timed and edited regularly scheduled news programs and documentaries. This is not to imply that censorship is a premeditated practice in the daily news programs or occasional documentaries (although the strictures of time and commercial advertising in themselves often act as censors), but prejudice, selectivity and timidity are all operative in these matters. There are conflicts and contradictions also between hard-hitting journalism and cautious policy (a consciousness that Big Brother in government is looking over the broadcaster's shoulder). These factors are apparent particularly in television's coverage of the war in Indochina—a war which television has brought to the dinner table in an indigestible package with the seven-o'clock news, and then repeated on the eleven-o'clock news for waking nightmares. This is how CBS's Morley Safer described television at war:[3]

> This is television's first war. It is only in the last few years that the medium has become portable enough to go out on military operations. And this has raised some serious problems—problems, incidentally, which every network correspondent and cameraman in Vietnam is acutely aware of.
>
> The camera can describe in excruciating, harrowing detail what war is all about. The cry of pain, the shattered face—it's all there on film, and out it goes to millions of American homes during the dinner hour. It is true that on its own every piece of war film takes on a certain antiwar character, simply because it tells it that way. It also tells what happens to civilians who are caught in the middle of battle. It tells what happens to soldiers under stress of the unreal conditions in which they live.
>
> The unfavorable has always been reported along with the favorable—but television tells it with greater impact. When the U.S. blunders, television leaves little doubt. So when a government official, either in Saigon or Washington, denies what television plainly reports and then attempts to give verisimilitude to his denial by damning the reporters—at best that is pure humbug.

A supreme example of humbuggery, in which the government impugned the integrity not only of reporters but also of a network itself, was given in the spring of 1970. It was also an example of how effective the adversary role of the media can be when one segment of the media refuses to yield ground to the censor.

The antagonists in this case were Clark Mollenhoff, a special assistant to the President, whose duties were in effect to be house detective for the administration, and CBS-TV. Mollenhoff for years had been an investigative reporter for the *Des Moines Register* and the *Tribune*, Cowles morning and evening newspapers, and had earned a reputation as a righteous scourge of government bureaucrats. His approach was sometimes characterized as a "Mollenhoff cocktail."

This particular cocktail party had its origin in a CBS-TV broad-

[3] *In Dateline 1966: Covering the War*, an anthology published by the Overseas Press Club, New York.

cast from South Vietnam on November 3, 1969, curiously enough the same day as President Nixon's controversial report to the nation appealing to the "silent majority" for support on the war. The TV film clip, narrated by CBS correspondent Don Webster, showed a South Vietnamese soldier stabbing a prisoner to death. Shortly thereafter the Pentagon requested out-takes of the broadcast (film taken but not shown). CBS refused. The Pentagon seemingly lost interest in the matter, but not Clark Mollenhoff. In May 1970 he leaked a White House memo to columnist Jack Anderson (700 papers) and to columnist Richard Wilson (60 papers), a former colleague on the *Register* and the *Tribune*. Both Anderson and Wilson then published stories alleging that the stabbing shown on the CBS broadcast was merely a training exercise (the prisoner, according to this version, was already dead, and therefore presumably legitimate practice material), and that CBS had staged the incident, just as it had staged "police brutality" in the streets of Chicago during the 1968 Democratic National Convention.

On May 21, soon after the leak ("plant" would be a more apt description), Walter Cronkite, in an unusual seven-minute segment of the *CBS Evening News*, said:

> For reasons not entirely clear, the White House has engaged in an undercover campaign to discredit CBS News by alleging that the story was faked. . . . We broadcast the original story in the belief that it told something about the nature of the war in Vietnam. What has happened since tells us something about the government and its relations with news media which carry stories the government finds disagreeable.

Correspondent Webster on the same broadcast offered a detailed refutation of the government's allegations, named the South Vietnamese sergeant responsible for the stabbing, and in an on-screen interview with him elicited the admission that he had indeed stabbed a living man. The sergeant, who was later named "Soldier of the Year" by the government in Saigon, remembered the CBS-TV crew's being present.

The White House made no direct charge against CBS, nor did it bring the matter to the attention of the Federal Communications Commission. Had it done so, CBS would have had a formal oppor-

tunity to defend itself. Immediately after the May 21 CBS broadcast, both the White House and the Pentagon disclaimed
responsibility for the leaked memo. White House Communications Director Herbert Klein, according to *Newsweek* (June 1,
1970), did not even know of the leak until CBS called him and
suggested he tune in on the Cronkite broadcast May 21. Klein's
ignorance was difficult to swallow.

Ten days later Mollenhoff announced his resignation from government service to become Washington bureau chief of the *Register* and the *Tribune*—an offer "too good" to be turned down. It
was clear that Mollenhoff had become a liability: he was clumsy
with his cocktails.

Cronkite was painfully accurate in noting that the incident told
us something about the government. But what about columnists
Wilson and Anderson, who published Mollenhoff's concoction
without checking with CBS? What about the other networks,
which remained silent on the matter, and the newspapers, which
saw no reason for editorial comment? The post-Agnew tremors
were still apparent.

"If it had just been a single episode," said Cronkite, "I think it
could have been forgotten. But it represents a continuing attitude
and a threat to all of us in the media." Senator J. W. Fulbright,
chairman of the Senate Foreign Relations Committee, thought so,
too. He commended CBS in a letter to the network published in
Variety but, as far as could be ascertained, in no other newspaper
of general circulation. Fulbright said:

> Never before have our democratic institutions—whether the
> Congress or the free press—been so seriously threatened by an
> administration experienced in the techniques of mass advertising,
> and uninhibited in presenting inaccurate or misleading information
> in order to sell official policies. It is not by chance, I believe, that
> the Vice-President's campaign of intimidation and criticism is now
> followed by specific attacks by the administration on specific tele-
> vision networks or newspapers on specific stories.

Another specific administration attack on CBS occurred some
months later, early in 1971, involving the CBS-TV program *The
Selling of the Pentagon*. This was a documentary film demonstrating that the Defense Department, contrary to law, was conducting

lavish propaganda programs directed at businessmen and civic groups in support of its policies in Indochina. This time the assault came from both the White House and the Congress and culminated in a demand that CBS turn over to the House Commerce Committee both the raw material of the telecast and notes on the editing procedures used in producing the film.

Dr. Frank Stanton, head of CBS, refused (CBS, to its credit, broadcast the film a second time), and the committee voted to ask Congress for a contempt citation against Stanton. On June 25, 1971, Stanton declared: "There can be no doubt in anyone's mind that the First Amendment would bar this subpena if directed at the editing of a newspaper report, a book, or a magazine." The response from a committee member was memorable. "We are not interested in the First Amendment," said William L. Springer, Republican of Ohio. "We are interested in deceit." The remark was all the more incredible because it was made in the midst of the furor about monumental governmental deceit then being exposed through publication of the Pentagon Papers. In July, in an action undoubtedly influenced by the Pentagon Papers exposure, Congress refused to cite Stanton for contempt.

Now the remarkable thing about *The Selling of the Pentagon* is not that it was produced, but that this kind of program is so rarely produced. It is the type of documentary the television networks should be making continually to keep the public informed about the government's lapses, breaches of ethics and unnecessary secrecy.

There was an interesting footnote to *The Selling of the Pentagon* which created little comment. Among the personalities appearing on the program to make brief but stirring speeches about the nobility and invincibility of the American war machine were two television personalities. One was Chet Huntley, of the Huntley-Brinkley NBC News team, who has since retired. The other was Walter Cronkite.

Cronkite is a star—our man in China, our man on the moon (almost), a household name, a newsman as newsmaker. But others fashion the news, too, anonymously or unsung in the television newsrooms, and their experiences offer perhaps an even more consistent exposition of the failure of television as an information medium. Consider the history of Arthur Alpert, with whom I spent several hours to obtain a picture of how a newswriter and reporter works—or seeks to work—in the medium.

Alpert was first a newspaper journalist with the *New York World-Telegram & Sun* from 1960 to 1962. When his mortal reviews of the nightclub circuit caused him to be transferred to the obituary desk, he quit and found a job at WABC-TV, the "flagship" of the ABC network, where he became a writer on the original local news team. He remained for four years as a writer and producer of documentaries and public-affairs programs—a thin field at WABC.

There were two shocks in the transition from print to electronic journalism, he said: the good pay and the obligation to leave out of a story almost everything that should go into it. His fascination with film enabled him to go along with the routine of producing entertaining and fast-paced programs without major internal disturbance. Then one day his boss said to him: "Boy, Art, that show really moved!" and something snapped in him. It meant that he had become a master at packaging things neatly, making them short and entertaining, and providing a lively surrounding for the commercial spots. Local television news programs are big moneymakers because their large audiences attract advertisers. Most profitable of all for the networks are the so-called O and Os —the local stations owned and operated wholly by the networks, such as WABC-TV and WCBS-TV in New York.

Alpert was neither a radical nor a political activist. His views had been shaped at Brooklyn College during the McCarthy years of the 1950s, and he had emerged with an abhorrence of McCarthyism, a resistance to communism and yet with contempt for professional anti-Communists. The proper business of an American democrat, he felt, was to be more democratic, and "that's what democracy should be all about."

In 1965 he went to Vietnam for ABC to do a documentary which was successful "because we did not do much thinking." The crew shot precisely what it saw, and in 1965 most Americans were not yet aware of the reality of Vietnam. Response to the film was favorable from both doves and hawks, and it jolted Alpert into an awareness that there must be something wrong with his own beliefs. It was a situation that required not balance but a definite attitude. With that realization came a revelation: the requirements of the system made it impossible for him to present the kind of news programs he wanted by that time to do.

Had there been any overt pressures on the job? I asked. He replied:

Not many. If in fact you do your job within the corporate requirements, you need not be admonished. Once or twice there were suggestions that shows were "too black." The years 1962–63 were the beginning of the so-called black revolution, and there were many demonstrations and protests; but no one was covering them extensively yet. The programs were mostly concerned with the complaints of black and poor people, and that of course made them less entertaining. There was reaction too from what since has come to be known as the "silent majority." People would call in to denounce the programs. So there were hints from management that we might go a little bit softer, be a bit more entertaining. It was not so much that we were being urged by conservatives to be a little less liberal, as that we were being urged by businessmen to be a little more entertaining.

The syndrome at work in television in the mid-1960s was "corporate liberalism," Alpert said. Most of the executives were traditional liberals. They favored the civil-rights movement and there was a "moral presumption of the innocence of victimhood." The executives assumed that black people had a just cause, and that was reflected in the programs. But there was a more important ideology, the corporate one, and that means "not only that we must make more money but we must be safe."

That was understandable as far as the executives were concerned, I said, but what about the men and women who put the programs together, the ones on the lower levels? Alpert responded:

I think their conflict is resolved by a mechanism which in our time we call "alienation." Journalists are idealists. They go into the business because they want to help solve the problems of society and the world. And when they find frustrations there, they rant and rave briefly, but eventually find that the enemy is not attackable because the enemy is not a person. I found myself yelling at a succession of bosses, but it finally occurred to me (after three bosses had come and gone) that "the boss" was not the bastard; rather, it was a systemic problem. My boss was doing the best he could within the limits imposed upon him.

It is a lot easier to attack a bad boss, a conservative boss, than it is to attack something which until recently has been amorphous—a way of doing business. So when you can't grab, isolate, attack, you retire and try to enjoy what room there is left in the system—there is some—and essentially set up a wall between your professional role and your human aspirations—the desire to be rational, to serve yourself and others. When this had churned around in me sufficiently for me to understand, I quit WABC-TV.

A year and a half of freelance work followed, and then Alpert joined the experimental Public Broadcasting Laboratory in 1967. The Public Broadcasting Laboratory (PBL) was created as a two-year project with a ten-million-dollar grant from the Ford Foundation, under the direction of Fred W. Friendly, the foundation's chief television consultant and former director of CBS-TV News. The project was an experimental laboratory for a public broadcast system which Friendly hoped to project. Its goals and operating principles were to "reflect insights, approaches, and types of thinking not normally associated with television." The programs were broadcast on Sunday evenings over the National Educational Television network, marking the first time that a national noncommercial network had been set up on a continuing basis for simultaneous broadcasts. The project was marked by considerable bickering between PBL and NET, and by dissatisfaction among the more venturesome young persons on the PBL staff. PBL ended its operations in April 1969.

Alpert was attracted to a project whose aim was to bring together the aspirations of noncommercial television and the skills of commercial broadcasting. But he discovered it was not exactly as described. PBL's purpose, in the short run, was political—to persuade Congress that, if money was forthcoming publicly for a domestic satellite scheme, noncommercial television could produce valuable programs in the public interest. In practice, Alpert said, because of lack of planning and disharmony, the PBL operation was chaos. But he himself was pleased to have produced the only program he was proud of during his television career—a critique of journalism. For one of his programs he sought to demonstrate the deficiencies of coverage by the general media of antiwar activities, and he selected the demonstration in Washington in January 1968 of the Jeannette Rankin Brigade (named for the former congresswoman):

The women were demanding that the funds for conducting the war in Vietnam be turned to domestic requirements. For the first time, as almost nobody perceived, there were "respectable" women present—religious groups, and many others, perhaps the first demonstration in which so many socially conservative people took this liberal and even radical tack. I examined the coverage by NBC, UPI, the *Washington Post* and the *New York Times*, and came up with the finding that, except for the *Post*, the others missed most of the story. Analyzing why, I concluded that the villain was objectivity—corporate objectivity.

I had a heck of a time getting it on the air because PBL had its own problems with conclusions like that. But we did get it on the air, after some amendments, and after bringing in Joseph P. Lyford from the Ford Foundation in Santa Barbara. And that's an interesting point. Lyford had an important position and standing in the journalism world, and he could shoulder responsibility. This is what I call the "authority phenomenon." In television, you don't say anything dangerous, but if you have to say it, you find someone in authority to say it for you. And in this situation it was quite clear: Arthur Alpert, producer and reporter, could not say on his own hook that these people had missed the story in the guise of objectivity. You bring in an authority to act as a lightning rod in case anyone gets struck.

The PBL experiment, Alpert felt, was a failure because of the élitist character of the organization. It was, he said, devised by the Ford Foundation and executed by people, himself among them, who did not represent society as it actually existed: "We needed more women and black people. We had lots of young people, but they did not have enough power." PBL sought to recreate CBS in public television, and since there already was one CBS, why another? According to Alpert, Friendly might reply that it was not the CBS of Edward R. Murrow that he had directed. True—but that CBS also had its limitations. There was in addition at PBL a "crisis of leadership that intersects with politics but is not in itself political. Foundation-sponsored projects tend to be irresponsible in the original sense. The foundation tries desperately not to shape the project, and nobody else wants to either, so it lies there, without a rocket." Alpert continued:

So what we came up with was one or two programs which were so shocking to the educational stations around the country that we promptly climbed down. Education TV is run by boards of trustees who are conservative socially, and often politically as well. They may be liberal in context of their home towns, but not in terms of New York. I think it would be fair to say that their idea of good programming would be 24 hours of the Boston Symphony. When they saw our kind of liberalism—it definitely was not radicalism— they were aghast. So we departed from that tone and proceeded to combine the best and worst of the worlds of commercial and public broadcasting, and it was disastrous. When people ask what PBL was all about, the answer is that it was for liberals hiding in the hinterlands. It was their connection with the world.

When we saw that PBL was going to die or be replaced, several of us on the staff sought a voice in the decision-making process. Fred Bowen, who had succeeded Av Westin as head of PBL, and Fred Friendly were importuned to allow the people who make the programs to have a voice in shaping the organization and the kind of programs to be produced. We were treated politely, listened to, and ignored. It's odd, because many of the people involved with the Ford Foundation are aware that institutions are at issue in the country today, and that they must be changed. But it is much easier to advocate reshaping an institution you're not working for.

After another period of freelancing, Alpert was enticed—against his instincts—to join WCBS-TV. The siren was John Wicklein, a colleague at ABC and PBL, who had been hired as manager of news broadcasts at WCBS-TV. Wicklein had worked also for the *New York Times*. A serious and able newsman with a strong moral sense, he wanted to turn WCBS News into a real digging operation and persuaded Alpert that he would have the latitude to accomplish this. Alpert joined him in October 1970. Eleven weeks later Alpert was fired, along with Michael Keating, WCBS-TV news director, who had been sympathetic to the Wicklein idea. Wicklein himself was fired shortly thereafter.

"Wicklein," said Alpert, "is an old-fashioned applecart upsetter. I tried to get into problem-solving journalism. We both missed. We were fired." Programs about abortion, the reasons for the failure of Wall Street firms and the background of suicides at the Tombs prison made the top brass uncomfortable because they made actual and potential advertisers uncomfortable. CBS had turned itself into a conglomerate with the purchase of the New York Yankees baseball club, Holt, Rinehart & Winston publishers, Creative Playthings and Fender Musical Instruments, among others, and was hurting financially because of the failure of these nontelevision enterprises to show a big profit. It leaned heavily on the proceeds of WCBS-TV, and venturesome journalism in that situation was risky. So the stable was cleaned out.

On the basis of his commercial and noncommercial experiences, Alpert has developed some theories about the operation and impact of television:

> TV and radio, as we set it up, are honest brokers between the people and the people. They go out and look at some of us in some context, and then report back to the rest of us. I think there is some validity in that concept, and I would not like to see it go altogether. But something has happened in the United States in the last few years. People are beginning to appreciate the fiction of the melting pot and of assimilation, and they are realizing that this is a pluralistic society with many diverse interests. They would like to argue it out on that basis. If that is the case, then our electronic media need a lot of diverse voices, not necessarily defined along political lines—chess players, by gosh, and John Birchers, and people who like Chinese pottery. I am not suggesting that we eliminate the networks and radio stations. I am suggesting that they move in the direction of giving access, free uncensored access, and that we use cable television[4] for access for everybody. The only way to do this is to set cable TV up along lines diametrically opposed to the existing system.
>
> At present, a man or a company using the public airways is responsible to the Federal Communications Commission, which is

---

[4] See Appendix B.

responsible to the President. The FCC serves the industry, and when by accident it tries not to, the industry hits it on the head. I think we need to establish cable as a common carrier—as a means of communication open to everybody on the same published rates. That is, if you or I want to telephone, we are in the same class of users, we pay the same, and we cannot be refused service. The common carrier is in the business of carrying your message from point A to point B, and it has nothing to do with the content of the message. Thus the message and the means of communication are totally different. Now if you apply that to television, it would mean that for the first time the man who owns the means of communication will have nothing to do with what is being communicated. That should be our aim.

In practice this would mean that if a person wanted to present a program—say, a review of the media—he would pay for the time, on a published scale, and the time would be his without interference. Of course, money would still be a restricting factor. If persons wished to respond to the program, they in turn could purchase time at the same rates. In this manner, both would have access to a neutral system—unlike that at present.

Proponents of the common-carrier approach assert that there will no longer be any need for "equal time" regulations or "fairness" doctrines. These regulations and rules, they say, reflect the present situation, which is scarce channels. If there were a free marketplace of ideas, the regulations would be excess baggage. In Alpert's view, they have operated to stifle free discussion.

Would a change in the national administration improve matters with regard to FCC operations? Not likely: the FCC has for the most part—and despite the dissent of some dedicated commissioners—operated throughout its career in behalf of the television industry and will continue to do so, whatever the administration. But as cable TV becomes a force to reckon with, things can be done to achieve changes in television programming, and the first step is educating the public to the fact that it is entitled to access and should form pressure groups toward that end. Responsibility for launching that campaign rests to a large extent with the people working in the television medium. The public does not know what is *not* on television; it knows only what *is* on. The media people know both what is and what is not on. Ultimately, the struggle enters the political arena, and while it would be futile to expect major reforms, certain alterations in current patterns can be made through organized pressure groups.

The National Conference on Citizens Rights in Broadcasting made a start toward this end at a convocation in New York in April 1970, and even the organizers of the conference were surprised that 1,200 persons turned out. But the character of the convocation was élitist, with big names vying with one another for the microphone, and wealthy operators of cable-television companies getting more than equal time over less experienced minority groups.

What about extending First Amendment protections to the radio-television industry? I asked Alpert. Would that encourage the managers of the industry to resist government pressure and to give greater access to the public—particularly dissenting sections of the public? Alpert answered:

If you give television journalism the same protection that is given to the print media, then in fact you are saying we are going to change the whole system, because you can't have First Amendment protections and still maintain licensing. What you're saying is that we are going to abolish the FCC, and come up with some other system. There are two problems here: one is the fear the government or big business will intimidate television—government especially—and I don't see how this can be solved so long as government issues licenses; the second is that you don't really need government to intimidate television journalism because it is shaped essentially by the corporate interests of an industry whose main purpose is, first, the maximization of profits, and, second, enlarging its power, which it does through advertising. This means that it has a vested interest in having the broadest appeal possible, and in being inoffensive.

Protecting television journalism against government is a desirable goal, but that still leaves the problem of protecting it against the television industry. There is very little good journalism on television, and it comes to us as a shock when it *is* presented. It is not that the people who work in television journalism don't want to undertake it: they try hard, and in the beginning they care desperately—even some of the executives. But the combination of the profit motive, monopoly conditions, and government regulation makes it almost impossible to do much within the existing system. You can say to government: Keep your hands off!, and of course they won't. You can say to the owners of the industry: Shape up!, and that would be silly because they are shaping up to the needs of their system. I would suspect that the real victims here are people like Dr. Frank Stanton of CBS, a bright and sophisticated man who cannot possibly watch television because if he did, he would be bored stiff. If he watches his news programs, he must see how superficial they are, because he's been around a long time. The poor man is exploited by the system, just as we are.

Would it not be more accurate to call Stanton a participant rather than a victim? I asked. If he were a victim, as we are, would he not be motivated in a different way? "We are all participant victims," Alpert replied. "One wishes Stanton and the others would think differently, but the man who benefits from the system in the way of power and prestige is also a victim, because the system does not permit him to express his most human desires."

Nor does the system, with its competitive nature, permit a common front in the industry against governmental harassment. Support for CBS during *The Selling of the Pentagon* furor was certainly not so great as it was (as Fred Friendly noted in an article in *Harper's* magazine) when CBS and Edward R. Murrow were under fire during the McCarthy era. In 1971 the other networks perhaps were waiting to see whether advertisers would punish CBS by placing their advertising elsewhere—that is, with the other networks.

In the lower echelons of television, Alpert said, the attitude toward CBS and the Pentagon program was mixed because the world is more complicated than it was in the days of Ed Murrow:

> For example, years ago, I would have said: Right on, CBS! But today, I will say: OK, CBS, I'm with you, but I know now that I am not defending "the truth" but the lesser of two evils, or attacking the worse of two evils. So a lot of us rad-libs are not as enthusiastic as we once were about joining this kind of fight. Yet it is terribly important that we join the fight. Things like *The Selling of the Pentagon* and the fuss in its wake prove that the system is not entirely monolithic. It is still too monolithic for my taste, but a lot of decent

things do get through, and it is important that we preserve that freedom as a basis upon which to build more.

Sensing Alpert's ambivalence and seeming contradictions about
both his work and the media which he was criticizing, I put a
final question to him: "How do you, at age thirty-nine, in between
generations—with one foot in the younger generation and the
other in the elder generation—how do you see your own future?"
He replied:

> Schizophrenia would be a relief. I have about five phrenias. I am
> part of a swing generation, and I am torn between working within
> the system to change it, and getting out of it to change it, and I
> guess I have been moving steadily and slowly out. Mostly because
> I did not work very well within it. Like most people of my genera-
> tion, I have been supported by the very organizations I have been
> complaining about, and I am addicted to that support. So I think
> I'll be slow, but I think I will reach a point just outside the mass
> media where I can make a rational and radical criticism of the sys-
> tem, which may help. Because people older than I am are not
> aware of the deficiencies of the media, and people younger than I
> am tend to throw the baby out with the bath water, I want to be
> a little bit of a bridge between them. And that's a good place to
> shut up.

Alpert, however, did not shut up—and he did find a bridge on
the fringe of the mass media. In July 1971 radio station WRVR-FM,
New York, owned and operated by the Riverside Church, took
on a new general manager to convert the station from an essentially music station to one of news and public affairs. The new
manager was John Wicklein, Alpert's colleague at CBS, and once
again Wicklein asked Alpert to join him. Alpert did, and thus the
two were together again, but under entirely different auspices.

Control of the station (until that time noncommercial) was
shifted from the Riverside Church to a Riverside Broadcasting
Corporation, whose trustees were affiliated with the church. In
a policy statement on assuming his new role, Wicklein said:

> We want to be a force for constructive change in this community.
> We will seek out problems that should be brought to public atten-
> tion. We want to raise controversy on these issues, on the theory that

questions concerning the welfare of the public are best thrashed out in public. When we do that, we expect to be challenged. When we are, we will put the challengers on the air to rebut the stands we have taken. We will also open up the public-affairs programs for telephone call-ins, so that you can question people in the news and present your ideas on community problems.

In order to have an effective democracy, there must be public forums in which the people can present opposing points of view on controversial issues of the day. I believe strongly that freedom of speech is essential to improving the quality of our lives. For this reason, the station will support the free expression of ideas and oppose the suppression of dissent. We will be particularly on guard against government suppression of news and commentary on television and radio, and government attempts to silence the press.

The station will not restrict its reporters' independence in digging into controversial stories. Nor will we permit pressure from business, government or community groups to restrict that independence. In our news and public-affairs programs, we hope to offer an alternative to the pap that passes for news and the pallid comment that passes for analysis on many radio and television stations in New York.

For more than a year WRVR has lived up to its credo. It now takes advertising, but there is no evidence that its programs have been influenced by this fact—and the advertising is presented quietly and without the idiocy accompanying most commercials on the regular stations. The news reporters do dig, and discussions are frank—about prison conditions, welfare problems, housing, consumer affairs and just about everything that concerns the New York metropolitan community.

And Arthur Alpert? He is director of news for WRVR-FM and has his own program one evening a week. The title? *Inside Media.*

CHAPTER IX

A QUESTION
OF COLOR

THE reporter slowed his car as he approached the walled estate on Long Island, 30 miles from New York City, where his assignment had taken him. Cars were parked at odd angles near the gate set back from the road, and men and women stood in an irregular semicircle, some talking idly, others peering about. Photographic equipment lay nearby. News people.

The reporter drove his car past the group down the road and parked it on a shoulder. He trudged back toward the gate, and as he came within hearing distance of the group outside he heard a voice say: "Finally, here comes someone to park our cars." The reporter was black.

Later, inside the house, when the press was entertained in the library, the reporter was overwhelmed with offerings of food and drink from his white colleagues seeking to redress a grievous offense. That, of course, simply compounded the offense.

When Thomas A. Johnson of the *New York Times*, the reporter of the scenario, told me this story, he smiled broadly. I smiled, too—narrowly. But whatever embarrassment and dismay I felt on hearing the story could in no measure match the emotions that Tom Johnson must have suppressed that day, or the feelings of his black colleagues of the white press on countless other days of assignment in the white world.

Johnson is a leading member of the Three Percent Club, a non-existent organization I have conjured into being for the purpose of

162

this report on the presence and progress of the black journalist in the white media, with some excursions into the state of the black media, and the coverage of news of the black community. The "three percent" represents the number of black and minority personnel on the editorial staffs of the communications media of the United States. The precentage varies in certain areas, but generally averages out to three.

The rise of the black journalist in the white media is a phenomenon of the last decade and particularly the last years of the 1960s. Until then, some big newspapers had one token black editorial person, a rare few had two or three, most had none at all. At the *New York Times,* for example, black maintenance workers (under Newspaper Guild jurisdiction) numbered in the hundreds; there were one or two blacks in editorial positions.

Two factors were basically responsible for an abrupt, if limited, shift in hiring policies in the 1960s. One was the expanding market for goods in the black communities, which at the same time were becoming increasingly resentful of lily-white products and packaging—including news products.

The other and perhaps more persuasive factor was the influence of the black freedom movement, which had helped to build in black communities an atmosphere of hostility that made it virtually impossible for white reporters to come in and gather news there. At the Conference on Recruitment and Training of Minority Employees sponsored by the Newspaper Guild in New York in April 1971, Eleanor Holmes Norton, chairman of the New York City Human Rights Commission, said: "It was undoubtedly the black rebellions which shut white reporters out to which we owe almost all of the modest growth in minority reporters, in particular. The daily media learned quickly that access to a growing population of hostile blacks depended upon the recruitment of more black reporters."

Today there is hardly a big-city daily newspaper or television news program that functions without black writers or on-camera reporters. But while the change in complexion appears to be sharp, in terms of numbers and percentages it is not. The Newspaper Guild undertook a racial employment survey in the spring of 1971, with queries to 89 Guild units in 41 cities in the United States and Canada (80 were below the border). Seventy-five responded. They reported 23,112 professional (editorial) employees, of whom 97.7 percent were Anglo-Saxon, 1.5 percent black, 0.4 percent with Spanish surnames, 0.4 percent Oriental, and 0.1 percent Indian. Translated into people, this meant 235 blacks, 32 Spanish, 22 Orientals, 2 Indians. Of these, slightly more than half were reporters, copyeditors or photographers. Most startling statistic of all: one-third of the Guild units reported no minority personnel at all.

If percentage points are boring, turn for a moment to a statistic come to life. Dianne White made her debut as a "weather girl" on KSD-TV in St. Louis in August of 1961. Her hiring broke the color bar, and other things besides the weather heated up in St. Louis that summer. Ray Karpowicz, the station manager, recalled almost ten years later: "We had the first Negro in town. It wasn't a popular thing to do. We got a lot of criticism from both the public and the sponsors. But we stuck it out."

Miss White, a former fashion model, was brief and precise in her recollection: "You need a stiff back. I was a kind of commodity. But it's been an even exchange. I learned a lot. I'm not a commodity anymore."

Very few black journalists were meeting one another in St. Louis, however, through most of the 1960s, and the unwillingness to hire more blacks left Miss White an oddity if not a commodity. But in 1968 things began to change. St. Louis had emerged almost unscathed from the ghetto uprisings of the preceding years, but the powers in the city saw the writing on the walls, particularly in the newsrooms. In March 1968 the Report of the National Advisory Commission on Civil Disorders (the Kerner Commission) pinpointed a cause of the nationwide disorders. It said:

> Important segments of the media failed to report adequately on the causes and the consequences of civil disorders and on the underlying problems of race relations. They have not communicated to the majority of their readers—which is white—a sense of the degradation, misery, and hopelessness of life in the ghetto. This failing must be corrected and the improvement must come from within the industry.

Talks were initiated between the news executives of St. Louis and the black community, and the editors were told that the city's newspapers were afflicted with "tired blood." A transfusion of blackness was firmly suggested. The suggestion was adopted, and by 1970 the St. Louis media had formed a Five Percent Club. In ten years, to be precise, the percentage of blacks in the media rose from zero in 1960 to five percent in 1970. There were seven (out of 166) on the *Post-Dispatch* editorial staff, three (out of 135) on the *Globe-Democrat,* five (out of 36) at KSD-TV and radio, and five (out of 47) at KMOX-TV and radio.

That may read like real progress—until another statistic drives home a realistic point: St. Louis within a few years will have a black population of 50 percent. The same holds true for the urban centers of Chicago, New York, Philadelphia and Los Angeles, among other cities, where the pattern of black hiring is similar to that of St. Louis. When this prospect is absorbed, it becomes apparent that the "showcase black" syndrome is still prevalent.

Confronted with this firm evidence of tokenism, news executives acknowledge the figures but protest their characterization. "You have to understand," they say earnestly, "that the supply of *qualified* black journalists is limited. You don't know how *much* we wish there were more of them" (the word "black" in this context is interchangeable with "Puerto Rican," "Chicano," "Oriental" or "Indian").

For most publications and TV stations the action rarely gets beyond the wishful stage. A reason for the failure of minority recruiting methods—or lack of them—was offered in the related field of advertising, but it was applicable to the communications industry also. Paul Lavenson of the Hotel Corporation of America told the American Association of Advertisers that there was a 0.7 representation of black professionals in the industry nationwide at the end of 1969.

"I suspect," he said, "that the 'let's employ more blacks' memo comes down from the president's office and the personnel guy goes through the standard channels and comes up with zero. If you're hunting deer and you really want to bag one, you don't use buckshot. You use a special rifle, a telescopic sight, and most importantly, you go where the deer are. Damn few deer ever wander right into your kitchen, no matter how many times your mouth waters for venison."

One can be horrified at the bloody metaphor, and the memory of blacks being hunted down for reasons other than prospective employment, without rejecting Lavenson's point. It was a point made even more recently in the news industry itself by Norman Isaacs, former executive editor of the *Louisville Courier-Journal*, a past president of the American Society of Newspaper Editors, and now a resident adviser at the Columbia Graduate School of Journalism. He told the Newspaper Guild Minority Group Recruitment Conference in April 1971: "We on newspapers are responsible for the present state of affairs. We had a closed-door policy toward all minority groups up until the recent past." Newspapers, he said, have only themselves to blame for the short supply of minority personnel, and "editors and their city editors and their copydesks and good large parts of their staffs are well behind their communities" in this area.

Both the ASNE and the American Newspaper Publishers Association, he said, have considerable power to change things: "I wish to hell they would use it. The publishers are not your problem. They are nobody's problem. It is the editors and managing editors, and once their disposition is correct, proper, right, and they want to get it done, they will get some hiring done."

One thing they could do is abandon the "qualification" standard, which is rarely raised when a bright, talented, untutored *white* youngster comes along and they are challenged to take a chance. While professional standards obviously have changed, and college degrees seem almost mandatory for a newspaper or TV editorial job today, there was a time when no-degree Italians, Jews and Irish developed into some of the best-known bylines in the newspaper industry. But they were white. There are no rules to prevent similar experiments with black youngsters—particularly when on-the-job training programs have come into fashion—except the unwritten rules or prejudice in the minds of editors and their assistants.

Even granting the validity of the requirement of educational qualification, the increasing number of available young black college graduates renders invalid the "lack of supply" argument. What has been in large supply, however, is the distrust among young blacks about careers in the white media. The reason is not difficult to determine: it stems from the persistent disappointment and rejection experienced by black job applicants not only in journalism but in most areas of professional life.

Several worthwhile and untokenlike efforts have been undertaken in the last years to break down the mistrust among young blacks that there can be a departure "from that terribly un-American horizontal life pattern," as Eleanor Holmes Norton described it.

The Newspaper Fund, sponsored by Dow Jones & Company (*Wall Street Journal* and *National Observer*), in 1968 established an Urban Journalism Workshop in Washington, D.C., in a project which has now been expanded to finance workshops in 12 areas of the country. Yet by mid-1971 only nine workshops had been established and, although the money was available, the search was still on for three newspapers to co-sponsor the remaining workshops.

The *New York Times,* the *Washington Post,* the *San Francisco Examiner* and other newspapers have training programs, and the Ford Foundation, with matching funds from the Columbia Broadcasting System and the National Broadcasting Company, has sponsored a summer program in broadcast journalism at the Columbia Graduate School of Journalism. The Ford Foundation has also financed an on-the-job training program at United Press International.

The Newspaper Guild has authorized the institution of a National Minority Skills Bank to serve as an informational center and referral service for all minority training programs in the Guild and for the dozens of private and public job-training programs. The Guild has also determined to seek fixed "minimum percentages" of minority employees wherever possible "to remedy past and continuing inequities," and to seek scholarships for minority groups funded by the Guild and newspaper managements.

At predominantly black universities, where there has been a marked absence of journalism courses, the number of journalism programs has risen from only two in the mid-1960s to 40 in 1970, according to the United Negro College Fund. More students are enrolling in these courses, although their skepticism about careers in the white media remains high. The preference is for broadcast journalism or noncommercial public relations rather than newspapers. In the *Columbia Journalism Review* (July/ August 1971), Roger M. Williams of Time-Life News Service wrote: "Significantly, many black students intend—or say they intend—to work in 'white journalism' only long enough to acquire the experience and skills they need to undertake the same sort of work in the black communities."

They know they are not being hired into "white journalism," in most cases, with any degree of enthusiasm; the attitude of their editors and many of their white colleagues often is transparent. At Clark College in Atlanta, Alan Bussel, director of the expanding journalism program, declared that white editors disguise their motives poorly. "I get calls from editors who want 'a colored writer,'" he said. "They say they are not under pressure to get one, but you know that some of them are. I don't think many of the students will stay after they get there."

But what about those who do stay and are still coming in? Have they been able to affect significantly the coverage of news of the black community and the racial attitudes of their editors and white colleagues? For answers to these questions I turned to several black reporters, in particular to Thomas A. Johnson of the *New York Times*, the man who didn't park those cars on Long Island.

At forty-one, Johnson is a senior citizen among black reporters. After leaving Long Island University in 1955, where he studied journalism under a GI Bill grant, he couldn't find a job. He went to work for a small public-relations firm and, when that folded, opened his own one-man agency. He wrote his own stories, took his own pictures, then peddled both to the black press—sometimes for five dollars a combination.

In 1963 he got a call from William F. McIlwain, then an editor on *Newsday* on Long Island. "He comes from North Carolina," Johnson said, "and when his voice came at me I thought he was a brother. He said, 'How would you like to be in the newspaper business?' He said everybody was talking about doing something for the Negroes, making a big thing about civil rights and all that, but nobody was giving Negroes any jobs. It sort of disgusted him, he said, when he looked around the newspapers and saw not a single Negro. He wanted one at *Newsday*."

Johnson joined the staff and covered general assignment until

another call came, in 1966, from the *New York Times.* They
wanted one too, so he left Long Island for Manhattan. For the
Times Johnson has covered uprisings in the ghettos, Adam Clayton Powell, Jr., on Bimini, the progress of black cultural movements, the war in Vietnam and the condition of black troops in
Europe. For a series in 1968 about the black soldier in Vietnam
and his prospects on returning to civilian life, Johnson received
two distinguished journalism awards. He has an appropriate sense
of the significance of his own career, a quiet and easy manner, a
careful speech and a splendid sense of humor. What follows is a
synthesis of my conversation with Johnson and other black
journalists. The formulations and opinions are largely theirs, interspersed with some opinions of my own.

There are three categories of black journalists in the white
media. The senior ones, such as Johnson, mostly in their forties
or older, worked first in the black media before or during the
mass demonstrations that marked the integrationist civil-rights
movement. When the white media decided they needed some
blacks on their staffs, they were readily available and made the
transition. They regard themselves for the most part as interpreters of the black experience.

The second group, now in their thirties, moved directly from
the universities and schools of journalism into the white media—
without experience with black publications. Like their elders,
they sought to be journalists first; craft was what they sought.

But the youngest ones, now coming along, regarded journalism
as a tool for social activism. They want to revolutionize the
media. Too young to have been part of the sit-ins and freedom
rides of the 1960s, they nonetheless have been deeply affected by
a decade of social turmoil on the campuses and in the streets, a
pervading sense of which they have brought to their work.

The oldest black journalists may have compromised a bit in
the sense that they have accepted certain rules by which to live,
to earn a living, to determine the degree of one's activism. A
lawyer, they say for example, does not picket a company against
which he is bringing a case the next day. They have had some
experience of the system, and while they might like to go to work
for the Muslim weekly *Muhammad Speaks* or the Black Panther

paper, they are at the same time confronted with the fact of families who require a take-home salary of decent proportion. The younger people object to this life-style, and the differences have caused certain frictions among the black journalists. The older group is not devoid of this activist drive, but it has resolved in itself for the most part the question of journalism first, activism second.

What motivated the older group to turn to the white media was partly economics and partly the creative excitement of the black movement that carried them along toward the idea of social, occupational and racial integration. Thus, with Johnson's generation, the goal was the *New York Times,* and that held true to a large extent for the second wave of black journalists emerging just before the shifting tide in the black movement away from integration.

But the youngest group questioned and for the most part rejected racial and social integration. Why should they be contributing to the success of the white media? they said. While many were going to the *Times,* CBS and NBC, others wanted to do a "black thing." They took jobs with the Community News Service, a New York–based outfit covering black and Puerto Rican news, or the *Race Relations Reporter* in Nashville or with the more militant black press. But often, perhaps within a year, they accepted bids from the white media. They are, said Johnson, doing in one year what it took his generation seven or eight years to see: that you can starve to death financially and emotionally on a black plantation as well as on a white one.

There were, in addition, young people who had taken jobs with black newspapers, who had sat at their typewriters hour after hour rewriting the *New York Times* and the local white daily, never able to do what they had come to do, and who finally left in disgust.

They had color in common with their publishers but little else. With exceptions such as the *Baltimore Afro-American,* the *Chicago Defender,* the *Michigan Chronicle* and the *New York Amsterdam News* (since the newspaper came under new management in mid-1971), black newspapers were operated by businessmen interested primarily in filling pages with advertisements and disinterested in covering the black community.

With a sharper concept of themselves as human beings than their elders, the young black journalists moved to the *Times* or the *Washington Post* or NBC and discovered that they could work there; that while they were not going to radicalize the white institutions, they were able at times to do the things they wanted to do—to reveal a hidden truth in a controversy, to provide some coverage to an area which would go uncovered if they were not there.

That is the kind of gratification that makes it somewhat easier to get past the insults and affronts—the times when the black reporter is taken for a messenger boy or a janitor, or asked to show his credentials at a press conference when no white reporter is similarly challenged; or when he asks a question on camera and the person addressed replies right through him to the white cameraman. The black reporter consults with a white editor before going into the black community on assignment and reports back to a white editor. And there is the problem simply of getting used to living with white colleagues in the newsroom.

Drawn together by color and common problems, the black journalists shy away from integration in the newsrooms. "We meet all the time," said Johnson. "We stand around talking together in the newsroom, and a white colleague will walk by and say: 'Plotting a revolution?', and one of us will say: 'We are deciding whether you're going to put out a paper.' It happens just about every day. The whites are curious, a bit suspicious, perhaps, when I think of it, which I don't do very often. But there are whites I gravitate to on an individual basis, and talk about work, how it went on that story yesterday. But I could probably miss talking to whites three or four times a week and not even think about it."

Melvin Mencher, an associate professor at the Columbia Graduate School of Journalism, drew some revealing comments from black journalists during a 16-week cross-country survey for the school's Interracial Reporting Program. In Connecticut, a black radio newsman told him: "Right after I went to work, I was introduced to every one of the people in the place, the first time that had ever happened. I was the only reporter taken to the state broadcasting association dinner."

That kind of mascot approach smolders. In Kansas City, Melvin Lewis, a general assignment reporter on the *Star*, told Mencher: "Look, I'm black. I know I have to be better than the average guy. I have to show I'm better here. I have to get out on stories to show them. But even when I do, I know they're saying, 'That's a pretty good nigger.' Or else they say, 'He's a good boy.' Boy, boy, boy. I'm 'boy' to them. They'd like me to spend my life going around kissing whitey's ass. I'm not built that way."

Bob DeLeon of *Newsday* stated the problem less pungently but no less accurately. He said:

> When blacks joined the media and other newspaper staffs, they were told, "You will not be treated differently from any white member of our staff. We want you to remember that you are a journalist who just happens to be black." Today, more than ever, black journalists everywhere are having serious doubts about the validity of that assessment. The doubts are being raised by the journalists themselves in terms of the kinds of stories they choose or are assigned to cover by their various publications—and by members of the black community—a constituency that black journalists must serve.
>
> With the thrust of black consciousness and the undeniable swing away from integration efforts toward a black cultural nationalism, black journalists have been placed in a position that is not easily defended. On the one hand, they must fulfill obligations to their brothers and sisters in the community, and they must, on the other hand, fulfill certain obligations they have made to their prospective employers.

To deal with this dilemma, organizations of black journalists have come into being. The first was Black Perspective, in 1967, designed primarily to influence the media to improve their coverage of racial news, to help bring about a greater understanding in the media about the black freedom movement, and to maintain a liaison among black journalists throughout the country. Among the initiators were Robert Maynard of the *Washington Post*, Claude Lewis of the *Philadelphia Bulletin* and Johnson.

How would they go about accomplishing all these goals? I asked Johnson. "We're still trying to find out," he said with a smile tinged with rue. But he proceeded to demonstrate that things were being done.

If a newspaper is guilty of ignorance or misinterpretation in a story dealing with the black community, Black Perspective members on the paper ask for a conference with management, not on an organizational basis, but as individuals. This is the after-the-fact approach. Before the fact, Black Perspective seeks to make other black journalists aware of their own strength within the media—both white and black—and aware of the group strength of Black Perspective.

In June 1970 the first National Conference of Black News Media workers was held at Lincoln University in Jefferson City, Missouri, where Dr. Armistead Pride more than 30 years ago set up the first journalism curriculum in a black university. Out of the conference emerged a National Association of Black Media Workers with several regional chapters.

These moves to organization have inspired the birth of black newsletters on individual papers such as *Umesika* (Swahili for "Have you heard?") at the *New York Times*. And the new journalism reviews have devoted increasing attention to the problems of black journalists and the coverage of black news. In Denver and Los Angeles, for example, the stress is on Chicanos as well as blacks; and in the East there is emphasis on Puerto Ricans.

One topic of frequent discussion among black media workers is the question of assignment to purely "black" stories as against general assignment. In the early days, Johnson said, the process worked like a sponge:

> The editors would send their black man out to absorb everything that was going on and when he came back they would squeeze him out like a sponge. This is what black reporters resent most, and it is why many of them insist on staying on to watch the copydesk, and until the first edition comes out, to make sure that what they put down *on* paper comes out *in* the paper.

As an example, he said he was preparing a story about the increase in crime in black neighborhoods, "or rather the increase in the number of blacks in the more profitable areas of crime." He was doing it, he said, because "if I didn't, some white reporter would grab it and do a story that would say essentially, 'Look at them niggers up there robbing and stealing.' I show the reasons why this increase in crime is taking place. I don't think the white reporter would have the background or the interest."

So the conflict about assignment persists, a mixture of protectiveness, pride and concern—and resentment, too. Reporters with established reputations (such as Johnson, Robert Maynard of the *Washington Post* and L. F. Palmer of the *Chicago Daily News*) for the most part choose their own assignments and have considerable leeway with time and travel. But, said Johnson, "you have to go up to the man and tell him that you want to do this kind of thing, and in that sense there is a measure of psychic justification for your existence in the white media."

There is conflict on the question of assignment not only within the reporter himself but between him and some elements of the black community. From time to time editors feeling guilty about only black assignments for black reporters may send one off to do a poverty story in the suburbs ("It's a white story," said Johnson, "because it's the suburbs"). Observant white colleagues will come by to congratulate the black reporter on the assignment. But then a call will almost surely follow from the director of an urban poverty program (black) saying: "What are you doing covering that kind of a story when we've got all these problems among our own folk?"

There are many such pressures, particularly upon the younger black reporters, from civil-rights groups. To Johnson the pressures were understandable but shortsighted. He said:

I think the time is approaching—though still somewhat distant—when the young black reporter is going to have to have the general freedom that a white reporter has—at least on the papers not run by the Neanderthals. A time when they will want to be just journalists. It is a long-range goal we have to work toward. Now most of us, and particularly my generation, which may be becoming expendable, are fighting a psychological battle: every black today feels a push toward doing the black story. He almost feels that he is denying his community if he avoids it.

There are many pressures on the young black reporter, so much so that he has all he can do to get his head together. He has to be very strong to resist these pressures, which come from people like myself too. For example, in my course on Race and the New Media at New York University, the students are impressed simply because I am Tom Johnson, foreign correspondent without a beat, traveling around the country and around the world. That impresses them. But at bottom the story is still Old Sam, still the nigger.

The talk turned to the black press again and its influence within the black community. There are today more than 200 black newspapers in the United States with a combined circulation of about two million. Only two are dailies: the *Chicago Defender* (33,000) and the *Atlanta World* (25,000). Of the older established papers, the *Afro-American* alone, with editions in Baltimore, Richmond and Washington, D.C., has maintained a steady circulation (137,000). The new leaders are *Muhammad Speaks* (400,000) and the *Black Panther* (110,000 in 1970 but certainly less today because of the split in the party). These figures in themselves bespeak the changing attitudes in the black communities and a militant orientation away from the traditional black press.

Among the reasons for the decline of the older newspapers is the inroad of television and black radio. Inner-city blacks, said L. F. Palmer of the *Chicago Daily News*, are "audio-oriented." A Chicago editor added: "The four black radio stations here reach more listeners in an hour than the black newspaper has readers in a month."

More significant, however, is the fact that black newspapers have not been either able or willing to keep up with the rapidly changing moods and the decline of patience in the black communities. They are more parochial than their nationally circulated forebears, and they emphasize social news for the middle-class and sensation for the casual reader.

Hoyt Fuller, managing editor of *Black World*, took note of the cleavage between the black militants and the black press which, he said, "represents essentially the interests of the black bourgeoisie." The problems of the black press, he conceded, were compounded by the infinitely greater resources of the white press now available to black journalists working there. He did not regard the increased and improved coverage of the black com-

munity by the white media as a "fad that is going to pass." He
said:

I don't think the white press is going to return to its prior position
of ignoring the black community. But I do think the black community is turning inward and is no longer interested in having its
activities interpreted for it by the white press. It is no longer interested in having anything interpreted for it by the white press, and
that is why blacks will turn more and more to their own newspapers.
The black press must perform its job, and I put the responsibility on
the black press to be not only relevant but first rate in all that
it does.

This view was echoed by Johnson, a product of the black press.
He said: "They are not all bad, but most are bad because they
have no concept of journalism, or right or wrong, or the need of
the community to know. They had a tradition of crusading but
they don't crusade anymore."

He was infuriated by a recent convention of the National Newspaper Publishers Association (black) in Atlanta at which several
awards of about 1,000 dollars each were given to black journalists
—all awards sponsored by Coca-Cola, Liggett and Myers and
other giant corporations. "I thought it cheapened the whole
thing," he said. "It would have been better to have given a seven-
dollar award on principle, with the money collected from the
hardware store around the corner. The black press has not taken
the lead in the struggle to change America. The lead has come
from elsewhere."

But he felt changes were being made in several of the larger
papers, and they are apparent in New York since the takeover of
the *Amsterdam News* by an enterprising group of black investors
led by Clarence B. Jones, Jr. Circulation in a few months rose
from 80,000 to 93,000 and was continuing upward. The paper has
established an editorial board of prominent blacks in all en-
deavors, extended its cultural coverage and improved its investigative reporting, an ingredient painfully missing for years
in the black communities. Further, the group is seeking to create
a loose national network of black communications media for an
interchange of ideas and facilities, and to broaden coverage.

Johnson spoke with some ambivalence about black magazines

with large circulation, such as *Ebony*. He said he was appalled at times by some of its features and cited one in which the magazine sought to demonstrate that black women were becoming prettier—ostensibly because they were becoming whiter. "I'd like to burn the magazine at times," he said, but almost immediately thereafter he was warm with praise for the work in *Ebony* of Lerone Bennett, whom he characterized as "one of the most influential black journalists of our time."

From my conversations with Johnson and the other black journalists, I came away with a complicated set of reactions which were entirely appropriate to the subject of black journalists in the essentially white media. If the black journalists had mixed feelings and misgivings, they also had a tremendous sense of achievement in a period that spanned less than a decade. There is no question that the coverage of the black community, while still woefully inadequate, has finally emerged from its swamp of prejudice, arrogance and fear. And the improvement must be attributed almost entirely to the work and spirit of the black journalists such as Johnson and his younger colleagues.

"One thing you learn from the white mass media," Johnson said, "is the inescapable necessity for good, effective black publications. Because no matter what the media, I don't think they will take the time to do the job that needs to be done in the coverage of black news."

Fuller, Palmer, Johnson and the others have set high standards of journalistic quality for the black media. No black journals at present meet their standards. Nor will the best of the black journalists, or the black community, be satisfied with a foothold in the white press, however beneficial that may be at present.

If and when the young black journalists of the white press, with their accrued experience and knowledge of the operation of the white power structure, accept the challenge laid down by the future, a new black press could emerge which would be not only relevant and first rate, but above all, a unifying and activating force of tremendous power for the black community.

CHAPTER X

THE NEWSROOM
AS MEN'S ROOM

"THE thing that was surprising to find," said B. J. Phillips, "is that if you scratch a woman, you find a feminist."

B. J. Phillips's visitor, sitting in the small, untidy, but workmanlike office on the twenty-fifth floor of the Time-Life Building, thought fleetingly that he might not have put it that way; but after one hour he knew that was the only way to put it. And if he had had another word for "workmanlike," he would have used it.

For B. J. Phillips is a woman—young, straightforward and committed to the cause of equality of women in the communications industry. She is a writer for *Time* (you knew it was a writer's office, and not a researcher's, because it had windows). That should hardly be a breathtaking fact, except that it was: she was one of the few women to be hired by *Time* as a writer. *Time* was 48 years old in the year of the interview, 1971.

Since the spring of 1970, there has been a feminine ferment in the newspaper and magazine offices of the nation—and now beginning in the television studios—which is reshaping the character of editorial staffs, the content of the publications and the outlook and approach of the Newspaper Guild, the chief representative of editorial and commercial employees of newspapers and newsmagazines.

The main beneficiaries of the ferment—some were beginning even to concede the benefits—were the newspapers of Washington and New York, the newsweeklies and the big, slick women's magazines with headquarters in New York. But the radical and so-called underground publications, many of them with adolescent attitudes toward women and sex, also were caught up in the winds of change.

The preliminaries are told best in B. J. Phillips's own words, and here they are, as they evolved in a long conversation, with the questions implied:

The whole thing didn't start in Washington, but it was the place where it came together. It was especially gratifying for me because I had the image of being a young Turk, a troublemaker. And it was good to find really respected newspaperwomen respond—people like Frances Lewine of the Associated Press, Helen Thomas of United Press International and Sarah McClendon of the Texas newspapers, the ones who really cover what's going on in Washington.

It started very casually. I was working in the Style Section of the *Washington Post,* and we were covering the women's movement. In a deeper sense we women reporters were affected by it. As women, we had the problem of discrimination as third-class citizens. As professionals, it took more training, more qualification to get ahead in the industry than it took for males. Editors always say: We're looking for *qualified* women or *qualified* blacks. That's so hypocritical. You never hear them say: We're looking for *qualified* white males.

It was and still is very difficult for a woman to obtain broad-range credentials. We had to be superqualified, like the blacks. We had to be "super-nigger," as the cartoons say. Women are shunted off to the women's page, or become obituary writers. Rarely are they given a chance to cover the general news, as men are.

Maybe it's true that there is not a woman qualified to be managing editor of, for example, the *Washington Post.* Why not? The answer is that in the history of the press women never had a chance to make themselves qualified.

What really put it all together was the demonstration at the Gridiron Club in March 1970. I was sitting in the newsroom with two other women and said: "It's Gridiron time again. . . . Those exclusionary bastards! You know, we ought to picket them." Someone else said: "Hey, that's a pretty good idea."

So we spent four hours on a Saturday afternoon talking about it and calling people up. We really struck a responsive chord, particularly among people who had been in the business a long time. When I called Sarah McClendon (I had never met her) and told her what we were going to do, she let out a yell and said: "I think that's the best thing I ever heard. I'll be there!"

Then what became clear to me was that these women had been eating this shit 20 years longer than I had. For every horror story I could tell, they had 20 more years of them.

Along came Gridiron night. I went down about 5:30 P.M. and found about 30 women already there outside the Statler-Hilton. One woman photographer had liberated some mounting board for picket signs. My favorite was "Free Kay Graham." [She is the publisher of the *Washington Post.*] The day before, Nicholas von Hoffman had written a column in the *Post* about the Gridiron Club, saying what a bad scene it was. But otherwise it had been helter-skelter, no other publicity.

So there we were in our long evening pantsuits, feather boas flying in the wind, cops moving us around all the time. What amazed me was that all these women who came out had never been on a picket line before, except perhaps for a Newspaper Guild strike. It was, among other things, the world's only self-interviewing picket line. We were walking around interviewing one another because most of the women there had to cover Mrs. Nixon's press conference.

We also went up to the doors and held them open for all those nice liberal editors and publishers. We really embarrassed them, and it's going to be an even greater embarrassment to them. The only thing the media can't stand is media coverage of itself. In the last analysis, that's what's going to do it.

There's a parallel with the black movement, with the fact that white reporters are not welcome in the black communities. That's coming true in the women's movement, too, as far as men reporters are concerned. It may not be the best way of doing things. Anybody ought to be able to cover any story at any time. But if it has to be done, women are going to ram it down editors' throats.

After the Gridiron, things began to snowball. A meeting was called at the home of another woman reporter for which signs had been posted in the women's rest rooms at the *Post* and the *Star*. We talked about existing inequities, problems of assignments, the excuses for not allowing women to cover night assignments on the ground that the streets of Washington were not safe at night. That may be true, but it never applied to those of us who were covering *parties* at night, when it was just as tough to get a cab in the back streets of Georgetown as it was in some downtown areas. Editors have chivalry about your personal safety when it is convenient to them. Otherwise, it's tough old turkey.

What came out of our meetings was that we began to see the media as reinforcing attitudes that were part of the problem. It does not report about the problems as much as it reinforces them. And it cannot therefore be considered as part of the solution. Because of our profession, we felt we had an opportunity to do something, and not only for ourselves.

Word of our meetings got around the *Post*. We took a lot of crap from the guys on the copydesk—you know, about whether we were studying karate every Wednesday night. But the brass was getting nervous. And by the time we finally went in to see them, they were so worried about what we might do that they were very receptive.

Before we went in, we had drawn up a position paper—two women from the *Post* and two from the *Star*—and everyone went over it word for word. But there were very few changes. We asked for an interview with Executive Editor Ben Bradlee and Managing Editor Eugene Patterson. As it turned out, it was for the morning when the kids were killed at Kent State. At the *Post* we sent the paper in ten minutes before the meeting to give them a chance to think about it, but no opportunity to wriggle out. The position paper opened this way:

> The news media are powerful shapers of public conscience and awareness. No segment of the population suffers the ill or good of media characterization so intensely as do minority groups. It is not an overstatement to say that the minute the old Negro stereotypes left the pages of American newspapers, a large step was taken toward recognizing the dignity of black Americans.

Likewise we feel that the media should take the first steps in recognizing the dignity of women if they are to discharge properly their peculiar mandate for leadership. Newspapers must purge themselves of the sexual stereotypes if the climate of the society is to change in the area of women's rights. An awareness of women as people must start here.

Accordingly, we believe it is time for Washington's newspapers to examine the characterizations, identifications, and attitudes toward women that routinely appear in the news pages.

In the area of women's news we insisted that newspapers "assure that no part of the paper becomes a dumping ground or 'women's place' for such stories."

On discrimination in coverage we noted the frequency with which women have been barred from covering assignments because of their sex, including the all-male National Press Club, cited the protests against this by the Newspaper Guild and the lack of action by the newspapers themselves. We asked the Washington newspapers to "use all available resources" to make sure that women "are not barred from covering news events on the basis of sex."

On stereotypes and identifications we said that women suffer as much from unconscious discrimination as from overt anti-feminism. We listed headlines such as "Grandmother Named Ambassador" (no one writes about the "househusband" who has taken up politics). A woman who is divorced should not be stigmatized forever as a "divorcee." Her ex-husband isn't. Also, the "transformation into nouns of adjectives denoting hair color is as good an example as exists of the woman-as-horseflesh attitude. Blond, brunette and redhead, like roan, chestnut and bay, do not tell anything beyond hair color." Particularly offensive, the position paper said, "is stigmatizing women as freaks because they have done something—anything—that doesn't fit the male myth about them. This pseudo-achiever syndrome is central to the problem of women's rights."

We spoke of the "tired adjectives" used to describe women (a choice of about six) and ended with a few notes on the future:

Women's-rights news is very big news at the moment. No self-respecting publication is without its cover story, series, or analysis.

But there is, by definition, an element of ignorance in all media discoveries—blacks, Indians, the poor. Such issues would not be hot news if they were understood and reported well all along. Our purpose is to fill in some of these areas of insensitivity and ignorance which have led to the present problems. The result can only be better newspapers.

The women of the *Washington Post* offered a graphic example, on the eve of Women's Strike Day in August 1970, of what they objected to in print. It was done in reverse English in a broadside circulated at the *Post* and at other papers. It read:

We all know that tomorrow is the 50th anniversary of women's suffrage, but it is also the birthday of Benjamin Bradlee, The Post's executive editor. In recognition of this astounding juxtaposition, some members of the Style Section have prepared the enclosed news bulletin.

Ben Bradlee, slim, attractive, but complex executive editor of the *Washington Post*, is 49 years old today, but he doesn't look it. How does he manage to combine a successful career with the happy home life he has created in his gracious Georgetown home?

In an interview today, pert, vivacious Mr. Bradlee revealed his secret. He relaxes after a day of whirlwind activity of the newspaper world by whomping up a batch of his favorite pecan-sauerbraten cookies for his thriving family.

Father of seven, youthful-looking Mr. Bradlee quips, "I enjoy working for the *Post*, but every family needs a strongly based home life."

"Sometimes," he sighs, "I almost wish I could work part time. After all, the public's trust in the newspaper is great, but my azaleas are dying."

What does Mrs. Bradlee think of her debonair husband's flair for journalism? "I think it's great," she said. "Every wife should let her husband work. It makes him so well-rounded. Now he has something to talk about at the dinner table."

She appreciates the extra effort he takes to maintain his youthful looks and figure despite his busy, busy day. Mr. Bradlee loves his work, but he is aware of the dangers involved. So far he does not feel that he is in competition with his wife.

"When that day comes," he said with a shudder, "I'll know it's time to quit."

Mr. Bradlee's quick and easy recipe for pecan-sauerbraten cookies appears in tomorrow's bulletin.

We found that the *Post* management was agreeable to our position paper, but the thing was to pin them down. We wanted a memo, and a few days after I left to take the job with *Time* in New York, it came down. And do you know, it was a paraphrase of our position paper. The same thing happened at the *Star*, where the meeting was held a couple of weeks later.

We talked with management about other things, too—hirings and promotions and salaries, more women as summer interns. We wanted them to *seek out* women. After all, if women are going to be able to be qualified for a tryout, you've got to give them a chance for internships while they are still at college. We also agreed that whenever we felt we had found something wrong, we would send it in and then talk about it.

The women have remained organized in the time since the agreement. We call ourselves the Newswomen's Caucus, I guess you'd say. We made a point not to have leaders. Of course, a couple of people are always more involved than others and have taken over the . . . uh . . . leadership.

The position paper became a model. A few weeks later someone reminded us that the Newspaper Guild would soon be holding its annual convention in Seattle. We knew that the only power we had was intimidation—the threat to make trouble, to file a suit. In the last analysis, the real power is to threaten the power of the newspapers—the threat to strike. As staff members, of course, we don't have access to what's in management's books, the codified salary lists and all that, but the Guild, of course, is a party to these things. So we decided we'd give the Guild whatever *help*, you know, that we could.

It all came through the Washington-Baltimore local of the Guild. We drew up the original draft; a delegation of women went to the executive committee of the local and, in effect, said: "Well, fellows, here it is. We expect you to take it to the convention and lead the floor fight." The resolutions covered various things, from the nebulous business about how women don't get a fair shake, to specifics that would be included in a model contract.

They *did* go to Seattle, they *did* take our recommendations, they *did* lead the floor fight, and it was the biggest single issue of the convention. Maybe it's too much to say that we were the main inspiration for the changes in the Guild and the *Guild Reporter;* but we were the first people actively to press the issue in a highly codified and organized way to management and to the representatives of the employees.

It was the first time that anybody just got it all together, and just didn't maybe poor-mouth it at a Guild meeting, or gripe around the newsroom. For a group that didn't have a name or a leader, we really organized the stuff, knew what we wanted, went after it and got it. I think it was a little bit incredible. It just goes to show what you can do when you get your shit together, as the kids say.

Why did I leave the *Post?* Well, I was in the Style Section, couldn't get a transfer to the National Section, and *Time* offered me a job in *their* National Section. I don't think I would have left the *Washington Post*—it's a good paper, and you think twice about leaving—if I did not think I had a better future somewhere else. It would have taken me much longer if I had remained at the *Post*, and one of the reasons is the fact that I am a woman.

I'm single. But take the situation of a married woman at the *Post*. There was an opening in the New York bureau of the *Post*, and a woman editor on the national desk proposed the name of a married reporter, primarily so that a woman would have a shot at the job. Management's reaction, of course, was: "But she's married." They never asked her whether she was interested, or whether her husband might be able to make the move, and it just so happens that his work enabled him to move freely. She was never even considered. If they ask a *man* if he wants to make a move, they don't bother to ask whether his wife works or would even object.

I recall so vividly in those early days that everyone took our activities as a joke. It really was a laughing matter to them. I was told that at a meeting of the editors one prominent person there said, in the best locker-room tradition: "I think these women have a point. The least we can do is to lower the seat on the toilet."

For chrissakes, what kind of a response is that? Here are these guys sitting around telling dirty jokes. As if you didn't have enough problems, you have to fight this stuff. And then you hear them saying, some of them: "What do you want to do—get into the men's room?" I've never given a thought to men's rooms, but I'm convinced now that the hypersensitive reaction indicates that there must be some highly esoteric sex stuff going on in there. Otherwise, why so worried? There really is nothing going on in the women's rooms, I can tell you.

You ask about actual cases of discrimination. There are hundreds of them. I know a woman in Atlanta—she's not in the newspaper business any longer—who started as an obituary writer on a paper there at the beginning of World War II. By the end of the war she had moved from obits to general assignment to assistant city editor. And when the boys came back, what do you think they did with her? Let her keep her job? Not on your life! They dumped her ass back on obits. Now, if this woman was qualified, as she had proved, surely there must have been some other place for her. She quit.

But for every one who says, "Screw you, I will not be exploited, I will not be kicked in the teeth," there must be hundreds who suffer in silence, who stay in the equivalent of Siberia. There are thousands of stories like this.

The oldest bugaboo, of course, is that women leave to get married. At the *Washington Post* we did a study of this, because several women who had babies had had incredible hassles with the personnel department. We found the turnover rate of men in the years surveyed was higher than the turnover rate of women. We discovered also that the paper had lost more man-hours from men serving military obligations than from women with maternity leave. Guys were going off for six months with the National Guard. Women would take a month off to have a baby. Every guy under thirty in the newsroom took two weeks out every summer, in addition to regular vacations, for the Guard. But God help you if you got pregnant! Statistics just don't bear out the myth about women and marriage and babies. And women journalists marry other journalists. The rate is very high. They just don't go any place. They stay.

About the future? There is no going back to the old way of

doing things. Absolutely not. The word "optimist" may be too strong, but I am confident that eventually there are going to be major and long-lasting changes.

I don't see it coming any time soon, just as I don't see racism ending soon. In the same sort of long-term struggle, the problems that women have as women in the industry arise out of the same problems that women have generally in society. Until that is substantially changed, we're going to continue to have problems. The media are part of the system, part of the power establishment. To change things, one of the places you have to start is the media— because the media's ability to shape and mold public opinion is crucial.

Until you change this, there's not much hope for the rest of society. That's why these early things are so important. Quite frankly, the whole of society needs some consciousness raising, and the main thing that is capable of effecting this is the media. This is the main tool. Things have to change here.

The "alternate media" is only partially the answer. I feel it has its limitations. We have got to get through to the networks, to CBS and NBC, to the advertising agencies. We have to erase the scuff marks from the minds of women who have been told over and over again that a woman's be-all and end-all is to have a smooth, shiny, unmarked floor.

The really important battle must be won here.

That's the end of B. J. Phillips's story, but it was only the beginning of the action.

In the fall of 1970 the National Press Club of Washington— which for 63 years had refused to admit women to membership— conducted a mail ballot on the issue. The vote was 522 to 243 to admit women; but because the "yes" vote fell short of the required two-thirds of the 1,063 active members, the prohibition remained. A petition was circulated for a meeting in January 1971 for a new vote, requiring a two-thirds majority of only those attending. (Meanwhile the National Press Club of Canada in Ottawa and the Winnipeg Press Club ended their ban against women.)

The January debate in Washington was heated. The opposition was led by Ralph De Toledano, a columnist for King Features

Syndicate, biographer of Richard Nixon and indefatigable hunter of Reds. His mind was both above and below the belt. "If God had wanted something other than the two sexes," he said, "he would have created a unisex. . . . They're burning their bras, and now they want us to burn our jockstraps."

On the other side, Richard Starnes of the Scripps-Howard papers spoke of De Toledano's "sleeve-garter mentality." This, he said, "has made the Press Club a sepulchral deadfall fit only for troglodyte special pleaders with hobnail livers and ethical infrastructures that could cause a wave of revulsion in a Scranton parlor house."

Elimination seemed much on the *macho* minds of male journalists throughout the women's drive, and stout ramparts were thrown up outside the men's rooms. In a two-page spread of cartoons showing how the nation's press depicted the Women's National Strike of August 26, 1970, *Editor & Publisher* reproduced eight representative cartoons under a headline reading: "Cartoonists strike while the women's lib iron is hot."

Among them was one by Valtman in the *Hartford Times* portraying a group of six women (bucktoothed, bespectacled, unattractively miniskirted and panted) driving a battering ram against a door marked "Gentlemen," as two frantic men fled out the back door. The cartoon was captioned: "The Last Citadel."

But one citadel did fall: the National Press Club voted 227 to 56 to admit women to membership. A move to keep women out of the taproom, cardroom and pool hall failed. The "last bastion" was gone, said Robert Tate Allen of *Washington Religious News*, in an uncharitable statement. Several women reporters who had been covering the proceedings (from the outside) were invited inside by their male supporters for a drink at the men's bar. De Toledano objected that the house rules had not yet been changed. The women asked for a ruling as to whether they might finish their drinks.

"I rule that you may finish your beer," said James Srodes of McGraw-Hill, "or I'll punch him [De Toledano] in the mouth."

The rules, however, had not yet been changed at *Editor & Publisher*, where women had always been "gals." The headline over the story about the vote read: "Press club barriers down; gals' feet on brass rail." An era of "male journalistic camaraderie has ended in the nation's capital," the obituary concluded.

When Sarah McClendon, scourge of Presidents, got her press-club card, she wept. "Honey," she said, "I can't tell you the snubs I've endured. I worked in a tenth-floor office in the National Press Building for 12 years, and I couldn't come up here to the thir-teenth floor to have a hamburger."

Three days before the vote, the Women's National Press Club voted to open its membership to men.

In March 1971 the Gridiron Club again held its annual ritual at the Statler-Hilton in Washington, and this time there were many more stags at bay. The arriving guests found that the pickets in evening attire had doubled over the previous year to 60 and that they had been joined by 20 men. The picket signs were more pointed: "Teddy, Women Vote Too." When Senator Edward M. Kennedy arrived, he got out of his car, walked to the line, where he shook some hands, and then entered the hotel. He was joined by Chief Justice Burger, Henry Kissinger and Vice-President Agnew, among others.

The women said they had sent 125 letters urging invited guests to stay away but only four agreed: Senators McGovern, Muskie and Mansfield, and Walter Washington, mayor of Washington. President Nixon also was absent, but his press secretary, Ron Ziegler, said it had nothing to do with the women's protest.

The most cynical comment of the evening came from Senator Charles Mathias of Maryland. He told the women he would have respected their picket line, but "I'm not a Presidential candidate this year." The remark may one day return to haunt him: on December 4, 1971, the Gridiron Club voted to admit women to its annual spring dinner. But the membership remained all male.

There were activities in New York in the spring of 1970 which may well have eased B. J. Phillips's transition from the *Washington Post* to *Time*. In May 1970 the attorney general of the state of New York, acting on a complaint by 35 percent of the women employed by Time, Inc., as "professionals," filed an action on their behalf with the state's Human Rights Commission. The charge was that Time, Inc., employed women exclusively or predominantly as researchers, or in low-paid jobs with little chance of advancement.

A preliminary hearing on June 10 found probable cause for the complaint and a public hearing was ordered. To avoid publicity and any semblance of guilt as to the charges, Time, Inc., agreed to conciliation and in February 1971 reached an agreement with the women employees of *Time, Life, Fortune* and *Sports Illustrated*.

The agreement covered new employment for women by integrating all job categories, salaries and advancement without regard to sex or marital status. Complaints would be investigated by a committee composed equally of women staff members and management, and there would be periodic compliance reviews. Job descriptions for about 150 women on all four publications would be full and accurate, and training and tryout programs would be instituted.

During the negotiation period the status of several women was improved. Four *Time* researchers were advanced to associate editor, and women were promoted to senior editor and associate editor at *Life* and *Sports Illustrated*. The masthead, in which researchers would henceforth be termed "reporter-researchers," was altered to reflect these changes.

Although the first newsmagazine agreement was reached at *Time*, the first moves were made at *Newsweek* in March 1970, when women staff members announced they were filing discrimination charges with the federal government. The announcement, at the offices of the American Civil Liberties Union, coincided with the publication of an impressive issue of *Newsweek* with a cover story titled "Women in Revolt."

The *New York Times* reporter covering the press conference was still bemused by prevalent chauvinism. He reported an unusually large number of women reporters present, among them one he described as "slim and miniskirted . . . wearing a field jacket." By contrast, the *Newsweek* women were "neatly and conservatively dressed." Among them was "a bespectacled brunette."

Osborn Elliott, *Newsweek's* editor-in-chief, denied any discrimination and said that researchers were women because of a "newsmagazine tradition going back to almost 50 years." But "a change in that tradition has been under active consideration." The complaint was never put to the test because the press conference elicited negotiating signals from the management, and a "Memorandum of Understanding" was worked out and signed on August 26, 1970—Women's Strike Day. The memorandum was similar to *Time*'s agreement, but it did not have the same policing force.

While the statements read smoothly, they entailed months of difficult negotiation both among the women at each newsweekly and between the women and management (there was a first-rate report about this by Lilla Lyon in *New York* magazine, February 22, 1971). The results thus far have not greatly impressed the women employees.

A check of the mastheads at *Time* and *Newsweek* in March 1972 showed one woman—Ruth Brine—listed as a senior editor at *Time*. *Newsweek* had none. *Time* had one woman general editor (out of 23), and *Newsweek* had one woman associate editor (out of 20).

The annual convention of the Newspaper Guild in Seattle in July 1970 was indeed a watershed. The theme of women's rights dominated the proceedings for the first time in the Guild's 37-year history. In August Guild president Charles A. Perlik announced a Guild-wide conference in Chicago for the following November to coordinate Guild action to end sex discrimination in the newspaper industry.

Participating in the Chicago conference were 117 representatives from 34 locals, overwhelmingly women. Eleanor Dunn, secretary of the Ottawa local (Guild membership includes Canada), who was named interim coordinator, reported later that she had been "shocked by the anger of some of the women." A wide-ranging series of recommendations was adopted in Chicago. Among them: special training and recruitment programs to increase the number of women in upper-level jobs; campaigns to eliminate discrimination against women in press clubs and sports press boxes; child-care centers for working parents in all Guild shops; abandonment of separate "male" and "female" help-wanted ads; an end to discrimination in job assignments and the labeling of newspaper sections as "women's" or "society" pages; broadening of maternity and paternity leaves in Guild contracts; opportunity for advancement of women in all categories of Guild leadership.

Caroline Bird, author of *Born Female*, told the conference: "The worst sexists in America today are the craft unions which are trying to protect women against getting paid for lifting weights no heavier than a child or a grocery sack, or out of jobs carrying overtime." She derided the "myth that jobs have sex, that a job is either a little girl or a little boy." This, she said, is reinforced by another myth. "that women are back of, behind, and under men because that's where they want to be. . . . Just as we have had to compensate by seeking out and promoting blacks, so we have to rescue women from the myth that they can't do or won't do by systematically recruiting and encouraging them."

There was an ironic footnote to the conference. Among the delegates was Lisa Hobbs, a feature writer for the *Vancouver* (B. C.) *Sun* and author of *Love and Liberation*. A foreign correspondent for many years, she is an Australian citizen.

The day after the conference concluded, she left for Washington for a reunion with her brother, a newspaperman stopping off at the capital on his way back to Australia from an assignment in Europe. The Australian embassy press attaché had arranged for a luncheon meeting for them, but Mrs. Hobbs was unable to join her brother at the appointed place. It was the dining room of the National Press Club, at that time still off limits to women.

One off-limits sanctuary was invaded by more than 100 women on a day in March 1970 in New York: the office of editor John Mack Carter at the *Ladies' Home Journal* (circulation seven million). It was a carefully planned action by ten women's liberation groups which had been meeting for weeks. The encounter began at 9:00 A.M. and ended at 8:00 P.M. and, except for the liberation of some of Carter's cigars in a symbolic gesture and a bum's rush for an offensive TV cameraman, was conducted without nonverbal incident. But tempers ran high.

The sitters were protesting "a publication which feeds off woman's anger and frustration." What the women sought was "articles which deal realistically with our lives." They pelted Carter with such questions as: "Why do you shellac ham before photographing it? . . . Why has there been only one article about black women in the previous year? . . . Why do you print ads which degrade women?"

Carter sat stoically on the edge of his desk throughout the meeting; at his side, carrying the brunt of the confrontation for management, was Lenore Hershey, the only woman senior editor on the magazine. The original demands were for Carter's resignation and the assignment of an entire issue to the liberation movement. But they were refined at the end of the 11-hour siege to an agreement to permit the women to plan, write and edit an eight-page section for August. The *Journal* organization was shaken, from editor Carter to the women clerks and stenographers in the outer offices. These employees were at first hostile to the invaders, but came around during the day to neutrality and even support.

The eight-page August section carried a disclaimer by Carter that "we" do not agree with many of the assumptions presented about marriage, sex, childbirth, job discrimination and child care. But there was no question that they would jolt the readership with their unaccustomed views. The magazine's 10,000-dollar fee was donated by the women to liberation causes.

After the sit-in in March, Carter had said: "I had little patience with suggestions from nonprofessionals. Now I have none at all." After the issue was produced, he said he felt the readers of the *Journal* would not so much identify with the women's liberation position as they would understand better what the women were talking about.

That change might be characterized as all deliberate speed. But the women's march down Fifth Avenue on August 26 produced a great leap forward by the seven big slicks—the *Journal*, *Family Circle*, *Good Housekeeping*, *Cosmopolitan*, *McCall's*, *Redbook* and *Woman's Day*, which together sell 40 million copies a month.

While economic factors may have been more than coincidental in producing the changes (*McCall's* reportedly lost four million dollars in 1970 and *Good Housekeeping*'s advertising was down 14 percent), the magazines began in earnest to make innovations to keep pace with changing times.

By February 1971 Carter was conceding that "some of the complaints made about our magazines by the women's lib types were right. There has been a lot of silliness cranked out to sell products and life-styles to women, but it will never happen in this magazine again. The *Journal* will not be guilty of any stereotyped formula or position concerning women."

Early in 1971 *McCall's* engaged Betty Friedan as a columnist, and Shana Alexander, editor of *McCall's*, was saying: "Now I feel a general function of a woman's magazine is to be not only a voice speaking to women, but the voice of *women* speaking to women."

In January 1971, after a four-month boycott of *Cosmopolitan* by the National Women's Strike Coalition, the magazine opened a column each month to feminists. The boycott had been called because of *Cosmopolitan*'s "commercial exploitation of sexual differences" and because it was geared to selling women as "sexual objects." The new column was to be 1,500 words long, open to all women and untouched by *Cosmopolitan*'s editors. Proceeds would go to the Women's Strike Coalition for their programs of abortion counseling, child care and general organizing.

The rush of articles in the slicks about abortion, careers for women outside the home and sexual freedom bore a worried mark of concern about the marketplace. But it was also a recognition of women's increasing resentment of the plastic image of women being presented in four colors in the magazines and on millions of television screens. There was a dawning appreciation that women just might rise in revolt against being pictured as making love to cans of floor wax and room disinfectants; that beneath the deodorized and sanitized skins there might be human beings who were concerned about the conditions under the floorboards of America that were producing a national smell.

The newspapers were sniffing too, but not hard enough. Women's demonstrations, such as the annual march in New York and elsewhere on August 26 (Women's Equality Day), were widely reported, but on other days of the year women's concerns fared less well. Serious issues such as abortion and job equality were mostly ignored or received superficial treatment except, for example, when suit was filed in New York demanding civil rights for the fetus. That guaranteed page one news.

Major changes, however, were taking place in what once was known as the "women's pages," now given flaring titles such as "Style" (*Washington Post*) or "Family • Food • Fashions • Furnishings" (*New York Times*). In these sections articles concerning women often did receive full and fair treatment. But, said Ruth Rovner, a freelance journalist, in the *Philadelphia Journalism Review* (September/October 1971): "Women's pages serve a special function by focusing on features rather than news. 'Hard news,' whether made by women or men, belongs in the general news hole. And that's where women's liberation suffers journalistic abuse."

In the pages of many newspapers brides were being discarded along with the wives of no-hit pitchers. Society news was being renovated with touches of camp and alleged spoofing, making up a potpourri of radical chic for the wasteland minds of "the beautiful people" and titillation for readers who, in editors' eyes, read the items with longing for a world they would never make. This was hardly enough, said Jean Sharley Taylor, women's editor of the *Los Angeles Times:*

> There is little doubt that the newspaper's inner filling, the old women's section, will be packaged more seductively in the future, geared to people rather than pies. That we will be increasingly conscious of the need to tell the truth in whatever we do. And to see fresh vision. New forms. To live in the world of this minute and to try to capture some of its wonders and pain. But we are changing without research.

Miss Taylor, in an article in the *Bulletin* of the American Society of Newspaper Editors (October 1971), placed the blame directly upon the organization that published the *Bulletin.* She wrote:

> There is only one place that the basic thinking about women's news coverage can begin to refocus: at an ASNE convention. But not a half-hour's worth. Not 45 minutes of gleeful chuckles with comfortable Willie Snow Ethridge and earth-mother pithies with Pearl Bailey. What you should give us is the whole damn week. The first look since the invention of the printing press. Because two things are true:
> The first is that it is becoming increasingly impossible to separate the women's rights issue from the issue of reshaping women's pages to contemporary power—since those sections are the direct products of the discrimination which spawned the rights fight. The second is that women's pages are what they are because editors are the most enthusiastic protectors of male supremacy in journalism. ASNE is a male country club that defies the intruding thought of women's pages. It resents any discussion above a B-cup level.
> And that image—molded in the minds of publishers and top edi-

tors—is carried through the ranks to city editors, to reporters, to desk men, to copy boys, and it permeates the wire services. It is an essentially silent fraternity—although nightside on the copydesk is less silent than the brass—that emotionally supports any blows leveled by any member against the encroachment of women.

That was strong language, but well-merited, as any male operative in a newsroom who has championed the cause of women's liberation will attest. The characterization of newspaper editors applied equally to the managers of broadcast journalism, particularly as it concerned the employment of women on editorial broadcast staffs. The "weather girl" syndrome was giving way in many cities to the hiring of women reporters for general assignment; but many women on the network staffs still felt they were regarded as "house chicks." "Everybody's got a woman," said reporter Christine Lund of San Francisco. "It's like having a dog."

Since 1969 big-city stations have increasingly assigned women to serious reporting. In Boston two network affiliates which in 1967 between them employed one woman reporter had five by late 1971. There were 11 women correspondents then in Washington's five television stations—eight hired in the previous two years. Even Houston's three stations had hired one woman each. There was a curious twist to the hiring policy, however, rather like killing two birds with one stone. The women being hired were mostly black or Puerto Rican.

In New York, at the headquarters stations of the three major networks, there were seven women covering local news—five black, one Puerto Rican, one white. Three of Cleveland's five women reporters were black, one of two in Detroit and two in Boston. In Boston one of the two black reporters said she felt her race *and* sex "absolutely" guaranteed her job. Nancy Dickerson, who had become CBS's first woman correspondent 11 years earlier, said: "Every station in America feels it must have one black and one woman. With a black woman, they take care of their tokenism in one fell swoop."

"They will always come up with some theory about why it cannot work" for women to serve in the same capacity as men, said ABC's Marlene Sanders, who for a short while held the exalted position of "anchor woman" on the *ABC Weekend News*. (Weekend news time, generally with the smallest audience of the week, is the favorite token ground for black anchor men, too.) Validating Miss Sanders's statement, Reuven Frank, president of NBC News, foisted his own resisting chauvinism on the public. "I have the strong feeling," he said, "that audiences are less prepared to accept news from a woman's voice than a man's."

There was unconscious corroboration of Jean Taylor's sharp criticism of her male colleagues in an article in *Newsweek* (August 30, 1971) about the progress of women in broadcast news. The writer, never at a loss for an adjectival cliché, described New York's Gloria Rojas (Puerto Rican) as "vivacious," CBS's Pia Lindstrom as the "svelte" daughter of Ingrid Bergman, and Honolulu's Linda Coble as a "stunning blond who favors pink muumuus."

As B. J. Phillips said, there will be no going back to the old ways. Few women will be conned into accepting token concessions. Yet what most women journalists still feel today was summed up by a sign carried by a Gridiron Club dinner picket in 1971:

"*Who's* come a long way, baby?"

CHAPTER XI

THE ARMED FORCES
UNDERGROUND

ONE of the largest and least-publicized media monopolies in the world is based in the Department of Defense in the Pentagon. It is the Office of Information for the Armed Forces, part of the Office of the Assistant Secretary of Defense, Manpower. It supervises the work of 400 radio and television stations in 29 foreign countries and nine United States territories through the Armed Forces Radio and Television Service; the preparation of films and literature for internal guidance; the European and Pacific editions of *Stars and Stripes* (the armed forces newspaper) and the Armed Forces News Bureau.

This vast news and information network operates officially under a Freedom of Information Memorandum of the Department of Defense—the so-called McNamara Doctrine—issued in May 1967. It states:

> Members of the armed forces constitute an important segment of the American public. They are entitled to the same unrestricted access to news as are all other citizens. Interference with this access to news will not be permitted. The calculated withholding of unfavorable news stories and wire service reports from troop information publications such as *Stars and Stripes* or the censorship of news stories and broadcasts over such outlets as Armed Forces Radio and Television Service is prohibited. . . . News management and meddling with the news will not be tolerated, either in external public information or internal troop information.

That was May 1, 1967. Six months later a confidential report was obtained by columnist Jack Anderson disclosing that the management of the armed forces network had bungled its operations so extensively that the network's image was "on the brink of international ridicule." The report was intended only for the eyes of John Broger, the network's director in Washington, and a few other Pentagon officials, and nothing was done about it. In the fall of 1969 a similar report was pigeonholed.

Late in 1969 charges of censorship in the armed forces news service were becoming increasingly frequent, particularly in Vietnam. (Radio broadcasts there had begun in 1962 and were augmented in 1966 by television programs, first transmitted from an airplane in flight.) Several enlisted newsmen were transferred abruptly to "nonsensitive" jobs after seeking to present unadulterated news about operations in Vietnam.

Specialist/4 Robert O. Hodierne, a *Stars and Stripes* reporter and former war correspondent for United Press International, was quoted in a *New York Times* dispatch from Saigon (January 5, 1970) as saying: "You are on pretty shaky ground when you can't tell your troops the truth about the war for fear they wouldn't fight if you did."

That remark had been prompted by an incident the night before. That incident provided proof of not only shaky ground but also large gaps in the communications ground rules for enlisted newscasters who sought to present the facts or were bold enough to say the facts were being withheld.

The televised news on the night of January 4 was being read over the Armed Forces Vietnam Network (AFVN) by Specialist/5 Robert Lawrence, a soldier for seven months and a former manager of a radio station in McRae, Georgia. His news file completed, he looked straight at the camera for a "closing note." Projecting himself in the decade ahead, he said that as a newsman he was dedicated to telling the truth at all times, whether in the military or as a civilian. Then he said:

In the military in Vietnam I have found that a newscaster at AFVN is not free to tell the truth and in essence to tell it like it is. MACV [Military Assistance Command Vietnam—the United States command] and the MACV Office of Information [MACOI] have seen to it that all those newscasters who are dedicated to their work are sent away to other areas, in some cases off the air completely. . . . We have been suppressed, and I'm probably in trouble for telling you tonight the truth. I hope you'll help stop censorship at AFVN and any American station under military rule. Thank you, and goodbye.

The farewell was prophetic. The next day Lawrence was driven to the office of the Army inspector general, where he was subjected to sharp questioning. He asked for counsel and was told he had no such right because he had not been charged with wrongdoing. But even without charge, he was told, an officer was "going to take you upstairs and interrogate you until you give us the information." The upstairs room was equipped with blanketed walls, tape recorders and a mattress on the floor. Lawrence later reported his reaction: "I don't believe this is happening." He refused to answer any questions.

The AFVN suspended Lawrence pending an investigation. It decided also that it no longer required the services of Corporal Thomas M. Sinkovitz, a Marine sports newscaster, who had immediately followed Lawrence on television January 4 and said: "Thank you, Bob, in more ways than one."

Since MACV insisted there was no censorship in Vietnam (the McNamara Doctrine was still operative), it found it difficult to prefer a charge against Lawrence, but it managed a pretext. It seems that on the night of December 29, 1969, while Lawrence was preparing a broadcast, the sergeant in charge of the news department at AFVN Saigon ordered him to drive a truckload of GIs to their quarters. Lawrence refused on the ground that he would not have time to complete his script. The sergeant, according to Lawrence, swore that he would see Lawrence in Longbinh jail "if it's the last thing I do."

On January 8 the Army announced that Lawrence would face a court-martial on charges of being disrespectful to a superior officer and with being absent without leave (from his assignment to drive the truck). The next day Lawrence and Sinkovitz were ordered transferred to other duties—Sinkovitz to the First Marine Air-Naval Gunfire Liaison Command and Lawrence to assist a chaplin in Kontum Province in the remote north.

Before departing, Lawrence enlisted the services of the National Emergency Civil Liberties Committee, an organization devoting much of its resources and legal services to draft and conscientious-objector cases and harassment in the armed services. The NECLC general counsel, Leonard B. Boudin, together with the GI Civil Liberties Defense Committee, took steps immediately to protect Lawrence's rights and demanded a transfer of the proceedings to the United States. Boudin also demanded and obtained assignment of military counsel to Lawrence.

The Army meanwhile spent two weeks investigating itself and emerged untainted: it found no substance to charges that it was censoring its news services. Quite the contrary. The investigators found, in Alice-in-Wonderland fashion, that Lawrence was being transferred for refusing to accept Defense Department policies—the McNamara Doctrine forbidding interference in news operations—"which are binding." Having pronounced itself above suspicion, the Army then ordered a withdrawal to a previously prepared position: on January 29 it sent a cable to Boudin informing him that charges against Lawrence were being dropped.

The retreat clearly was forced by militant protest in the United States and prompt and forthright legal guidance. But that did not mean that the Army had adopted a policy of abiding by its own directives and would henceforth stop meddling with the news and punishing newsmen upholding the principle that enlisted men enjoyed the privileges of the same Constitution as their civilian brothers and sisters. Rather, the Army's attention was being directed increasingly to a more virulent form of press rebellion in its ranks—the GI underground press.

The rise of the unauthorized media in the military was motivated by two sets of factors: (1) the increasingly oppressive atmosphere within the armed forces as a result of the war in Indochina—created by the unwillingness of GIs to serve in Vietnam, brutality by officers and "lifers" (noncommissioned career officers), particularly against black and Puerto Rican soldiers, and the gross inequities of the military code of justice; (2) the spread of the civilian war protest movement, augmented by an ever-growing number of young people—draft resisters, conscientious objectors, college students and returned veterans.

An overriding factor was the general dissatisfaction among the enlisted men with the authorized armed forces communications media. The GIs were weary of hearing that they had never had it so good, that the war in Indochina was "winding down" and that morale in the armed services was at peak level. News of the civilian protest against the war came in bits and pieces over the armed forces radio, in the press of Europe and Asia, and in letters and clippings from the commercial press sent by families and friends in the United States to GIs overseas.

There was a shift also in political attitudes at home. By mid-1968 it was apparent that the McCarthy-for-President campaign had been halted by the machine politicians in the Democratic party and the punishing elbows of Robert Kennedy. But unlike previous Presidential election years, when frustrated reformers withdrew into nonactivity, this time the antiwar movement was joined by young people in the universities and among the poor and the minorities—the potential casualties in Vietnam—and a surprising number of older people heretofore uninvolved in protest. Reports of record-high rates of Army desertions and refusal to respond to draft notices helped enormously to jolt the nation into articulate opposition to the war. This was the fertile ground in which the seeds of the GI underground press were planted.

The first newspaper published for GIs was the *Bond* in Berkeley, California, by William Callison, not a GI himself but a draft resister who understood the significance of the GI resistance movement. Between June and November 1967 he published 14 issues and distributed them to GIs at bases in Oakland and on the Pacific Coast generally. When legal actions involving his own draft resistance became preoccupying, he turned the *Bond* over to the American Servicemen's Union, founded in December 1967, largely through the perseverance of an Army private named Andy Stapp.

Stapp's own resistance to the war first came to public notice in October 1965 when he burned his draft card and was forced as a result to leave Pennsylvania State University. In May 1966 he joined the Army deliberately to continue his antiwar work. Within a short time he found himself in the stockade after a court-martial conviction for having refused to turn over "subversive" literature. Another trial for "breaking restriction" ended in acquittal.

After he founded the American Servicemen's Union, the charges became more severe. In February 1968 he went before a Field Board hearing on charges of "subversion and disloyalty." Fourteen months later the Army found him entirely intolerable and on April 19, 1969, sent him out with an undesirable discharge. April 19, of course, is the anniversary of the revolutionary Battle of Concord Bridge in 1775, when a shot was fired "heard 'round the world." Almost 200 years later Stapp may perhaps be credited with lighting the fuse for a similar explosion. And, like the band of eighteenth-century rebels who were once considered rabble, he also won respectability—by forcing the Army through legal action to remove the "undesirable" tag from his discharge papers.

The American Servicemen's Union, which continued to publish the *Bond* each month, was a union of rank-and-file men and women in the military with more than 10,000 members in 1972. It had chapters at 140 bases in the United States, 60 overseas and on 50 ships at sea. Membership was limited to enlisted personnel up to the rank of specialist 5th class, with the exception of low-ranking sergeants in the Air Force. ("It's not exactly like the officers are rushing to join," Stapp told me in an interview with him and his colleague, Terry Klug.) The ASU put forward an eight-point cornerstone program:

1. An end to saluting and sir-ing of officers as degrading.
2. Rank-and-file control over court-martial boards.
3. An end to racism in the armed forces.
4. Federal minimum wages for all enlisted men.
5. The right of GIs to collective bargaining.
6. The right of free political association.
7. The election of officers by enlisted men and women.
8. The right to disobey illegal and immoral orders.

From a few thousand readers in the winter of 1967–68, the *Bond* circulation grew to 100,000 in 1971. Its circulation was matched by the only other dissenting national service monthly, the *Ally*, associated but not affiliated with the national antidraft organization called the Resistance.

There were in addition 100 newspapers with about 80,000 readers published near various military bases in the United States and abroad, some by ASU members. These were concerned mainly with base problems, although all were opposed to the war in Vietnam, and some were airing the issue of racism in the Army. Over-all, there have been more than 150 base newspapers since the first two began publication in 1968. But, as Stapp said, "these publications tend to spring up and die away. Four guys get to-gether and begin to put out a paper. Then they are transferred or thrown in the stockade, and another group gets together and starts another paper."

The first base papers were *Fatigue Press* at Fort Hood, Texas, and *Fun, Travel and Adventure* at Fort Knox, Kentucky. The ini-tials FTA were soon translated into a three-word expletive describ-ing the feelings of GIs about the Army.

The names of the papers were expressive, bitterly humorous and determined. On the West Coast there were *Up Against the Bulkhead* (Berkeley), *Marine Blues* (San Francisco) and *Duck Power* (San Diego). Heading east were *Counter-Attack* (Colorado Springs), *AWOL Press* (Manhattan, Kansas), *Navy Times Are Changing* (North Chicago), *A Four-Year Bummer* (Champaign, Illinois) and *First Amendment* (Indianapolis). In the South were *Left Face* (Anniston, Alabama), *The Last Harass* (Augusta) and *Short Times* (Columbia, South Carolina). On the East Coast were *Open Sights* (Philadelphia), *Shakedown* (Wrightstown, New Jer-sey) and *Potemkin* (New York).

There were also GI newspapers in England, Germany, France, Sweden, the Philippines, Japan and Korea with names such as *About Face, Proper Gander, Venceremos, Freedom Rings, Kill for Peace, Semper Fi,* the *Whig* and *Paper Grenade.*

These publications were started for the most part not by people who were politically oriented or experienced but by people who had gripes and grievances on the day-to-day level. Through their activities and discussions, however, their political education was advancing and they were coming to see, more rapidly than they might have otherwise, that the war in Indochina was "a bummer." The Army was "always rotten," said Stapp, "but you didn't see all those papers in 1965, for example." It was clear that the antiwar movement outside the Army bases inspired those inside to com-plain about their grievances; and it was no wonder then that the greatest stimulus to the GI press occurred in 1968 and 1969, with the unprecedented antiwar demonstrations in cities throughout the country.

Perhaps the first disciplinary action against the underground service press was taken in the case of Pfc. Dennis Davis, editor of the *Last Harass*. He was given an undesirable discharge on April 14, 1969, three weeks before he was scheduled to leave the service. About the same time Pfc. Bruce Peterson went before a court-martial at Fort Hood, charged with possession of marijuana. He was the editor of *Fatigue Press*, but the Army professed ignorance of his antiwar activities.

A defense group at Fort Hood placed a full-page advertisement in the *New York Times* on April 12, 1969, insisting that Peterson's conviction on the marijuana charge was false. The ad said the Army reported finding marijuana in the lint of Peterson's trouser pockets, but regretted that the weed (the evidence) had been destroyed in the process of analysis.

At Fort Dix, New Jersey, the appearance of the first issue of *Shakedown* drew threats of confiscation and arrests by both military and local police. Company officers warned their men not to read the newspaper. In the *New York Times* of April 20, 1969, reporter Benjamin A. Franklin wrote: "In the rigid structure of the military . . . a very little dissent goes a long way. . . . The GI anti-war movement already is keeping the brass awake at night . . . . The fact is, if it lasts, that GI dissent could be the most effective form of anti-war protest thought up yet."

The military counterattack was sporadic until September 1969, when an increasingly concerned Army issued a "Guidance on Dissent" memorandum, an echo of the McNamara memorandum of 1967. It said:

Dissent, in the literal sense of disagreement with policies of government, is a right of every citizen in our system of government. We do not ask that every citizen or soldier agree with every policy of the government. Indeed, the First Amendment to the Constitution requires that he be permitted to believe what he will.

Army regulations provide that personal literary efforts may not be pursued during duty hours or accomplished by use of Army property. However, the publication of "underground" newspapers by soldiers off-post, and with their own money and equipment, is generally protected under the First Amendment's guarantees of freedom of the press. Unless such newspapers contain language, the utterance of which is punishable by federal law (e.g. USC Sec. 2387 or the Uniform Code of Military Justice), authors of an "underground newspaper" may not be disciplined for mere publication.

As with the McNamara Doctrine, there were wide gaps between the high-sounding principles and their application. Army regulations say that soldiers are allowed to possess one copy of an underground paper, but not to *distribute* copies. Those charged with distribution received punishment ranging from fines of 25 dollars up to seven months in the stockade. Base commanders have always been allowed to set their own scale of punishment. Wade Carson, a member of the ASU, for example, was given a sentence of five months at Fort Lewis, Washington, for distributing ASU literature.

Further, base commanders, with the active assistance of the "lifers," were circumventing the First Amendment protections against harassment by preferring charges having nothing to do with the publication or distribution of antiwar material. There was always an excuse for disciplinary action for breaches of strictly military regulations and these could be concocted in the traditional manner of the armed forces.

A major freedom-of-the-press case created a stir in the spring of 1969. Its First Amendment issue was clear-cut because the serviceman involved had a record of such impeccable behavior that no false charge could be brought against him. He was Journalist Seaman Apprentice Roger Lee Priest, assigned to the Office of Navy Information in Washington. Blond (short hair), blue-eyed, his uniform neatly pressed and his shoes shined to a high gloss, Priest was the unlikely-looking editor and publisher of an underground Navy newspaper called *Om*.

Its first number was published on April 4, 1969. Within two hours Priest was transferred from the Office of Navy Information to a "broom job" at the Washington Navy Yard. After the second issue, at least 25 investigators were assigned by the Navy to watch Priest. When the young seaman went to Cleveland to address a peace workshop, according to the *New Republic* (January 14, 1970), in the audience of 15 at least six were believed to be Navy investigators.

Om listed the addresses of organizations in Canada helping servicemen who deserted, and its articles urged general resistance to the war. But what riled the brass most was that *Om* described the Chairman of the Joint Chiefs of Staff, General Earle G. Wheeler, as a "pig," Secretary of Defense Melvin Laird as "people's enemy No. 1" and Representative L. Mendel Rivers of Georgia as a "hog mucking an otherwise clean stream."

Rivers, until his death in 1971, was chairman of the House Armed Services Committee and a man whom all generals and admirals addressed as "Sir," even during the rare periods when he was sober. Enraged by Priest's characterization, Rivers wrote to the Pentagon demanding that it "silence" the journalist seaman. The Navy responded by charging Priest with employing "contemptuous words" against Rivers in a wrongful manner. Later it dropped that charge, realizing that further publicity would prove embarrassing to Rivers. (For the same reason Rivers never publicly protested Drew Pearson's repeated description of him as an incompetent alcoholic.)

But the Navy pursued the case with vigor. It ordered a court-martial for Priest with eight specified charges, among them "inducing desertion, sedition and disloyalty among fellow servicemen." Priest's defense was assumed by Washington attorney David Rein, one of the most astute civil-liberties attorneys in the capital, who determined that the case involved a clear First Amendment question about the rights of servicemen: did they become second-class citizens once they entered the armed forces?

The Priest court-martial lasted two weeks. There were impressive defense arguments on behalf of freedom of speech and of the press, but the Navy for its part evaded the First Amendment issues and confined itself to proving that Priest was the publisher of *Om*—a fact which the defense had conceded from the outset. Priest was found guilty of a lesser charge—promoting disloyalty and disobedience among servicemen. On April 27, 1970, he was dropped to the lowest possible rank (E-1), a letter of reprimand was placed in his service record and he was given a bad-conduct discharge.

The case was appealed up through the military system, and on February 12, 1971, the Navy Court of Military Review reversed Priest's court-martial conviction. The decision was made on a technical point: the court determined that the trial judge had made an error in his instructions by declaring that "disloyalty to an authority of the United States is equivalent to disloyalty to the United States."

This decision meant that if the Navy decided not to pursue the matter further it would be forced to give Priest an honorable discharge, and the *New York Times* reported at the time that the Navy was not inclined to press the issue. Priest declared himself as "terribly relieved" and celebrated by getting married.

But the relief was temporary—the Navy was out for blood. It appealed the ruling, and on August 27, 1971, the Appellate Court, the highest military tribunal in the country, decided that the trial judge's instructions *had* been proper in the original trial and returned the case to the Court of Review. If the conviction was upheld the second time around, the only resort would be to the Supreme Court of the United States.

The vindictiveness of the military was clear. Without ever addressing itself to the fundamental constitutional question, it was determined to convict Priest and wash the "hog" off Mendel Rivers, who no longer even figured in the case. With the institution of a Nixon Supreme Court, the Navy's course would seem to have been made easier. But it also emphasized the urgency of the GI resistance movement.

What struck me about Stapp and his colleague, Terry Klug, as I sat with them in the office of the American Servicemen's Union, was their combination of toughness and sweetness, qualities which seemed to go naturally together in young men who had known the Army, hated war with an uncompromising fierceness, yet were able to regard their fellow GIs and their brothers and sisters in the antiwar movement with an equally uncompromising gentleness. There was no contradiction at all. Klug was finishing the remains of a salad lunch out of a plastic container as he began to tell me about himself:

> When I got my orders for Vietnam, I skipped the orders and the country, and went to France. That was 1967. The Servicemen's Union had just been founded when I met Dick Parent in Paris, and we were getting the *Bond*. We decided we'd put out a newsletter

called *ACT*, and used a lot of stuff from the *Bond* in it. We managed to get the newsletter into Italy, Switzerland, and mainly into Germany, where we have more than 100,000 men. We also got many into Vietnam, but it was tough.

The reaction of the brass? They hated it because it was a direct threat to them. We were fighting the oppression of the officer caste. But they couldn't take any action against us in Paris. The distributors, however, were harassed, charged with going AWOL, and court-martialed on any pretext they could stick them with.

They finally caught up with me. I received three years for desertion with intent to shirk service in Vietnam. I served two years before my appeal came through, and the charge was busted down to AWOL, which it ought to have been all the time. The maximum for that is one year, so I served a year extra. They owe me a year.

There is virtually no hostility toward the GI press from the GIs themselves. At the Servicemen's Union mail pours in each day with news, stories of harassment, requests for guidance and legal assistance—but no anger directed at the union or its newspaper. Similarly the union's representatives are received in the most friendly fashion at Army bases. Klug took up the narrative:

When we were in Washington, we heard that several units at Fort Meade in Maryland had been alerted for duty in Washington, D.C., for the demonstrations beginning April 24, 1971. So we got out a sheet explaining that the struggle in the streets and the struggle in the camps were one and the same thing. We told the GIs they should have nothing to do with the brass and with lifer orders to go into the streets to fight their brothers and sisters.

We took our leaflets and the *Bond* and went out to Fort Meade. Four of us spent three hours at night distributing the material, right into the barracks, stopping and talking when we could. So many of the guys wanted to talk. All that it would have taken was for one guy to go to the commanding officer and say: "There are four guys here, all in civilian clothes, distributing leaflets." In five minutes we would have had the MPs on us, maybe got arrested. But not one man did it. And that's been our experience pretty much on all the bases.

I've spent two or three days on a base, sleeping there even. When an officer would spot me, it was obvious I was not a GI, because I had longer hair and was not in uniform. So he'd say: "Hey, wait a minute. You're a civilian. You can't stay here." And a GI would say to the officer: "You'd better get out of here or you may get hurt." We were protected by the GIs. It was obvious that ultimately they had the strength.

The scene was reenacted at many bases, and the officers were acutely aware of the mood of the men. At Fort Meyer, Virginia, the colonel in charge assembled his men during the 1971 May Day demonstrations in Washington and said: "I know that two-thirds of you would rather be out there with the demonstrators than here in the Army." From the ranks came two voices almost in unison: "What do you mean, two-thirds?" Several GIs jumped the fence to talk to Servicemen's Union organizers and were forced back to their trucks by the sergeants.

As the ASU contingent left Washington after the May Day demonstrations, along with the troop convoys that had been placed on alert, a car full of civilians taking bundles of the *Bond* to Detroit pulled up alongside an Army truck. The GIs, members of the 82nd Airborne Division, began hauling bundles of papers onto the truck. This was repeated several times, on the expressway, with the *Bond* car almost grazing the speeding convoy trucks.

The main problems encountered by the union organizers were apathy and a degree of resignation and cynicism among young people who had been beaten down most of their lives—a sense that they couldn't fight the Army, couldn't win against the colossus. But even with this feeling prevalent, the hostility to the war in Indochina among the GIs was almost universal, particularly among black troops.

Unlike most of the individual base newspapers, the *Bond* continually stressed the pernicious effects of racism in the Army. Many white GIs who opposed the war nonetheless had difficulty connecting the struggle against war with the struggle against racism. But the black GIs, who had organized their own troops at the bases and were publishing their own newspapers, were a powerful educating force.

At a camp in Hawaii a Ku Klux Klan unit was formed in 1970. (Black troops have been attacked by Klansmen in the Army in Germany, and crosses have been burned on hilltops in Vietnam.)

The ASU chapter included at the camp more than 100 black members who met to devise a simple counter strategy to Klan threats. One night they hung rope nooses over the bunks of sleeping Klan members. When the sleepers awoke, that was the end of the Klan. It simply dissolved in the morning air.

One cure for apathy, the ASU organizers found, was time in the stockade. As Terry Klug phrased it: "If they didn't care what was happening to them before they went into the stockades, or they didn't understand, they surely found out after they went in there." The brutality of the racist guards, the filth and inhuman conditions were excellent instruction tools. And so were "political" prisoners such as Klug. He reported this episode:

> Right after Andy Stapp's *Up Against the Brass* was published, I was in Leavenworth prison, working in mental hygiene. "Mental destruction" would be more apt. A lot of antiwar literature would come in and they would just shove it in the incinerators. But I had a little guard who was friendly and he would salvage a lot of it for me.
>
> I got some radical papers and used to do a lot of reprinting, making carbon copies of articles I thought other prisoners could relate to. One day my guard friend came up with three copies of Andy's book. I was working with a black prisoner who had another friend working in the prison library. So we took the front and back covers off Stapp's books, reprinted the whole covers with titles like *Black Beauty,* put a library sticker on them, stamped them and started them around like other books.
>
> It really was great because, you know, in prison things can disappear, and we had to keep a tight rein on these books—three books for 1,500 prisoners. I'd give a prisoner a book and would ask for it back the next day so I could give it to someone else. Soon the guys were placing orders. I never had any trouble for the six weeks I was there, and I never lost a book. When I left, the books were still circulating. Several hundred guys had read them.

The effect of the GI papers, particularly those published by minority enlisted men, was noticeable in the increasing unity among the black, Puerto Rican and Chicano GIs. Since the antiwar movement was established within the Army, these groups have become increasingly militant. And where once the rate of reenlistment among minority groups was extremely high, primarily because of the paucity of self-respecting jobs in civilian life, it dropped by 50 percent in 1971—despite the increasing rate of unemployment in civilian life.

Stronger bonds have been created also between white radicals and minority groups within the armed forces. The basis for the new ties was a reasoning that any GI who was *for* the war almost invariably would have racial prejudice; any GI who was *against* the war would be more likely to have something in common with black or Puerto Rican enlisted men. But this was not taken for granted. At times the question of oppression of minority groups got lost in a rhetorical scramble; but increasingly many black GIs felt they could relate to white servicemen through their common opposition to the war, and hoped that white GIs could relate to them on a basis of racial equality. The camaraderie among black and white in the returned-veterans movement seemed to bear this out.

The civilian underground press and the GI press today enjoy cordial relations, but this was not always the case. In the early days of the civilian underground press, a lack of maturity and political common sense combined to portray everyone in the Army as the "enemy." But this attitude changed as the antiwar movement grew within the armed forces, and young radicals enlisted consciously in order to continue their antiwar work within the service. This new relationship was demonstrated in a report by the editors of the *Fifth Estate*, a Detroit underground newspaper, in the summer of 1971. They wrote:

> The *Fifth Estate* has been giving free subs for over three years [to GIs in Vietnam] and we feel we have had at least a minimal impact on GI readers. We get numerous letters telling us how our paper is read by "20 Marines" or by "our whole company." Some GIs even sent it to other bases and areas when they were finished with it. This says more for the state of consciousness of the GIs than it does for our paper. GIs are exceptionally eager for radical, anti-war, anti-brass articles and we should be in the process of giving it to them.

The underground press does carry considerable news of antiwar activities, of course, and publishes guides to GI newspapers and coffeehouses springing up near Army bases. But the main source of "anti-brass" news remains the GI publications, distributed at the coffeehouses, at airline and bus terminals, and circulated quietly on the bases themselves. A mood of rebellion and defiance is found in every one, whether the publication is crudely mimeographed or neatly printed.

In the upper right-hand corner of page one of the *Bond* (and many local base papers) a legend appears: "This paper is your personal property. It cannot be taken away for any reason." In the same spot in *Rough Draft*, published in the Tidewater area of Virginia, the editors state their purpose: "To expose those in authority who have betrayed the trust of the American people by using their power to deprive men of their constitutional rights."

In pungent and simple language—but never condescending— the publications tell the GIs where to go for help if they need a lawyer; how to cut through red tape to get to the inspector general's office; what demonstrations are being planned nearby; examples of resistance at other camps which might be duplicated.

Conditions in the stockades come in for much comment. A two-part series on the stockades at Fort Knox was published in *Fun, Travel, and Adventure*, written by a former GI who had firsthand experience. He wrote: "There was an IG [Inspector General] inspection. . . . Hundreds of prisoners were 'paroled' for the day so that the inhuman overcrowding wouldn't be noted as a gig. . . . The next day the prisoners were stuffed back in the stockade."

The regular press generally confines itself to publishing the findings of such an inspection, but, as one GI editor put it, "What the hell will the brass show you in a conducted tour through a stockade that a guy who's been in one won't tell you more honestly?"

Much space is devoted in the GI press, particularly the two national publications, the *Bond* and the *Ally*, to letters from GIs. These are a remarkable blend of news, moods and cries of anguish about everything ranging from latrine duty to the pernicious effect of widespread use of drugs. The language is colorful, colloquial and entirely irreverent. Above all, the letters demonstrate the hunger of the servicemen for the comradeship of like-minded persons, a desperate longing to know that someone cares about them in a godforsaken mudhole in the northern tier of South Vietnam, and a sense of amazement and revelation that such publications as the *Bond* and the *Ally* exist.

Distaste for the war is manifest in almost every letter. *Rough Draft* published on page one a letter from Vietnam whose sentiments have been echoed in letters to similar publications throughout the world: "I tell you in all honesty that out of the hundred-plus men here at HQ, you will not find one man who would state we are right in being here."

In the March 18, 1971, issue of the *Bond* this letter from Fairchild Air Force Base in Washington appeared:

I was an apathetic person without any strong views on any subject dealing with peace, war, oppression, rights, etc., until I was sent to Vietnam in January of '69. While "serving" my country in that crime of illegal involvement I saw the people of Vietnam degraded, cursed and humiliated almost daily. I saw the way NVA prisoners were treated by our "wholesome" American soldiers (usually lifers). Most of all, I talked with the people of Vietnam and heard what THEY wanted and how they felt about U.S. involvement.

I came back a changed person, no longer apathetic, sickened by the war and what it was doing.

At the present time I am on the editorial staff of a recently started underground newspaper and I am very interested in starting a chapter of ASU here at Fairchild and totally agree that the enlisted man's [and woman's—Ed.] strength lies in organization and solidarity.

This letter from Thailand, signed "Paul and all the heads," was published in the July 1971 issue of the *Ally*:

I am writing you for the sake of my sanity because the Pigs here at 815th B Company are driving all us heads mad. They have brought a CID [Counterintelligence Division investigator] here to try and bust as many of us as they can, but we had our shit together and they only got a couple of us. Every Article 15 that is given to a head is a farce but we have no way of fighting it because the Pigs threaten us with keeping us past our [discharge] time.

I fear if things don't change and the Pigs don't lay off we are going to be forced to kill a few of them by fragging. The Pigs hassle us so much that most of the heads have turned to Junk to relieve the tension. They refuse to let us talk to a lawyer if we get busted and we are so far out in the boonies that it's impossible to find anyone with a good understanding of the law. We need help but we don't know who to ask.

The same issue of the *Ally* published this poem by G. T. Long, titled "Military Tradition":

> Walking down a hall where I work I noticed
> Two latrines, one said "Officers" and the other
> "Airmen" and I couldn't help wonder if the Air-
> men's shit feels discriminated against.

In an appraisal of the GI press in the fall 1970 issue of the *Columbia Journalism Review* Murray Polner wrote:

> In the end, the GI papers remain amateurs, for now at least. Their content is uneven, their style sometimes turgid, their humor often simply not funny. But they have wit and sensitivity. Their writers are angrier than any other generation of conscriptees. Their future, of course, is impossible to predict, but this much is clear: so long as the war grinds on endlessly and men are compelled to join, and so long as the mass media pretend that military life is like a television serial, the GI press will continue to thrive in circulation and influence. Given no responsive media outlet, men—young or old—will conceive and nurture their own.

As usual, the nonresponsive media react long after the fact and seek to woo back an audience they have lost by default or never really had. In January 1971 the Army initiated a pilot program to revamp post newspapers. Fifteen were selected for the project, whose slogan was "Communicate!" Formats were changed, use of pictures increased, column measures widened and headlines brightened. Space for letters to the editor was greatly increased, and "Action Line" columns added. Photographs of officers pinning medals on one another vanished, and "Man on the Post" inter- views about troubling questions began to appear. In *Editor & Publisher* (September 25, 1971) the Army's aim was summed up in an article by Gareth D. Hiebert, a columnist for the *St. Paul Dispatch*, who is a lieutenant colonel in the Army Reserve information office. He wrote: " 'Telling it like it is,' within the bounds of good taste and propriety, is a trend in the Army press that has sent many traditions into limbo. The platitudes and official language are giving way to action and plain talk. . . . Army newspapers, if not in the midst of a revolution, are at least in the process of reformation."

The role of Martin Luther, in the Army press reformation, unfortunately fell to William C. Westmoreland, the Army Chief of Staff, who had to approve the guidelines adopted in the pilot program. The final proclamation was hardly as compelling as the theses nailed to the church door at Wittenberg. The guidelines stated: "Army newspapers should examine their format, style, and content to insure that they generate maximum reader interest. . . . Today's young soldier prefers content which addresses problems which he must face, using the deliberate informality and the language style of young America."

The implementation of the guidelines, however, was something less than freewheeling. The new look was carefully circumscribed by rules set down by Major General Winston Sidle, Army Chief of Information. There would be no compromise with "standards of good journalism," he said—no sensationalism, offensive words or pictures, nothing irresponsible. The latter category, according to the article by Gareth Hiebert, would encompass material attacking "American principles and system of government," or advocating "ideologies and forms of government hostile or contrary to the interests of the United States." Nor would there be any "lambasting" of key personalities. And while "discussion of relevant issues and controversial topics by Army newspapers is encouraged, this approach must be closely monitored."

The approach was similar to that of the regular civilian press imitating the style and form of the underground press. Stress was on "eye appeal," not mind appeal. Just a touch of "candid comment" on such bravely innocent questions as "Do you think there is discrimination in the Army?", gripes about off-duty KP, and the prohibition of cut-off trousers (as against Bermuda shorts) in Consolidated Mess Hall No. 1 at Fort Belvoir.

It was not that the Army had missed the point of the GI dissident press. Quite the contrary: if the Army press followed the line of the GI press politically rather than semantically (and it wasn't quite up to that either), there would indeed be revolution and not reform in the Army.

The publishers of the general commercial press were not nearly so nervous about the GI underground press as the Army brass. And if they were at all uncomfortable about it, they relieved their discomfort by ignoring it almost completely. There were reporters working on the general press who had established cordial relations with the staffs of the GI press; but their efforts to break through into their own newspapers with articles about the GI movement were largely futile.

There was one major breakthrough during the early days of May 1971 when the returned veterans staged their demonstration in Washington, D.C. Oddly, the commercial press coverage was heightened by a bungling and obtuse government which vacillated over permission for the veterans to honor dead servicemen in Arlington National Cemetery and to camp overnight in public park areas. The affront was so enormous that the press could not ignore the events, and television, live and searching for a change, trained an accusing spotlight on the nation's capital. When the effort to disrupt the life of the capital was made, and the massive arrests took place, the press almost universally reverted to its law-and-order syndrome, and the sympathy disappeared.

The military forces have shrewdly used thousands of small daily and weekly newspapers for news stories about hometown boys in uniform, designed to keep alive the old notion that the Army trains men for useful and interesting careers. News releases are produced on a simple formula by the tens of thousands, telling that Private John Doe, the son of Mr. and Mrs. Richard Doe of Doe Corners, has recently completed a certain training course or is enrolled in one.

Because local names almost always get space in a local newspaper, these news releases are printed so widely that the paper they consume must level a small forest each month. The number of military men engaged in grinding out these bulletins can only be guessed—certainly the total annual costs would run well into the millions.

A typical local newspaper, the *Daily Free Press* of Quakertown, Pennsylvania, printed six of these releases on February 9,

1972. They filled just over a column. Readers discovered that Private Randy L. Brensinger of Mertztown had learned at Aberdeen Proving Ground, Maryland, how to "conduct operational tests on burners, fire units, heaters, sewing machines, and shoe repair equipment to determine their condition and operational efficiency." At Fort Dix, New Jersey, Private Thomas Snider, Jr., of Sellersville had completed eight weeks of basic training and "received instruction in drill and ceremonies, weapons, map reading, combat tactics, military courtesy, military justice, first aid, and army history and traditions."

If a hometown boy were thrown into the stockade for passing out copies of an underground paper, this truly newsworthy item would probably not be judged fit for the space given to instruction in drill and ceremonies. The armed forces have built a happy marriage with the nation's small newspapers, and there is a cordial understanding with the big dailies.

I asked Andy Stapp about the attitude of the GI editors and movement organizers toward the establishment press. He replied:

> A lot of stuff gets published, but not one-tenth of what could be. Half of what goes into the *Bond*, for example, could be considered page one in the regular press. Take one case: the *Bond* publishes a story about a petition circulating among the men in Vietnam demanding that we get out. Now I can see that deserving at least column 3 on page one of the *New York Times*. Or we have an item about a general who drives around the post all day, and if he finds a GI with his uniform wrinkled, he throws him in the back of the truck. And he does nothing else all day long. I can see an item in the *New York Post*, at least, saying: "General Goes Berserk." Now all the papers get the *Bond*, but they rarely touch our stories.

The GI editors have little respect for the press as a whole. For individual reporters who try genuinely to cover the activities of the GI resistance movement, they have both affection and respect. Stapp singled out the *New York Times* for particular comment:

> The *Times* is one of the worst offenders by far because they calculate every single word that goes into that newspaper of record. They think that's living history. Like the Fort Dix struggle. These trials [of 38 enlisted men on charges stemming from a stockade

insurrection] were heavily covered in the *Times*. We sent out a press release every day to the *Times*. Yet in six months the name American Servicemen's Union never appeared once in the *Times*.

That's because the *Times* is so pompous it thinks that if it doesn't print our name, then the ASU doesn't exist; if they do print it, they call it into being. Also, and more basically, they apparently don't want to publicize the fact of our existence, because if they did, more GIs and the public in general would want to know more about us. It's OK to report a spontaneous rebellion; it's another thing to say that there's a working organization of dissenting GIs.

Now you take the *New York Post*. That's a big paper, but it's schlepp stuff compared with the *Times*. The *Post* once ran an editorial about us—you know, aren't we cute, a GI union. But you will never get anything like that in the *Times*. The *Times* reasons: Now, wait, every member of the Indian Parliament gets the *Times* in the morning. We can't have stuff like that in the paper. I think that as far as political news is concerned, the *Times* is the most tightly controlled organization in the country.

About the coverage of news from Indochina, Stapp was grimmer:

We know that the reporters there know a hundred times more than they report. Everything is screened by the military there, and a lot of reporters hang out with the officers at their clubs and get their news from the generals. They don't sleep in the barracks with the GIs, and they don't go to the GIs very often for their stories. The television crews in the field are more venturesome, though. But in general the newsmen in Indochina do not want to or are afraid to report things back.

Stapp commented also on the considerable evidence that the Army was becoming increasingly worried about the *Bond* and other GI papers turning up in Indochina:

There recently was a big flap about subversive literature coming into Vietnam. Now in World War II, there was censorship. Every piece of mail was read. But there is nothing like that now. I guess they wish they had done it, but it's too late. They've got their hands full, and besides we're not officially at war. But they are stopping mail—even first-class stuff. If a wife or a girl friend has put a peace sign on the back of the envelope, they will stop it. We have to take all kinds of steps to circumvent this kind of interception to get the papers into Vietnam.

What will happen, I asked, if there is a complete withdrawal of American troops from Vietnam—would the GI press go out of business? Stapp replied:

We should not assume that they are getting out of Vietnam. But even if they do go, we have a perspective not just against the war but against imperialism. And white racism will continue. In the Army, the kangaroo court-martials will go on, as will the oppression against the enlisted men.

There are potential revolutions in Latin America and elsewhere. There are potential revolutions of troops in Korea, for example, and thousands in Europe. The troops were put on the alert in Germany in the winter of 1970, and so was the 82d Airborne, the air wing in Greece. In Germany last year, the ASU leaflets did not deal with Vietnam but with the oil companies in Saudi Arabia. The big issue there was Jordan.

There's constant oppression against black and third-world people in the United States and we're organizing to fight that. The black GIs in Europe are forming their own organizations, and while they are, of course, opposed to Vietnam, they are concerned with the oppression against the rank-and-file soldier by the brass, who are the representatives of the ruling class.

Words such as "ruling class" and "imperialism" and "oppression" were not offered as remote rhetoric. These young men of the Servicemen's Union knew precisely what they were talking about. They and their colleagues had served in the United States Army in Alabama, Korea, Germany, Indochina and Fort Dix in New Jersey. They were not repeating by rote polemics from tracts published by a political party, whether American, Russian, Chinese or Vietnamese. They had been part of an imperialist army, had seen the effects of imperialism on the persons and properties of people of color, and their experiences had moved them to a study of why these things were taking place and how they might be prevented. They were seeking to join their experience to the lessons of the past and to develop from their theoretical studies a basis for future thought and action.

In their newspapers and their movement their approach was simple, patient and respectful, but above all engaged. They related to the problems of the servicemen in the smallest detail and the largest philosophical aspects. In all their work the style and idiom were peculiarly American, but mood and feelings were distinctly international: all victims of war and racism were brothers, whether they were the potential killers or the killed.

They supported draft resisters and deserters, and while they understood the significance of the resistance movements in the high schools and universities and among young workers, they concentrated their organizing activities among the servicemen. In all their work they sought and welcomed the support of civilian groups.

Interest abroad in the work was great. Articles from the GI press were reprinted widely in Europe and Asia, and programs involving dissident servicemen were presented frequently on television in Western Europe. The editors of the GI press welcomed the publicity. They understood, however, that it was generated primarily by revulsion against the war in Indochina and American policies generally, and not by a radical strain in foreign journalism. They were aware that the communications media of Europe and much of Asia would react very much like that of the United States if the resistance movements were indigenous. In mid-1971, however, there were the beginnings of links between American troops and the indigenous movements of the countries in which the troops were based, particularly Japan.

By the fall of 1971 there were nine GI newspapers being published in Japan, and a new publication was being born quietly each month. Because United States servicemen were liable to prosecution for distributing their newspapers, the services of Japanese students as distributors near United States bases were offered by Beheiren, the largest protest movement in Japan against the war in Indochina. A group of Japanese soldiers even established their own newspaper.

At Yokosuka naval base near Tokyo, a Marine wrote in the *Yokosuka David:* "Maybe through a joint effort on the part of all us peons, someday we'll see where a general shines his own shoes and drives his own car."

The biweekly *Semper Fi* at Iwakuni air station, where several aircraft were crippled by sabotage, was joined by a newsletter, *Thursday in the Belly of the Monster,* and by *Stars-N-Bars,* prepared in the brig and smuggled out by civilians for publication off the base.

Semper Fi has been a particular thorn in the side of the brass, and even though in the last two years full sets of editors have several times been shipped out, the paper keeps coming out. The latest set of four editors was shipped out in December 1971, and one, Paul Neighhorn, was separated from the service, after an incident ·in which the editors were not involved. It was clear that the Army was using the incident in an attempt to silence the paper.

The spark was a speech on the floor of the Japanese Diet on November 16 by a member, Yanosuke Narazaki, maintaining that he had proof the United States was storing nuclear weapons at the Iwakuni base. This would be in violation of the United States–Japanese Mutual Assistance Treaty. The charges rocked the Sato government, and embarrassed Army officials arranged a rare inspection tour of the base by the Japanese Defense Agency to disprove the charges.

There were reports that Narazaki had received his information from GIs stationed at the bases. Right after the speech the four editors of *Semper Fi* were taken into custody. They were not charged with involvement in the incident, but with being present at an antiwar demonstration off base on October 3, 1971. But it was obvious that the Army was using the Narazaki speech to get at the newspaper. *Semper Fi,* however, kept right on publishing after the editors were shipped out.

Because money is hard to come by, Neighhorn said in an interview after his return to the United States, only about 1,000 copies of *Semper Fi* are printed, but it gets passed from hand to hand and most of the 7,000 men stationed at the base see it as least once a month.

Semper Fi's coverage, Neighhorn said, was

half international, half local. We try to relate the two, make people understand why things are happening, try to give them background. I mean, they know that Vietnam's going on, but we try to let them know what Standard Oil's position in it is. These GIs haven't been exposed to that before, and once they are, they start thinking and asking questions and reading anything they can get ahold of.

Many of the American editors in Japan were Vietnam veterans. Typical was James Williams of Monroe, Louisiana, whose year's work with war casualties at a hospital on Okinawa and 15 months in Vietnam had turned him solidly against the war. He became an editor of Camp Drake's *Freedom Rings,* and in the fall of 1970 was the first GI in Japan to denounce the war publicly at a news conference.

From Japan the GI press network spread out to Okinawa and the Philippines. Black GIs at Kadena Air Force Base on Okinawa launched the publication *Demand for Freedom,* which became concerned with not only the grievances of the black GIs but also those of the Okinawa Military Workers Union, comprising Japanese who worked at the base. These moves toward alliance between Americans and Japanese infuriated the Army brass.

At Clark Air Base in the Philippines, the *Whig* exposed military police terror against Filipino base workers, forcing Philippines President Ferdinand Marcos to order an investigation and the disbanding of the "Red Patch" MP unit responsible for the terror (it was revived under another name).

Events such as these, although known to the correspondents of the general press on the scene, were rarely reported or transmitted. If they were transmitted, they were rarely published. But they became known at least to the readership of underground and college newspapers in the United States in reports distributed by Dispatch News Service International, a Washington-based news-gathering agency; Pacific News Service of San Francisco, and Liberation News Service of New York.

Newsworthy stories of underground efforts to reach the servicemen frequently appear in *Variety,* the show-business publication which covers the field of radio-television more thoroughly than any other newspaper in the country; but even the *Variety* stories are ignored by the general press. In its issue of December 2, 1970, *Variety* reported on Specialist/5 Steve J. Oreskovich, master of ceremonies for more than a year on the program *Underground,* a disc-jockey show broadcast by the American Forces

Network to GIs in Germany and to the German civilian audience. Emanating from Frankfurt, it offered progressive rock music and sprightly comment.

When Oreskovich was discharged from the service, he left behind a final prerecorded midnight show. The program was put on the air, and listeners were astounded to hear antiwar folk songs, clips of Vice-President Agnew's speeches critical of "longhairs" and liberals, and a description of a scene in which a Quaker war protester set himself afire outside the Pentagon and burned to death.

"I wonder," said Oreskovich's voice, "if little children in North Vietnam hurt when they die." The program proceeded for 20 minutes before the shocked directors of the network were able to pull it off the air and substitute another show. Yet no charges were brought against Oreskovich, presumably because the authorities decided that the ensuing publicity would compound the damage already done to "morale." Presumably also that was the reasoning of the general press in the United States, which did not consider the story worthy of publication. No radio or TV correspondent sought out Oreskovich for what could have been an enlightening interview.

A cover story in *Newsweek* magazine early in 1971 spoke of the "flakiness" of the American troops in Vietnam and said they had lost interest in their mission because they had been taken out of an active role in the war. David Cortright of the GIs for Peace, who had won a court fight against his transfer from Fort Bliss for political activities, disagreed. In the Spring 1971 issue of *Liberation* magazine he wrote:

> I would contend that the reverse is true. American GIs were taken out of the war because the policy makers could no longer consider them politically and militarily reliable. From the incidents of Hamburger Hill to widespread reports of "fragging" to the recent stories of 53 GIs refusing to advance near Laos, the evidence is strong that large numbers of American servicemen will no longer risk their lives in a cause they do not support.

For this new awareness, much credit must be accorded to the GI press and its courageous editors and distributors. In *Semper Fi*

"Tom Paine" wrote: "To defend one's homeland is one thing; but to send 500,000 men to oppose a people fighting an anticolonial war just so Nixon won't be the first President to lose a war is a nation's disgrace." And an airman at the Itazuke Air Station wrote in the GI newspaper *YAND*: "Killing for peace makes about as much sense as copulating for chastity."

This is the kind of comment that hits home with the servicemen. Their response often takes two directions. One is despair and resort to drugs as a blotting-out "release"; the other is an emotional and intellectual awakening and a new recruit for the GI movement.

Much has been written about the depths to which morale has dropped in the United States armed forces. But in the sense that servicemen are becoming aware that they can be a lever for the success or failure of American imperialism, morale in the military has never been higher.

The rebellion manifests itself in many ways, most of its positive, but some of it—such as the spreading use of hard drugs—negative. Desertions, according to an article by Ed Sherman in the *Nation*, were at the rate of 250,000 a year—the equivalent of ten combat divisions. Throughout America the underground communities were being joined by young men who had broken with the war syndrome.

This rebellion, and not the obviously contrived "Vietnamization" policy, is to a large degree behind the systematic withdrawal of ground troops from Vietnam and the decision to replace ground troops with increased air power. Desertions, refusal of GIs to enter combat, the organization within the ranks of militant black servicemen and the corrupt unwillingness to cope with the drug problem—all these elements which are exposed in the GI press have created an insoluble dilemma for the policy makers in Washington.

These are factors behind the revised war plans in Washington. The policy remains unchanged but the strategy has undergone major revisions. Yet the fact remains that despite improved technology which can eliminate manpower and despite advanced methods of killing, ground troops will be a necessary element in Washington's plans to hinder other national liberation movements throughout the world. And where American ground troops are stationed, anywhere in the world, the myriad problems of an imperialist army multiply.

Hundreds of thousands of American troops have come to understand the evil of American policy, its impact on their own persons, and its effect on "enemies" who have no desire to be enemies. Where once men such as Captain Howard Levy and Andy Stapp and the Fort Hood Three stood in courageous isolation from the mass of compliant servicemen—and with only a small group of civilians supporting them—now thousands of GIs at bases throughout the world have joined in organizing the fighting men themselves as a barrier to further adventures in killing. And they are joining their efforts to an ever-growing civilian protest movement which in turn has become influenced by the growing radicalization of the American serviceman.

It is a mighty combination which could become the best hope for educating the whole American public to the disaster of American policy.

Part Three

TURMOIL
WITHOUT

CHAPTER XII

NATIONAL
GUARDIANSHIP

IT MAY be difficult for Americans in 1973 to believe, but an American Socialist publication at one point in its 27-year career was the most widely read newspaper in the country. It was the weekly *Appeal to Reason,* the most successful and influential radical publication ever published in the United States, which once reached a circulation of over a million. At the height of its influence, it maintained a circulation of 400,000 for many years. A chief reason was Eugene Victor Debs.

Appeal was founded in 1895 by Julius Wayland, an Indiana Republican who had grown wealthy as a printer and real-estate man, and then had become an advocate of the socialism of Edward Bellamy (*Looking Backward*). Historian Ray Ginger relates[1] that the William Jennings Bryan "craze" of 1896, which demolished the populist movement in the Democratic party, almost extinguished *Appeal* at its start. After a temporary suspension, Wayland renewed publication at Girard, Kansas, and by 1899 had 100,000 readers.

Debs joined William D. (Big Bill) Haywood and other labor leaders in founding the Industrial Workers of the World in 1905. In December of that year, Frank Steunenberg, former governor of Idaho, was killed by a bomb, and Harry Orchard, a member

---

[1] *The Bending Cross,* by Ray Ginger (New Brunswick, N.J.: Rutgers University Press, 1949), an excellent biography of Debs and his place in the American political and labor scene.

of the Western Federation of Miners, was arrested and "con-
fessed" to Pinkerton detective agents. Orchard said he had been
hired by Haywood and Charles Moyer, leaders of the Western
miners, and George Pettibone, a Denver merchant and former
blacklisted miner, to kill Steunenberg because Steunenberg, as
governor, had called in federal troops to break the great Coeur
d'Alene strike in 1899.

Debs wrote a protest and sent it to *Appeal*, but it was so in-
flammatory that *Appeal*'s editor asked publisher Wayland for a
decision before printing it. Wayland looked it over and said:
"The only question I want you to settle in your mind before acting
is: will it work to the best interests of socialism?" The editorial appeared on page one under the heading "AROUSE, YE
SLAVES!" It said:

> There have been 25 years of revolutionary education, agitation,
> and organization since the Haymarket tragedy,[2] and if an attempt is
> made to repeat it, there will be a revolution, and I will do all in my
> power to precipitate it. . . . If they attempt to murder Moyer, Hay-
> wood, and their brothers, a million revolutionists at least will meet
> them with their guns.

From then on Debs wrote weekly about the case in *Appeal*
and it was at this time that the paper passed the million mark
in circulation. One single issue, Ginger wrote, required "ten bar-
rels of ink, six carloads of newsprint, three thousand mailbags,
and ten United States Mail cars." The arrangements for the trial
of the IWW leaders dragged on through 1906 and into 1907,
and by the time the trial actually opened in May 1907, Debs
had stung President Theodore Roosevelt into a personal verdict:
he judged Debs guilty—along with Haywood, Moyer and Pettibone.

In Boise, Idaho, the jury disagreed with the President, and
Haywood was acquitted. Moyer's case was dismissed, and Pettibone was freed later. But *Appeal* was subjected to vindictive
reprisal. Debs and Editor Fred Warren were indicted on charges

---

[2] In 1886 a bomb exploded in Chicago's Haymarket during a period of great labor
unrest, and several anarchists were arrested, tried and imprisoned in what was widely
regarded as a frameup. In 1893 John Peter Altgeld, governor of Illinois, pardoned
those who were still in prison.

of sending "scurrilous, defamatory, and threatening material" through the mails. Warren was tried first in 1909, convicted, sentenced to six months in prison and fined 10,000 dollars. An appeal was taken, and Debs and Warren converted the defense campaign to a subscription-building contest. *Appeal* circulation stood at 369,000 when they first went on tour; before the year was over it had reached 500,000.

Warren's conviction was upheld, and another national campaign was undertaken. President William Howard Taft, seeking to reduce the anger in the ranks of labor, struck out the six-month sentence, reduced the fine to 100 dollars and sent a pardon to Warren. The editor scrutinized the pardon, then sent it back with the request that a union label be added. He said he would pay the fine in *Appeal* subscription blanks. Taft, a more cagey politician than he was often credited with being, bowed out of the affair, and Warren never paid the fine.

Appeal, with Debs as chief editorial writer, went on to fight the conviction in 1910 of the McNamara brothers in the dynamiting of the *Los Angeles Times* building, in which 21 were killed. Debs charged that the owners of the *Times* themselves were guilty of the bombing. *Appeal* also sparked Debs's 1912 Presidential campaign, in which he got 900,000 votes on the Socialist party ticket. The Taft administration, retiring for the victorious Democrat, Woodrow Wilson, took a parting shot at *Appeal*. A new set of indictments was obtained against Debs, Warren and publisher Wayland growing out of a series of muckraking articles about the federal penitentiary at Leavenworth, Kansas. The indictments were never presented, but as a new frameup was being prepared against him, Wayland, then fifty-eight, went home one night, considered his situation and blew his brains out. In a much-read copy of Bellamy's *Looking Backward*, Wayland had stuck a note reading: "The struggle under the capitalist system isn't worth the effort. Let it pass."

Debs was heartbroken by Wayland's suicide and resigned his editorship at *Appeal*. A colleague wired Wayland's son: "We shed no tears of grief. Grief is for the naked lives of those who have made the world no better."

Appeal continued publication, with one interruption during World War I, and folded finally in its twenty-seventh year, 1922.

But until its publisher had been hounded to his death, *Appeal to Reason* had given the populists, Socialists and progressives of America just about the greatest run anybody ever got for his money in the press.

Appeal was the most exciting and widely read radical newspaper of the time, but the various factions of the Socialist party, with its membership at about 100,000 in 1912, published more than 300 papers and periodicals, among them five English-language and eight foreign-language dailies. The latter figure was a reflection of the increased immigration from Europe to the United States and the left-wing orientation of many of the new immigrants.

The Espionage Act of 1917, aimed at antiwar newspapers, successfully hampered the distribution of the Socialist newspapers by voiding their mailing rights. Among the victims were Victor Berger's *Milwaukee Leader* and the *New York Call*, which was still fighting as late as 1923 for its mailing privileges. Its petition was rejected by the Supreme Court, and after a brief spurt of life under the editorship of Norman Thomas, it died in the same year.

In the late 1920s and the depression years of the 1930s radical journalism never achieved a position commensurate with the organizing opportunities of the time. The Socialist party was in disarray and, at the height of the depression in 1936, was split in two. One reason was that the Socialists had become far more interested in propagating anticommunism than socialism, and the negative and sterile content of the party's program was reflected in its press. A few Socialist-oriented weeklies did have brisk but brief periods of popularity in the 1930s, but they soon faded. An exception was Oscar Ameringer's *American Guardian,* which reached a circulation of 40,000, largely because of the sharp and witty style of the editor and because it never succumbed to the virus of anticommunism.

George Seldes in his book *Lords of the Press* (New York: Julian Messner, 1938) notes that at the time the book was written there were 570 labor publications in the United States with a circulation of close to nine million. But they were not read with great interest, if they were read at all, by the majority of union members, nor did they exert any significant influence. Few union papers have been of high quality. Many have been puff sheets for union leaders, with pictures of officials on virtually every page; others have been dull, poorly written and atrociously edited. Professional journalists were not attracted to the labor field, and sporadic efforts to publish daily labor newspapers rarely persevered. The weeklies continued their plodding path, unread and unsung.

There have been exceptions, however. The *Seattle Daily Call*, followed by the *Seattle Union Record*, grew out of the great Seattle general strike of 1919 and gave a start in journalism to such brilliant radical journalists as Anna Louise Strong and Harvey O'Connor. The weekly *CIO News*, founded in 1937 under the editorship of Len De Caux,[3] was a distinctive publication during the rise of industrial unionism. There were two reasons for its high quality: De Caux's expert craftsmanship and humanism, and the fact that John L. Lewis and later Philip Murray, the first presidents of the Congress of Industrial Organizations, left De Caux alone. When the CIO began to purge left-wing unions from its ranks and joined the anti-Communist crusade, De Caux departed, and so did the *CIO News*'s effectiveness.

The *People's Press*, founded in the early 1930s, reached a circulation of about 250,000. It was an independent weekly of general interest, but was supported by the unions and published special regional editions in time of strikes and crises. The weekly *Labor*, established at the end of World War I, reached a circulation of 500,000, but its editor, Edward Keating, was unable to persuade Samuel Gompers, president of the American Federation of Labor, to sponsor a chain of labor papers across the country. This lack of interest was dismaying in view of the general press's unyielding hostility to labor's interests. Curtis D. MacDougall, in his book *The Press and Its Problems* (Dubuque, Ia.: William C. Brown, 1964), cites innumerable instances of suppression and distortion of news of labor during the 1930s and 1940s.

The most persevering antidote for the vicious presentation

---

[3] For a full description of the problems of labor journalism during that period, see *Labor Radical, From the Wobblies to CIO, A Personal History*, by Len De Caux (Boston: Beacon, 1970).

of labor news by the general press during these years was the Federated Press, founded in 1919 as a nonprofit news agency to serve the labor and radical press. FP was a mini-sized Associated Press, sending news and pictures by mail. It had originally a board of governors made up of representatives from all factions of the labor movement, and a managing editor—Carl Haessler— who had been a Rhodes scholar at Oxford, teacher, and prisoner (for actively opposing United States entry into World War I), and was passionately dedicated to labor's cause. FP had correspondents in the major cities and labor centers. On many occasions an FP "special correspondent" covering a major strike was a well-known staff member of one of the big daily newspapers writing under wraps. The agency survived for 30 years, finally yielding to the divisions in the House of Labor, financial pressures and political differences in its own house. Its closest counterpart today is Liberation News Service, which supplies news and graphics to the underground, alternate and college presses.

The most effective radical publication of the depression years was the *Daily Worker*, the spokesman for the Communist party of the United States. It helped spark the organization of the unemployed, campaigned against racism and mobilized assistance for the victims of racism in the South, supported hunger marches on Washington and fought against the rise of fascism both abroad and at home. It also took up vigorously the cause of industrial unionism, as against the craft unionism of the American Federation of Labor, and played a major role in the events leading to the founding of the Congress of Industrial Organizations. In the 1930s, when the membership of the Communist party was at its highest point—about 80,000—the *Daily Worker* circulation stood at 35,000. The weekend *Worker* reached 100,000.

Inevitably the *Daily Worker's* fortunes rose and fell with those of the Communist party, whose policies were strongly affected by the tide of international events and particularly events affecting the Soviet Union. Committed to the defense of the Soviet Union as the first—and at that time the only—socialist government, the party was severely affected by the Soviet-German nonaggression treaty of 1939 and the strong opposition to it in the United States. Its popular support declined further in the early years of World War II, which it characterized as an "imperialist war" before the German invasion of the Soviet Union in June 1941. Many Americans had difficulty reconciling the party's fuzzy calls for peace in 1939–41 (before the Nazi invasion of the U.S.S.R.) with its exhortations after the invasion for all-out war against Nazi Germany. This difficulty extended to members of the party itself, many of whom withdrew—not to join the anti-Communist crusade, but to continue as independent radicals hoping that at some future time they could come home again.

Compounding the *Daily Worker's* ideological and political problems were financial difficulties in the years following World War II and the paper's inability to attract to its staff professionally competent journalists—many of them sympathetic, but fearful of guilt by association. These factors, plus Cold War attrition, caused a further erosion of the fortunes of the *Daily Worker*. The party and its leaders bore the main brunt of the Cold War witch hunt of the late 1940s and the early 1950s, when first the Truman Doctrine and its loyalty oaths and Attorney General's lists, and then the McCarthy terror and the Korean War enveloped the country in a hysteria generated by the overall myth of the "international Communist conspiracy."

The *Daily Worker* was converted in 1958 to a weekly, the *Worker*, then published for a time twice a week. Finally, in 1968, it was renamed the *Daily World*, appearing with the most modern photo-composition and offset-printing techniques. The circulation of the *Daily World* in 1972 was 25,000. Unlike most of the publications of the New Left, it has paid consistent attention to labor problems and union affairs. Like the Communist party, the paper insists that the working class holds the key to basic changes in the American system. But also, like its parent, it continues to endorse Soviet foreign policy without deviation—particularly in regard to China—and its coverage of foreign affairs reflects this consistency.

Since World War II, a West Coast Communist newspaper has been published in San Francisco as the *People's World*, in turn a successor to the *Western Worker*. It was for many years a daily

236 DEADLINE FOR THE MEDIA

newspaper, but became weekly in the late 1950s. Originally it
had a more flexible approach than its East Coast counterpart,
but in recent years this flexibility has been less apparent.

The radical press of the post-World War II years mirrored the
polarization of political opinion on the left in the United States
and, to a large extent, the defensive posture of radicals. Those
who actively opposed administration policy were subjected to
not only the repressive countermeasures of government, but also
the hostility of the so-called democratic socialists, who believed
neither in democracy for dissenters nor socialism for the country.
So firmly were they in thrall to anticommunism that their press
at times was a virtual propaganda arm of Washington's foreign
policy. Because of their frozen attitudes, they were almost entirely immobilized during the McCarthy years (when they were
not actually abetting the inquisition), along with the fear-ridden
liberals longing vainly for a return to the days of the Rooseveltian
New Deal.

The chief rival to the *Daily World* for circulation and support
among radical activists is the *Militant*, weekly newspaper of the
Socialist Workers party (Trotskyist), which has been published
continuously (except for a two-year hiatus, 1937–38) since its
founding in 1928. Vigorous efforts by SWP members boosted its
circulation by 1972 to 30,000, although much of this is short-
term subscription. The *Militant* is very much involved in the
affairs of the radical movement, particularly peace activities and
racial questions, and publishes frequent analyses of the various
trends within the movement.

As with the *Daily World*, the *Militant's* effectiveness in
winning adherents to the radical point of view is diminished by
its extreme partisanship and rigidly held political theories. While
it is a valuable source of radical news, and many of its interpretive articles are well researched and sound, it countenances within
its pages only the rarest departure from its Trotskyist line.

Among the other radical weeklies of continuing circulation is
the *Weekly People*, organ of the Socialist Labor party, now in
its eighty-second year of publication, with a circulation of about
10,000. The *Weekly People* is sober and purist, declaring itself
to be the only truly Marxist publication in the country, according

to the theories of the party's most illustrious figure, Daniel DeLeon. It appears to have little influence among young radicals.

Two other political publications espousing Marxist theory are *Challenge*, publication of the Progressive Labor party, whose founders left the Communist party after a rancorous dispute in the 1950s, and *Worker's World*, published by a group which broke away from the Socialist Workers party. The PLP is particularly active among young people. It sits in severe judgment on socialist governments abroad and, at last report, had found the revolutions in China and Cuba both betraying Marxism. Newspapers are published also by several tinier Marxist sects, but none of them has any influence or attraction beyond its own severely drawn boundary lines.

A significant departure in American radical journalism took place at the height of the Cold War. It was the appearance within a three-year period of three independent publications, two of them weekly and one a monthly, all of them most accurately described as non-Communist leftist. Each evidenced dissatisfaction with what it regarded as the circumscribed publications of the existing parties of the traditional left and sought to find a readership and sphere of influence beyond it. The publications were:

National Guardian, founded in 1948 by Cedric Belfrage, author and journalist; John T. McManus, a newspaperman of many years experience with the *New York Times, Time* magazine and the experimental newspaper *PM;* and the author of this book. The subtitle of *National Guardian* was "Independent Progressive Weekly," although its content and editorial positions could more aptly be described as radical—a word rarely used at the time of the paper's founding.

Monthly Review, started in 1949 by Leo Huberman and Paul M. Sweezy, leading American Marxist teachers and economists, as an independent socialist publication. Since it never sought to become a newspaper, it is introduced here only because of the politically significant coincidence of its appearance.

I. F. Stone's Weekly, founded in 1952 and based in Washington, a nonconformist, muckraking publication reflecting the personal views of its editor (and sole writer), who described himself as an independent socialist. When Stone ceased publishing his *Weekly* (then *Bi-Weekly*) at the end of 1971, to become a contributing editor of the *New York Review of Books*, it had a circulation of 70,000—a phenomenal achievement for a left-wing publication without organized support or without staff beyond Stone and his wife, Esther, and an occasional assistant. The basic reason for its success and the esteem in which it was held was the indefatigable energy and acid but accurate commentary which Stone applied to national and international affairs. The acquiescence of the vast majority of the Washington press corps to the policies of government had given Stone a remarkably clear field of operation.

Since I was intimately involved in the founding of the *National Guardian* in 1948 and remained with the publication for 19 years until 1967, I can give a history of the purposes and problems of a radical newspaper which may be useful to younger journalists seeking to establish an alternative to the general commercial media. The founding principles and approach of the *National Guardian* remain valid today, in my opinion. This history by its nature will be more personal than other sections of this book, and for that I ask the readers' indulgence.

In preparing this section, I came upon a "confidential draft prospectus" for the *National Guardian*, dated June 1948, which opened as follows:

> The position of the Third Party [later named the Progressive Party] campaign and movement with respect to channels of public information is unique in political history. Poll samplings give 10,000,-000 as the number of Americans now expecting to vote for [Henry] Wallace. No election ever called on citizens to judge such manifold, complex life-and-death issues; and it is hardly likely that any majority of the 10,000,000 are clear about them.
>
> A broader disillusionment with old-style politics, going far beyond what this figure indicates, finds expression in nothing more than a general feeling of uncertainty, dread, and vague protest. The Third Party alone offers constructive interpretation of the issues, which are constantly developing and changing and in need of fresh analysis. Yet for all practical purposes no press exists to bring this interpretation to the 10,000,000—let alone the other disillusioned Americans who seek a program.

This situation is serious not only negatively because of the wall created between Wallace and his supporters, but positively, because red-baiting will be more and more used as a weapon against him. Wallace will not continue to get even the break he is now getting in the press. A clamping down on him, and intensified distortion of his policies, are to be expected. For purposes of the campaign, the need of at least one nationally circulated weekly—preferably not an official Third Party publication—is obvious. Perhaps even greater is the need of a paper as a continuing voice after November 1948.

The prospectus was prophetic in everything except the size of the vote for Henry Wallace—he received 1,157,000. But even that might have been predicted if the enormity of the press calumny of Wallace could have been accurately estimated, along with the fear of voters, in the privacy of the polling booth, that a vote for Wallace would be a vote for Thomas E. Dewey, the Republican candidate, and remove forever the hope that Harry Truman might reassume the mantle of the New Deal. As it turned out, the National Guardian long outlived the Progressive party.

The National Guardian published its first issue on October 18, 1948, as an independent and independently owned newsweekly which took strong issue with basic United States policy, both foreign and domestic. As radicals, its founders felt the need for a new publication dedicated not to sectarian polemics and opinion, as were the existing publications of the radical left, but to supplying factual news and interpretation in areas where the truth was suppressed or distorted.

In its early years, during which its editors and managers made half a dozen appearances before inquisitorial congressional committees—the House Committee on Un-American Activities, the Senate Internal Security Subcommittee (James O. Eastland of Mississippi, chairman), and the Senate Subcommittee on Government Operations (Joseph R. McCarthy of Wisconsin, chairman)—the National Guardian was variously described as "a virtual propaganda arm of the Soviet Union" (House committee report), and "the most flamboyant pro-Chinese publication in America" (columnists Rowland Evans and Robert Novak). But what motivated the subpenas and the epithets was not the idiotic allegations of adherence to the "international Communist conspiracy," but unyielding opposition to the United States policy.

From the beginning the small combination of professionally experienced and fledgling journalists who took part in the *National Guardian* realized that they could not compete with the news-gathering resources of the commercial press. There was rather a concentration on dissecting the existing press, following, unscrambling and analyzing its news and comment, and counter-posing in the *National Guardian* news and comment which the general press would not publish. In this effort, we had far more assistance abroad than at home. Many journalists in foreign countries, including some American political exiles, were eager to contribute to an American radical newspaper for very little pay. But except in the earliest days of the paper, journalists in the United States refused to write for it, even with pseudonyms. There were some splendid exceptions.

As the Cold War intensified, the *National Guardian* became a champion of its domestic victims, actual and potential. The great American witch hunt of the mid-twentieth century, of course, had its origins in the Cold War. The conjunction of events—the Truman Doctrine of 1947, the reactivated Smith Act of 1950 and the Korean War and McCarthy in the early 1950s—was not accidental. On the civil-rights front, the militant black freedom movement was not yet in existence, and there was a desperate need for journalistic campaigns for persons whose names are only dimly known, or not at all, to newer generations: Willie McGee, Rosa Ingram, the Martinsville Seven and the Trenton Six, all black and all facing death for crimes of which we were satisfied they were innocent. In its second issue the *National Guardian* took up the Trenton case as a new "Scottsboro Case," and in a campaign which eventually reverberated from Europe because of its articles, the newspaper helped win a new trial and freedom for the victims of a gross injustice.

The Cold War intensified in other areas, too. The Soviet Union in 1948 declared Yugoslavia's President Tito to be a renegade and revisionist, and adherents of the Soviet Union throughout the world almost unanimously echoed the charges and the judgment. The *National Guardian,* although it presented a sympathetic view of Soviet foreign policy generally, did not do so.

Rather it published several articles from Yugoslavia by Konni Zilliacus, maverick Labor Member of Parliament, presenting that country in a favorable light.

In the winter of 1949–50 Anna Louise Strong, the *National Guardian*'s correspondent in the Soviet Union and a world-famous journalist, was arrested in Moscow and expelled as a "well-known American espionage agent." Despite the patent absurdity of the charge, the Communist party of the United States and many of its supporters turned their backs on Miss Strong. The *National Guardian* rejected the unsupported charge and stood by its correspondent, despite harsh attacks from American friends of the Soviet Union. Cedric Belfrage and I, as editors of the weekly, undertook a quiet but persistent campaign of intervention with Eastern European diplomats to force Moscow to retract the charge. The Soviet government did—six years later. Miss Strong never renounced her faith in socialism, despite the bitterness of her experience. She went to Moscow to reclaim her possessions, then returned to China (from which she had reported years earlier about the Long March of the People's Liberation Army). She was received by its leaders, who were her friends, with great respect and invited to spend her remaining years in China. From Peking she continued to report regularly for the *National Guardian*. She died in Peking in 1970 and received a heroine's funeral service, with China's leaders in attendance. Miss Strong's reports from China to the *National Guardian* for more than a decade had been rejected by the general press in the United States as "propaganda for Red China." It is ironical that they were verified by the correspondents who accompanied President Nixon on his journey to China in February 1972 and by those who have reported from China since.

I dwell on these incidents because our method of dealing with such delicate issues set the newspaper's standard and tone. By a process of trial and error we settled on an approach through which we sought to make the paper as nearly as possible indispensable reading for any intelligent American who wanted to know what the left in America was thinking and who wanted also a fair presentation of the opposing forces in the world. Our second goal was to balance news of general interest with news of service to a predominantly radical readership—a readership which regarded the weekly as a communications center, almost as a political lifeline, in default of a cohesive and coherent radical movement.

Within this framework, the *National Guardian* became a counterweight to the general press, which accepted and disseminated American policy as demonstrative of the virtue of the capitalist system. The *National Guardian,* on the contrary, regarded United States policy and the system of monopoly capital as the chief sources of the world's problems. It did not advocate socialism as an alternative system for the United States, but insisted that it be discussed as a *possible alternative* and not as a horrid word. It offered friendly, or at least nonhostile, coverage of the socialist countries, while reserving the right to criticize at any time. It held that the peace of the world depended upon the people of the West accepting the fact that socialist countries were here to stay and that it was not the obligation of the United States government to destroy them.

The policy of the paper was to maintain a flexible approach so it could be a forum of the left. Adhering to this policy, it was able to count among its regular, and often critical, readers independent Socialists, Communists, Trotskyists, members of groups that had broken away from the left parties, liberals, and even conservatives who defended the right of a dissenting newspaper to publish, however critical it might be of established power. The editors rejected any approach which sought to cloak radicalism in another guise to achieve respectability. Rather, they insisted from the beginning that radicalism *was* a respectable political philosophy, in the best American tradition, and was entitled to its place in the American political debate.

It was this policy of flexibility, I believe, that enabled the *National Guardian* to persevere through a time when many left organizations and publications perished and to achieve the grudging respect of its opponents in the United States. Abroad, the respect was not grudging; *National Guardian* articles and editorials were reprinted not only in the socialist countries, but in Western European and neutralist Asian countries. If the newspaper was regarded by some as a prophet without honor in its own country, it demonstrated to the rest of the world that there was a core of sanity among the American people despite the overwhelming pressures of a predatory government and an acquiescent communications industry.

This approach to radical journalism, in my view, remains sound. There are, as I have noted, radical publications which champion one position or another in the debate that has been taking place for more than a decade in a divided international socialist movement (although there is a curious unanimity among otherwise hostile left factions in the United States today in their enmity toward China). It follows that the American radical community will be affected by the turns of the debate and its eventual outcome. Because of the intensity of the debate, however, and the emotions it stirs, there is a pressing need for an independent and flexible radical newspaper, national in scope, which could provide a forum for all points of view. An independent radical newspaper, in this sense, would serve as a unifying force rather than a divisive one. Its motivation would be against the splintering confusions of ideological discord that serve only to distract American radicals from their main task—the struggle against the proponents of war and racism in the country which is the fountainhead of both.

There were times in the *National Guardian*'s history when the coverage of news inevitably joined with journalistic campaigns to mobilize support for a particular situation or point of view. Three specific episodes come to mind: the Rosenberg case, which the *National Guardian* brought to world attention in a series of articles beginning in August 1951 that launched a worldwide effort to prevent the execution of the young couple who had been convicted on a charge of conspiracy to commit espionage; the Korean War, which the *National Guardian* had opposed from the beginning, and whose impact, along with the McCarthy terror, caused the circulation of the paper to drop from 54,000 to 22,000 in one year; and the assassination of President Kennedy, followed by a long article by Attorney Mark Lane (known as "A Brief for Lee Harvey Oswald," a documented study concluding that Oswald could not have been a lone killer). Lane's analysis was the longest article in the newspaper's history and certainly the most widely reprinted. The first two episodes had serious consequences for the *National Guardian;* the third had an impact in this country and abroad whose extent may never be measured until the truth about the assassination is revealed—if it ever is.

In May 1953, one month before the execution of the Rosenbergs at Sing Sing Prison, Belfrage and I were subpenaed to appear before the McCarthy committee in Washington (Belfrage then was editor and I was executive editor). The ostensible purpose of the summons was an investigation of United States government participation in the establishment of the new post-World War II press of occupied Germany, an operation in which both Belfrage and I had participated under the supervision of the Information Control Command of the United States Army. Actually, McCarthy concentrated not on Germany but on the *National Guardian* and its interest in the Rosenberg case.

As a result of our appearance, Belfrage, a British citizen, was arrested and held for deportation. He spent four months in prison, without being charged, in the course of a two-year struggle to reverse the deportation order. The effort failed, despite spirited help from much of the *National Guardian* readership, and Belfrage accepted deportation in 1955. From that time on, he was listed on the masthead as the editor-in-exile. I became the editor-in-residence, envying Belfrage's freedom to travel to almost any country in the world (including China in 1957) while I was bound to a desk in lower Manhattan.

The aftermath of the war in Korea brought new summonses— for General Manager John T. McManus and myself—to the Senate Internal Security Subcommittee in January 1956. Again the stated reason for the subpena was something other than our association with the *National Guardian*. Senator Eastland was angry with the *New York Times* for its editorials in support of racial integration in the schools of the South. (The famous Supreme Court decision had been handed down 18 months earlier, and the *Times* had kept a watch on the progress of integration.) In retaliation, Eastland sought to embarrass the *Times* by subpenaing present and past members of the *Times* editorial staff who might be suspected of left-wing affiliation. McManus and I both were *Times* alumni.

At the hearings, few questions were put to us about the *Times,* but there was a heavy concentration on the *National Guardian* and our publishing, a few years earlier, of the names of United

States prisoners of war in North Korea.[4] The names originally had been obtained from North Korean shortwave broadcasts and printed in the *China Monthly Review*, an English-language publication edited by John W. Powell, Jr., and published in Shanghai. The United States government, we knew, had also monitored the broadcasts, but had refused to make the names public. We did— and within a week were receiving hundreds of letters from wives and parents asking for information about men listed as missing in action and presumed dead. We supplied the information where we could and were able to establish that at least 1,000 men were alive. It was one of the most moving experiences of my career. For our efforts, however, we were denounced as traitors by several newspapers and narrowly escaped a charge of sedition arising out of the Eastland hearings.

The area that caused perhaps the greatest conflict between the *National Guardian* and some groups on the left, and surely produced the greatest turbulence in the letters columns, was domestic politics. A founding principle of the paper was the advocacy of an alternative to the two major political parties, which we regarded as essentially the same. We had supported the candidacies of Henry Wallace in 1948 and Vincent Hallinan on the Progressive party ticket in 1952 (the last year in which the Progressive party entered a candidate) and had rejected the "lesser evil" position of the liberals by refusing to support Adlai Stevenson, John F. Kennedy and Lyndon B. Johnson in succeeding elections. We did on several occasions, particularly in state or local elections, endorse a Socialist candidate if one was on the ballot.

This independent view clashed with the views of the Communist party. The party put forward the "mainstream" theory—that the bulk of working people were in the Democratic party, and it was therefore the duty of radicals to work within the Democratic party to urge it toward a more progressive position. We reasoned that radicals would be swallowed up by the Democratic party apparatus and would at best have only limited effectiveness. But

---

[4] The prisoner-of-war issue in Korea bears similarities with the situation of United States prisoners in North Vietnam, but unlike Vietnam, where the majority of the few hundred prisoners were captured airmen shot down over North Vietnam, the prisoners in Korea (numbering in the thousands) had been taken in land encounters with North Korean forces in both North and South Korea.

the lesser-evil theory had a tenacious quadrennial grip on the left-of-center electorate, and the debate among *National Guardian* readers and the shafts leveled at its editors became sharp indeed. After the elections, when the status quo was revealed to be untrammeled by the election results, and the canceled subscriptions were reinstated, the inevitable flood of letters poured in urging the *National Guardian* to take the lead in forming a third party. The reasoning ran thus: the newspaper had readers in every state who could form the nucleus of political clubs. There was no one else to do the job.

The hopes and frustrations of the readers were clear; the practical politics less so. No newspaper or publication can become a political party, nor can it be the main organizer of one. It can guide, instruct, encourage and inform, but it cannot substitute for an organization. A newsweekly with a small staff, however devoted and able, based in New York yet with three-fourths of its readership spread throughout the country and with obviously limited funds, can be a focal point and a clearing house for information and instruction for political organizers in the field. But the job of organizing is precisely there in the field—in the communities, with a regional or national apparatus functioning with a set of political principles, building a movement which a radical newspaper can publicize and support. The newspaper may even become the official organ of the party or the movement—although I would not recommend an existing independent publication taking this course—but there must first *be* a movement or a party already functioning.

When the Progressive party died and regional cooperating organizations such as the American Labor party in New York State were dismantled, it marked the end of political organizing on the left, outside of the small Communist party, the Socialist Workers party and some splinter groups. The persisting dilemma of the radical American opposition from that time on was that no party or organization came into being as a rallying point or organizing force. That situation persisted—with some temporary relief—through the rise of the New Left, and it prevails today. It is an illusion that *activity* on the left constitutes *organization*.

Accepting this reality, the *National Guardian* warmly welcomed and publicized every activity that could grow into an organized movement: the courageous vanguard of young black militants in the South leading to the Student Nonviolent Coordinating Committee; the activities in the universities leading to the Students for a Democratic Society and the DuBois Clubs, and the peace mobilizations against the war in Southeast Asia.

Young people increasingly turned to the *National Guardian* for news and guidance once their suspicions about its "Old Left" origins were dissipated. While they maintained their distrust of the organized forms of an older generation, they accepted factual news about their own unorganized activities. And while the editors of the *National Guardian* insisted throughout this period that unorganized and unstructured activity was far less effective than organized but unauthoritarian activity, they acknowledged the prevailing mood among the young radicals and agreed that it was for the younger generation to alter its course itself, if it would.

Internally, the problems of the *National Guardian* were exacerbated by the external currents on the left, particularly as they affected the housekeeping chores of a radical newspaper. It is an axiom that a tidy printed page hides a fairly untidy scramble to ensure survival. After the early euphoria of the Progressive party days and the expenditure of considerable sums in futile attempts to achieve mass circulation, we settled down to stabilizing what we accepted as a readership of respectable size and a financial condition of permanent crisis. Survival was guaranteed by involving almost the entire readership in the affairs of the paper. We barred cries of "Help!" in the pages of the paper as a public death rattle, but sent annual appeal letters to the readership and organized a "Buck of the Month Club," through which readers gave a dollar or more a month beyond their subscription price.

The problems of staffing a radical newspaper increased with time. The original staff—there was almost no turnover in the first 12 years—was made up largely of experienced newspapermen and women with considerable political background. Almost all had working wives or husbands who augmented the subsistence salaries of the *National Guardian*. When some of the staff left, primarily for economic reasons, our aim was to attract young people who might be trained for a future with the *National Guardian* or elsewhere in radical journalism. In the 1950s, in the wake of Joe McCarthy, few young candidates applied. But in the 1960s the situation changed dramatically: job applications poured in, and several young people were hired. This caused a sharp decline in the average age of the staff and a rise in conflicts between older hands with political experience of another era and younger hands with little political experience of any era, but with strongly held views about past and future politics. Interestingly enough, the debate soon crossed generational lines, and the divisions in the editorial conferences often did not conform to age categories.

These are some conclusions drawn from 19 years with a radical newspaper:

> An independent radical newspaper engenders hostility on the right, among liberals and, unfortunately, in some measure on the left.
>
> The editor of a radical newspaper cannot confine his work to editing a newspaper. He must in addition be a writer, copy reader, fund raiser, public speaker, traveler, teacher of journalism and sometimes a psychoanalyst willing if not always qualified to handle the problems of an often undisciplined and financially undernourished staff plus an articulate readership. It is not an ideal estate.
>
> Without the regular assistance of sympathetic persons who adhere to a political party or apparatus (and today perhaps even with them) there is little hope that a radical newspaper can achieve a mass circulation, or even survive without subsidy by its readership and larger contributors.
>
> The press of the nation, with rare exceptions, demonstrates a continuing hostility toward its radical brothers, to the extent of refusing to publish even startling new material if the source of the material is a radical newspaper.

In the special circumstances of the *National Guardian,* I had to cope also with two important departures. In the first instance, it was the exile of Cedric Belfrage, a close friend and collaborator whose mature presence was a sustaining force; in the second, it was the death in 1961 of John T. McManus, whose strength and optimism had maintained the security of the newspaper and the confidence of its staff through its most difficult periods. Neither Belfrage nor McManus was indispensable but each was irreplaceable.

Thus, through death and deportation, I became the sole owner of a publication which I felt should not be owned by one person. Despite the unsettling times and a growing indication that severe staff problems were in the making, I turned over to the staff in 1966 a 50 percent share of the ownership and control of the *National Guardian*. While I was then only dimly aware of the European precedents for such an action, I felt strongly that the newspaper should be legally what it had always been in practice —a cooperatively run and democratically administered enterprise. Every week since the founding of the paper there had been an editorial conference, with full staff participation, to plan each issue of the paper. Financially, the stock turnover meant nothing, since the paper had never shown a profit, and my salary was a token five dollars more than the highest journeyman rate on the paper. But psychologically and in terms of control the move was significant. It was my hope that this new sense of equality might persuade some of the more acerbic critics on the staff that there was no enemy within. It was my desire that in a very short time I might be able to relinquish some of the editor's duties and devote my energies to longer-range planning and writing.

Both the hope and the desire, however, were in vain. A large part of the staff held to the belief that the *National Guardian* could become a commercially profitable enterprise rather than substantially dependent on the support of its readers. The situation, according to this reasoning, had been created by the rise of the New Left. The prevailing staff view was that the *National Guardian* was a failure because its circulation remained at about 30,000 and that this failure was attributable to the editor's (and therefore the paper's) inability to be responsive to the hopes and aspirations of a "young and growing radical movement."

My position was that, while the potential of young radicals was self-evident and their searching independence should be encouraged, they had not in fact manifested themselves as a movement or even a cohesive force. I pointed to the prevalent "do your own thing" philosophy among radicals, the bickering among different factions of the New Left and a repetition of the failures of communication in the New Left, for which the Old Left had been denounced by the new noncommunicators. I felt further that, when young radicals had advanced to a stage of accepting a set of principles which they would apply to the practice of politics, they would seek unity with radicals of all ages—even with those who held differing views within the radical framework.

In such a situation, I felt, a newspaper such as the *National Guardian* should seek to be, as it always had been, the voice of an entire radical movement and not a segment of it. I was persuaded that young people expected of a radical newspaper what radicals of all ages expected of it—the most informed and expert news, commentary and service information available to advance their own ideas and to influence their fellows. Success for a radical newspaper could not be measured in terms of circulation. The respect and prestige which the *National Guardian* had already achieved, I felt, was based on two factors: that it was a newspaper first and a political entity second; that it maintained its policy of flexibility without yielding principles.

My fear was that the internal critics would seek to reverse the first factor—to put politics first and journalistic enterprise second—and that this group would seek to identify the paper, at a given time, with what it believed to be the most popular and successful faction of the New Left. There was clearly lacking among these staff members a sense of the continuity of history which would have demonstrated to them the inadvisability of such a course. Their rejection of the radical history of the previous generations struck me as unfortunate.

Months of discussion and argument took place in 1966 and 1967, and there was considerable agreement on certain changes in the paper which would make it more responsive to new currents in the radical ferment. But there seemed to be no possibility of agreement on basic differences—some of which were obscured by opportunistic argument—and the tone of the debate assumed a quality of personal venom that I found entirely out of place in an enterprise ostensibly devoted to the brotherhood of man.

In March 1967 I received a memorandum signed by several key members of the staff. It stated that the paper was "in crisis," and in effect presented me with an ultimatum to accept certain demands or face a general staff revolt. In response, I submitted my resignation on April 5, 1967, and was joined in this action by the paper's co-founder, Cedric Belfrage. I felt that a continuance of the debate would serve only to destroy the paper. I was willing to concede that my position might be in error and that my critics should have the opportunity to prove the wisdom of their approach. In my resignation I said:

> In one major sense, I do agree that the *National Guardian* is in crisis. But I believe the crisis is internal. I refer to the persistent bitterness and inability to find common ground which has undoubtedly been reflected in the work of the staff and the quality of the paper. Further, it has caused the voluntary departure of valuable staff members. If the rancor and division continue, the prospects for the *National Guardian* would be dim indeed. My departure is in accordance with a position I have expressed in the past—that if a majority of the staff expressed a lack of confidence in me, and I saw no hope of restoring a spirit of unity and harmony, I would withdraw.

The decision was painful after 19 years of participation in a project which had carried such high hopes. But there was, despite the pain, a sense of gratification for the years of work toward the goal of honest journalism and for the experiences which might be imparted to others.

The new managers of the *National Guardian* after some months of experimentation changed the name simply to the *Guardian*. Predictably they shifted their point of view according to the fortunes of dominant groups within the New Left—first rejecting the "Marxist approach" of the traditional left parties, then becoming virtually an adjunct of the Students for a Democratic Society, then veering away from a strictly New Left approach when SDS disintegrated into warring factions.

In the *Guardian* of December 14, 1968, following a turbulent meeting in New York marking the twentieth anniversary of the founding of the paper (and 18 months after I had resigned), an editorial declared: "The movement itself is split in numerous camps. There is no ideological cohesion. A relevant strategy for the next years has not been formulated."

I quote this not to vindicate a position or to take any pleasure from it. It was an accurate statement, verifying for the *Guardian* as well as for the radical movement as a whole that there are no miraculous shortcuts to "success." The *Guardian* has had two or three almost complete turnovers of staff since 1967. In 1970 a large part of the staff broke away to start the *Liberated Guardian,* and in 1972 a dissident group left the *Liberated Guardian* to form an "LLG group," presumably a *Liberated Liberated Guardian.*

The "old" *Guardian,* having exhausted the possibilities of a nearly defunct New Left, shifted back toward what it described as a "Marxist-Leninist" position and has settled down to a general approach very much resembling that of the *National Guardian.* Its circulation in October 1971 was listed as 14,000, less than half of the 1966 figure, and its advertising content was much thinner.

What happened in 1967 was not an isolated event but part of the convulsions that were shaking not only the American left, but also the nation as a whole and, in turn, many parts of the world. The cause of the convulsions was the youth rebellion against the strictures of stifling systems. In the United States it gave rise also to a new kind of journalism which had an exhilarating effect on young people and a discouraging effect on the circulation of radical political papers and, to a degree, of the general press. The new kind of journalism was the so-called underground press.

CHAPTER XIII

ROCK 'N' REVOLT

THE "underground press" (the term was devised by John Wilcock, one of the early journalistic rebels of the 1950s) began as a subjective protest against "the system." It advocated a life-style of drug euphoria, sexual freedom, liberation of the mind through rock 'n' roll music, long hair and bizarre dress—plus revolution. The kind of revolution was never defined, but it seemed to mean any activity against existing institutions. From its start in 1964 with Art Kunkin's the *Los Angeles Free Press,* the underground press had by the late 1960s surfaced as a political entity of considerable appeal, with an attraction for readers beyond "the underground" great enough to stir more than a ripple of concern in the established media.

In the spring of 1972 there were about 450 underground newspapers (even Wilcock dislikes the term as inappropriate to the very much aboveground concerns of the underground press). Most of them had replaced an equal number of defunct publications, and many had little hope of long life. But others have been publishing successfully for years, and the total circulation for the underground press as a whole is estimated by the most conservative analysts at three million. The *Los Angeles Free Press,* daddy of them all, reached a circulation of 95,000 in 1971—before intra-staff conflict produced a schism and a rival publication called the *Staff.* The only larger circulation (130,000) in the so-called underground is that of the *Village Voice* in New York, founded in 1955, but the *Voice* is not generally regarded as an underground newspaper. "The *Village Voice*," says Wilcock, who wrote for it several years, "ironically is in the position of a teacher outsmarted by its students. It was the *Voice*, with its pseudo-liberalism and willingness to print what at one time seemed far-out, that paved the way for all the underground papers that followed."

The early underground press appealed to an audience in its teens and early twenties which had become persuaded that the regular press[1] was neither accurate, complete nor candid in reporting about the educational system, the draft, economic opportunities and other concerns of younger citizens. The underground press was first staffed—and to a large extent still is—by young people willing to work for very little money or none at all, simply as a part of their life-style. Quite often, because of their admirable lack of avarice, they were exploited by a glib entrepreneur whose revolutionary conscience somehow evaporated whenever there was money in the house.

To the "straight" world, the sudden rush of the underground press seemed to presage revolution in the streets. Reputable citizens envisioned a vanguard of wild-eyed, long-maned young radicals, marching to the electronic beat of incendiary rock music, prepared to destroy institutional society and let anarchistic chaos reign. The presentiment was grossly exaggerated, largely because of the appalling ignorance of the established media and the skillful ability of some of the underground "heavies" to exploit the media for their own personal advantage. Abbie Hoffman and Jerry Rubin are excellent examples of such manipulative interplay with a media which soon warmed up to the sport. This interaction created a small but prominent group of household underground heroes who sought out TV cameras as a beagle follows a rabbit, and then produced, with the help of worshipful ghosts, best-selling books and recordings. The next step was lectures before adoring audiences from Berkeley to the Lower East Side. Thus was the affluent underground born.

The underground press was a new and spontaneous journalism attuned to the student rebellions, the protests against the war in Indochina and the militant black freedom movement (although

---

[1] The word "regular" rather than "commercial" is used here because many of the underground papers have become highly commercial—and some of them profit-making—through advertising.

few blacks were involved in underground-press activities). The development was facilitated by low-cost offset printing presses and by street venders who made above-average profits on sales—sometimes as much as 80 percent of the sale price. Supreme Court decisions against censorship permitted the use of language and art work that found a salivating market beyond the boundaries of the underground communities. The popularity of rock music made the underground press a thriving market for advertising recordings by big-name rock artists and groups. Robert Schwartz, president of Laurie Records, told *Business Week:* "The papers have a tremendous pass-along readership, maybe five or ten readers per issue. So the price per exposure comes way down. But more important, you know the readers are interested in what you're selling."

There was a market also in the underground press for head shops, the community stores offering all the accouterments to life in the underground, such as psychedelic art, theatrical costumes, incense and books on occult practices. The papers advanced the virtues of pot and "mind-blowing" drugs, carried long reviews of rock concerts and records, and glowing profiles of such rock idols as the Beatles, Bob Dylan, the Jefferson Airplane and the Rolling Stones. When the Beatles or Dylan composed new lyrics, underground analysts inspected them line for line to discern which way the wind was blowing and what revolutionary portents they contained. The incidental accumulation of millions of dollars by these rock artists somehow went unnoticed. They were, after all, the troubadors of a new life in a new world.[2]

This early psychedelic flamboyance was tolerated and even encouraged by the established institutions as a noisy but effective conduit away from political action. The establishment knew, of course, that social protest was the basic motivation of the underground press, but that, after all, was nothing new, and it could be contained or "coopted"—a New Left word for "taken over." The music and fashion industries were the first to move in, the one diluting with attractive financial bait the content of rock music, the other sending its scouts to copy the bizarre fashions which were later put on the market at grossly inflated prices in nonun-

---

[2] A first-rate account of the relationship of the underground press with the recording companies, by John Burks, appeared in the October 4, 1969, issue of the biweekly *Rolling Stone* (no relation to the rock group Rolling Stones).

derground shops. The art world and the advertising industry were not far behind. By the late 1960s, magazines, television commercials and, to an extent, newspaper display advertising took on the appearance of the lobby of the Fillmore East, the great rock emporium in Manhattan's East Village, as the real-estate interests euphemistically designated the Lower East Side.

There was, however, a persevering strain in the underground press that was geninely radical and could not be bought off, and it surfaced with considerable effect during the great protests against the war in Southeast Asia and the uprisings in the ghettos of the nation. In Detroit, for example, the underground newspaper the *Fifth Estate* published first-rate accounts of the Detroit riots of 1967 during which large sections of the city were burned down.

In the San Francisco Bay area, the *Berkeley Barb* and *Good Times* were turning their irreverent attention to local problems, as was the *Seed* in Chicago, *Kudzu* in Jackson, Mississippi, *Kaleidoscope* in Madison and Milwaukee, and the *Street Journal* in San Diego. The mixed feelings of some of the editors were expressed by the *Fifth Estate*'s editor Peter Werbe as he took a visitor through Detroit: "When it was burning, man, you could get up on the rooftops and see the flames in all directions. It was beautiful. You've never seen anything like it." Then, as though to make sure his visitor understood him precisely, he said: "I hate this fucking town so much." In the next breath, however, he talked not about destruction but about building: "We try to relate the paper to working-class kids. Those are the kids you want to reach. All you have to do is to look at the fantastic power the workers have got. They control the means of production."

Others were turned inward. In Washington, D.C., in 1969, a *Rolling Stone* reporter asked a staff member of the *Free Press* (it died in 1971) why an underground paper published in the capital paid so little attention to the inner workings of the vast government bureaucracy. The *Free Press* man agreed there was much to inspect, but noted that a reporter covering this area would have to get a haircut, wear a suit and a tie, drive a car and fraternize with reporters from the regular press. He said: "I'm not going to ask somebody to lead a false life-style just to get coverage of the fucking government."

At the *Great Speckled Bird* in Atlanta, one of the best of the persevering underground publications, there was concern about life-styles too, but in a more critical fashion. Miller Francis, a gifted writer about music, set down his impressions of a new recording by a rock group called MC-5. It was, he said, "a pasty-faced derivative of black music. They have simply wheeled their grimy Detroit vehicle up to a Black Power filling station and said, 'Fill 'er up.' They play with their hands and feet, not with their guts and soul. They are smug, not proud. That white radicals can be turned on by this farce demonstrates how far we must go before we can approach the problem of white racism in ourselves and in our communities without guilt or intimidation."

Counterposed against this comment was one from Steve Diamond of the *Dock of the Bay* in San Francisco: "Dylan and the Band are the key to it all, where it's all going. They're deep into rock. The ideal revolutionary device would be a duet between Bob Dylan and Jerry Rubin." Since both Dylan and Rubin seem since to have wandered far from the revolutionary ideal, the search for the dream duet will have to continue. Fortunately, the publications with staying power are seeking remedies for more immediate community problems. In Madison, John Kois, editor of *Kaleido-scope*, said in 1969: "We don't see ourselves as an instrument of the revolution, because we don't see any revolution. At this paper, we are almost traditional reformists—we pose alternatives and try to make them happen. We're gadflies." John Gwin of the *Great Speckled Bird* seemed to agree: "There's a good amount of this 'beyond politics' talk. But you know, life-styles are fine and everything, but there are all these stories about things that need taking care of in the South—voting rights, segregated schools, stuff like that. I don't care what else is going on. We got to take care of these things."

When they tried to take care of things, the real trouble started. Several papers came to the conclusion that millionaire rock groups were not the most dedicated standard bearers of social change and began to look elsewhere for solutions. Some even investigated socialism. The recording companies accordingly became less interested in the underground market and dropped much of their advertising. For many newspapers this was a hard blow, because few survived on circulation revenue alone. In the traditional pattern of affluent seduction, some underground newspapers succumbed to the dangling dollars and became plump with advertising and correspondingly listless in the quest for social and political change.

For the newspapers which maintained their radical principles, however, or began to adopt political ideals to replace the faded psychedelic fantasy, there was trouble of a different nature. Its origin was federal, state and local government, and their police and investigatory arms. The situation of the underground press of the South is typical of the experiences of other papers which have become increasingly concerned with political and social change.

Harassment and surveillance of the Southern underground is almost universal. A study in *South Today* reported that of all papers contacted by the Southern Regional Council, only the *Anvil* of Chapel Hill, North Carolina, escaped police harassment and arrest of staff members, publishers or salesmen—and even the *Anvil* reported vandalism of newsracks and threatening telephone calls, perhaps police-inspired. Employees of *Kudzu* in Mississippi have been charged with obscenity, vagrancy, assaulting officers, resisting arrest, criminal mischief, abusive language and obstructing traffic. The *Great Speckled Bird* successfully resisted two major prosecutions on charges of obscenity and profane language. It is not the alleged lewdness that bothers the authorities, however—some of the publications have become straitlaced enough to win the approval of Cotton Mather—but the sharp thrusts at authority itself, which the underground press regards as obscene.

In San Diego, home city of President Nixon's communications coordinator Herbert Klein and two dailies operated by the ultra-conservative Copley chain, the *Street Journal* has been continually harassed by city officials and the police. The *Street Journal,* remarkably free of four-letter words, was irreverent enough to confound its fellow undergrounders by lambasting the film *Easy Rider,* a visual tone poem to drugs, which had been canonized in much of the rest of the underground press. It has managed, as *Time* magazine put it, "to denounce pollution and corruption without invoking Mao Tse-tung." The *Street Journal* has suffered bullets through its windows, theft, smashed equipment, fire bombings and repeated arrests on charges subsequently thrown out.

The attacks on the *Street Journal* followed its publication of an unflattering two-page article about C. Arnholdt Smith, San Diego millionaire and political kingmaker. The *Journal* reported it had learned from an intimate of the Smith household that when Smith saw the article he called James S. Copley, owner of the San Diego media monopoly, and between them they agreed to "crush the *Journal*." The information, the *Journal* said, had been confirmed by a disaffected staff member of the Copley newspaper.

In Wisconsin the editor of *Kaleidoscope* was sentenced to six months on a contempt charge. He had refused to appear before a grand jury to disclose the source of a document, published in *Kaleidoscope,* attributed to a group claiming responsibility for bombing the Army Mathematics Research Center on the University of Wisconsin campus in Madison. The judge said the case was a clash between justice and freedom of the press. "Something has to give," he said. "What has to give is the First Amendment privilege—in the interest of justice." The editor later agreed to testify after having spent some time in jail. There are other cases of deliberate persecution:

In Cambridge street salesmen of Boston's *Avatar* amassed a total of 58 arrests for peddling "obscene material" before a judge ruled that the material was not obscene. By that time a number of newsdealers had been frightened into refusing to carry *Avatar,* and circulation dropped sharply.

In Montgomery County, Maryland, the editor of the Washington *Free Press* was sentenced to six months for publishing an allegedly obscene cartoon of a judge. In Chicago the editor of *Seed* was arrested for publishing a Christmas collage of nudes, police, skulls, sexual acts and lots more, in a pungent comment on American society. It was in the tradition of Georg Grosz, whose similar commentaries on German society are in the permanent collections of the great American museums. In Norman, Oklahoma, a judge dismissed charges of "selling pictures of sexual intercourse" against five staff members of the Norman underground newspaper *Jones Family's Grandchildren.* He did so reluctantly, on constitutional grounds, but urged the district attorney to appeal his ruling to a higher court. "Pictures of sexual intercourse," he said, "are the ultimate in obscenity." *Grand-children* had published the drawing, a tasteful one, as part of its New Year's greeting. The holiday notion cost 3,000 dollars in legal fees for the paper.

Another kind of intercourse got the *Los Angeles Free Press* into deep trouble. Editor Art Kunkin and a reporter were convicted of receiving stolen goods—in this case, information. The *Free Press* in August 1969 published the names and addresses of secret narcotics agents in the Los Angeles area, obtained from a photostat sent to the paper by a clerk in the attorney general's office in Los Angeles. After the conviction, on a felony charge, the *Free Press* settled out of court a civil action brought by eight of the narcotics agents. The price was 43,000 dollars—high even for a publication as profitable as the *Free Press* had become. The case had important implications for the press in general, but few newspapers reported or commented on the *Free Press*'s action or the court's verdict. Among those journalists who did was William J. Drummond, a member of the editorial staff of the *Los Angeles Times,* writing in the bimonthly magazine of the Public Information Center:

> Because the *Free Press* caters to a radical community and owes no allegiance to the conventional power structure, it often comes up with news that would otherwise go unpublicized. It was the *Free Press* and its sister papers in the underground that were calling for withdrawal from Vietnam long before the Establishment press. But the powerlessness of the underground press and its unpopularity with conventional society make it easy prey for zealous prosecutors. As Thucydides wrote, quoting a participant in the Melian Dialogue, "The strong do what they will, while the weak suffer what they must."

The diligence with which the government pursued the Los Angeles case made it clear that its main interest was in suppressing attacks on establishment practices. As for the obscenity charges against the underground press, there was a far riper area to explore: the wide-open pornographic publications on sale at thousands of newsstands and shops across the country. Yet these publications, except in rare cases, are allowed to sell mainly because they are almost devoid of political commentary. Further, they are purchased not by young people but by those generally characterized as Middle Americans. The youth rebellion has little need of pornographic material to stimulate a healthy sexual revolution.

For some of the underground papers, printing has proved almost as much of a problem as police, mainly because of printers' concern over the contents and unwillingness to grant credit. In New York the *East Village Other* and *Rat* (eventually taken over by a women's collective) were hard-pressed in 1969 to find a printer. Some underground publications have gone through as many as 50 printers during their careers. It was for a time a 75-mile trip for the editors of Seattle's *Helix;* the Phoenix *Orpheus* was printed in California. But perhaps the most poignant story is that of *Kaleidoscope,* or rather the man who printed it—William F. Schanen, Jr., of Port Washington, Wisconsin.

Schanen, a native of Port Washington, was publisher and editor of a weekly newspaper, the *Ozaukee Country Press,* and he owned two other small weeklies in nearby towns. As part of his job printing operations he took on *Kaleidoscope*—and that's where his troubles began. He had nothing to do with the content of *Kaleidoscope,* and most people in Port Washington had never seen the paper, but they had *heard* about it. It was, according to what they had heard, un-American and obscene. Schanen thought it would be un-American *not* to print it. "*Kaleidoscope* has journalistic merit," he said in the summer of 1969. "I don't agree with a lot of it, but what are we supposed to do, get rid of everything we disagree with?"

One man in particular thought that was exactly what Schanen ought to do. He was Benjamin Grob, a wealthy industrialist from Grafton, Wisconsin (where Schanen published one of his three weeklies), whose tool factory office wall held a large picture of the late Senator Joe McCarthy, a close friend. Grob sent out to 500 business groups and individuals a reprint of a *Kaleidoscope* article hinting at shady practices in some churches and describing some police actions as inhuman. Grob stated in an accompanying letter his intention of withdrawing advertising from Schanen's newspapers and ended: "Ladies and gentlemen, I am looking for company."

He got it. Merchants and industries rushed to pull their advertising out of all three Schanen papers in a boycott campaign to force him to drop the *Kaleidoscope* job. Schanen refused. When the Wisconsin Electric Power Company joined the boycott, it received hundreds of letters from angry customers who suggested that the company's job, as a franchised monopoly, was to supply power, not censorship. But the boycott held and Schanen's advertising revenue in the *Ozaukee Press* alone dropped from 3,000 dollars to 700 dollars a week. He estimated that the boycott would cost him 200,000 dollars in gross income in a year's time, but he would not yield. On the masthead of the *Ozaukee Press* he fixed the slogan: "The newspaper that refused to die." During the first week of the boycott Schanen learned that his newspaper had placed first in general excellence in the 1969 National Newspaper Association contest.

In October 1969 a fire caused 15,000 dollars' damage at a Grafton warehouse where Schanen's newsprint was stored. The fire chief suspected arson. Grob sent out a second, then a third letter, and most of the remaining advertisers canceled. The *Pilot*, the competing newspaper in Port Washington, supported the boycott editorially and grew correspondingly fatter. The FBI came around to talk to Schanen; it was not a friendly call.

When the boycott became 90 percent effective, Schanen was forced to sell two of his three newspapers, but held on to the *Ozaukee Press*. The Milwaukee chapter of Sigma Delta Chi, the professional journalism society, voiced its support, as did a few other SDX chapters. *Life* published a story; editorials in several newspapers denounced the boycott as a threat to freedom of the press. But nothing changed. During 1970 Schanen received 25 citations from various organizations, including the 1970 Elijah Parish Lovejoy award for courage in journalism. Still the boycott held.

"I couldn't believe it," Schanen told the *Life* reporter. "I was stunned. All these people, my friends, deserting like this. I'm not mad at them. Not even Grob. But I can't make any sense of it. Why they all quit. You have talked to them. What do you think they mean by it?"

The reporter fumbled for a reply, but he knew that Schanen knew the answer: a man in a position of power, stimulating fear and hatred—as his idolized senator had done 20 years before—among a people worried that the world "out there" would intrude to change things in Port Washington.

Schanen's newspaper, as he had pledged, did not die. But he did—of a heart attack in March 1971. He was fifty-seven.

For many editors of the underground press, conversely, William Schanen and his world were the "out there" for them. Holed up in their underground communities, they rarely ventured into that world, and as time went on they perceived it with increasingly romantic vision—rather like that of Don Quixote. An example of this vision was offered at a conference of underground editors at Ann Arbor, Michigan, sponsored by the White Panthers/Trans Love, a white group headed by John Sinclair, much given to revolutionary rhetoric, shock language and drug culture. The call to the conference read in part:

> This conference marks the turning point in the revolutionary media. This is the year—1969—that the revolutionary media will reach beyond the hip artistic enclaves of America out into the bowels of this society—to all our young brothers out there in television land, the school-jails, the factories and pool halls, to turn our people on to the truth about the problem—and the solution to that problem. This is the year we will transform our movement from an "underground press syndicate" to a functioning revolutionary brotherhood.

As it turned out, the main problem at the conference seemed to be the relationship of the underground press to Columbia Records. The panels were like nonfunctioning revolutionary committees, listing problems but unable to present even the vaguest beginnings of solutions. No one, it seemed, wanted to be regarded as a journalist. A further clue to the mood among a section of the underground press was offered by Peter Leggieri, publisher of the *East Village Other,* a moneymaking underground weekly in New York which generally gave the impression of having been assembled in an unmade bed upon which jars of paint had been spilled by frenetic body movements. "There's no agreement on how anybody in the underground sees anything," Leggieri said. "If the underground ever got charge of this country, there'd be a tremendous fight. It would make the revolution look small by comparison." [The *Other* ceased publication early in 1972.]

This underground viewpoint suggested that its exponents did not want to confront the world as it really existed—the world of the school-jails and the pool halls, of drafted men and draft resisters, poor people and oppressed blacks—and, everywhere, the living establishment which, underground, sometimes took the form of a threatening windmill or a hallucinatory nightmare evoked by a "bad trip." In 1970, among this group there was even nostalgia for the good old days of the 1964–66 period. This was expressed in clearly confused fashion by George Cavaletto, then on the staff of Liberation News Service, the news agency of the underground press:

> We're going through a lot of cultural crisis. A lot of papers are trying to cope with it. Three years ago there was something revolutionary in using drugs and sex and liberation, and dropping out was good. People were exploring different ways of relating to each other. In those days the papers were mainly turn-ons. What happened now is that that function has been taken over by the mass media. Drugs had a lot to do with placing people in a historical context—of placing people in a radical position. Using drugs was a revolutionary first step a lot of people took. But today we're beyond that, and today we're beginning to question confrontation with authorities as a way of life. I mean, you can't have a life-style based on constant theory and constant confrontation, because life isn't very satisfying that way. That's the crisis of the movement.

It was indeed a crisis which Cavaletto saw only dimly. He resented his dream revolution and life-style being "coopted" by the regular media. But if it was so easily coopted, it could hardly have been so revolutionary in the first place. Actually, what had been coopted was neither new nor revolutionary. It was something that had always existed in the "straight" world: the media simply gave it new coloration for the titillation of its audience. What Cavaletto could not absorb was another media message to the underground which said something like this: "We are taking away the toys with which you were playing Revolution. If you want to play the *real* game, your adversary is right here and waiting." For a part of the underground, the reality was too difficult to face, and it retreated deeper into the subterranean womb.

Others, however, took up the challenge. The turning point perhaps came in the aftermath of the great antiwar demonstrations of 1969 and the invasion of Laos in 1970, accompanied by the killing of the students at Kent State and Jackson State. When the Nixon administration made it evident that it would be moved by neither campus explosions nor street demonstrations, a new mood set in among the resisters. The returning Vietnam veterans began forming their own organizations—a development which would have been frowned on a few years earlier when the very word "organization" was anathema—and the Catholic resistance, as exemplified by the Berrigans, and the women's liberation movement were catching the imagination of the nation.

In September 1971 the *Berkeley Barb* came into possession of a Xeroxed copy of a newsletter called *Tupart Monthly Reports on the Underground Press*, published by National Media Analysis, Inc., of Washington, D.C., an organization which apparently made regular studies of the underground press and then sold them to interested parties—for example, the Central Intelligence Agency. The newsletter led off with some innocuous chatter— in clipped Kiplinger style—about the circulation, readership, scope of influence and content of the underground press. Then it got down to business with a warning in capital letters:

REVOLUTIONISTS GO BACK TO THE BOOKS

REVOLUTION! maintained its usual first place position in this month's analysis, often with what was little more than a reworking of the same rationale and slogans underground press observers have become accustomed to. Perhaps the most significant new thrust is a rather general "back to the books" theme. Both in articles and in display advertising there is added emphasis on the plethora of literature on revolution and guerrilla warfare which has been published in the U.S. in the past few years. There is also a call for emphasis on orthodoxy. . . . Atlanta's *Great Speckled Bird* said rather bluntly that it is well enough to make heroes out of Che Guevara, Ho Chi Minh, Mao and Lenin, but the serious revolutionary must study "the source of their ideas: the Marxist-Leninist tradition."

EDITORS SUMMARY—What the various radical and revolution-ist groups are saying is, "We have to get out to the people, and organize them—without so much rattling of our guerrilla bando-leers." This is what is happening with the underground press, it is spreading out the base with less noise and gore. We may even see a few nationally circulated papers fold, but at least, as we see it, their number has peaked. The increase will continue at the com-munity level. And there will be a continuing assortment of high school undergrounds—the high school underground press service in Washington claims they already number in the thousands.

There is a touch of nostalgia in the National Media Analysis report for the smashed windows and the seized university build-ings—things that were more tangible than the revolutionary guidance of *Das Kapital*. But the analysis is close to the mark in noting the trend in the underground press toward concentra-tion on the community. This trend is noticeable particularly in university areas such as Ithaca, New York (Cornell), and the Durham-Raleigh-Chapel Hill area of North Carolina. There the existing underground newspapers are either changing or yielding to a new kind of community newspaper in which both university people and townspeople participate. And the issues that concern these publications today are not so much the quality of the "grass" coming into the country as the price of bread in the local supermarkets, unemployment and welfare benefits, and housing crises created by the unprincipled university landlords who own much of the housing and land in their areas.

These new publications are making their way slowly, sometimes painfully. It takes time to break down the years of mistrust between "town and gown," but it is being accomplished. At Cornell, for example, the state-funded Council on Human Affairs operates under the aegis of the university, conducting classes and seminars in university buildings and offering courses for credit to townspeople who may one day decide to pursue their studies in a more formal fashion. For the local community people it is an opportunity to learn about the forces behind the experiences of their daily lives; for the university students and faculty, it is an opportunity to relate their theoretical knowledge to the practical experiences of their community neighbors. Most heartening of all, union members from local industry are joining the groups.

As the underground newspapers concentrate more and more on community affairs, they become increasingly dependent on Liberation News Service for reportage about national and international affairs. LNS was founded in the summer of 1967 by Ray Mungo, who had been editor of the *Boston University News*, and Marshall Bloom, who had been removed as an officer of the United States Student Association for his radical views. Both were in their early twenties, bright, freewheeling, very much involved in "the movement," and as much caught up with the Beatles' "yellow submarines" as with opposing the war in Vietnam. That combination was common in the middle 1960s and often was at the root of divisions that were to take place among movement people.

LNS set up shop in Washington with a few full-time workers and a dozen volunteers (unpaid), and began to service the growing underground-press movement with news stories produced in Washington and material received from stringers throughout the country—straight news, background articles, book reviews, poems and graphics. In 1968 the enterprise moved to New York and gradually became less interested in yellow submarines and more in nuclear ones, campus protests (it was the time of peak activities of the Students for a Democratic Society) and racism. Three packets of mimeographed LNS service went out weekly to subscribers among the underground press, college newspapers, some radio stations and even to the regular wire services and a few daily newspapers. Some of the articles were expertly written and contained information to be found nowhere else; others were sloppy, subjective and windy with rhetoric.

With the arrival at LNS of political radicals with professional training, the service improved in a remarkably short time. But the change was not pleasing to a segment of the LNS group which wanted the service to be less "vulgar Marxist" and more "flower people." This group left (with much of the organization's cash and equipment) to set up shop on a farm in Massachusetts, and after much bruising physical and legal hassling, each settled down to put out a separate LNS service. Few of the client papers became involved in the dispute and most published selections from both services. After a few months, however, the pastoral service dissolved with the winter snows, and by the time the spring flowers bloomed, there was only a New York LNS.

Today LNS operates with a budget of about 90,000 dollars a year, sending its service to more than 800 publications and organizations, and gathering its material from an increasingly professional group of correspondents in the United States and in such key areas as the Middle East, Southeast Asia and Latin America. The staff numbers about 15, living in small "collectives" where they share expenses (each staff member has a weekly salary of 35 dollars), and operating the service itself as a democratic cooperative. With efficient offset machines and a graphics shop, they are able to do job printing for radical groups to augment their income. Client papers pay varying sums for the service (when they pay); rates are higher for the commercial media on the reasoning that they can pay more.

A typical packet (now sent out twice a week) contains about 24 10-inch by 14-inch pages of cleanly presented news and art work (the graphics can be reproduced directly from the service file). It may include articles on China, a workers' protest in Uruguay, the Polaroid Corporation's activities in South Africa, land reform in Chile, a black boycott of high schools in Virginia, police brutality against Chicano militants in New Mexico, the formation of a prisoners' union in New York State, a review of an autobiography of Mother Jones (the famous labor organizer of the late nineteenth century) and photos from South Africa, Chile and Colombia.

The emphasis is heavy on so-called Third World countries and their struggle against American imperialism, mainly because that kind of material is more easily available than interpretive news and analytical commentary about domestic affairs. The staff of LNS (no editors are listed) is aware of this imbalance and has taken steps toward improved domestic coverage. The shifting emphasis in the underground press will help, as will the increasing interest among young radicals in American history and problems, and a new consciousness of the need for alliance with working people. There is also a refreshing decline in rhetoric and distorted news coverage.

The new earnestness and sense of commitment of the underground press to radical politics is evident in a regular department of LNS called "The Radical Media Bulletin Board—an internal newsletter for all LNS subscribers." Here newspapers and organizations present their problems, ask for guidance, announce important events of interest to other newspapers and set forth views about the movement and the various publications which they exchange. Addresses and telephone numbers are always supplied—a new and radical departure from the casual practices of earlier years.

A recent Bulletin Board led off with a message from the "LNS Staff Collective" itself:

> Underground press people are getting hip to the idea that an underground newspaper should not be anyone's private ego trip, but a revolutionary service to the people who read it. As more and more people try to grapple with that concept—and try to put out papers that not only decorate the world but aim to change it, that not only please their communities but aim to inspire them—each newspaper staff runs up against problems they never faced before. The letters we get from around the country make it clear that there are some pretty heated arguments going on in many underground offices about what to do next.

The arguments continue, perhaps with less heat but more light, as exhibited in an exchange in the LNS service between Jomo Raskin, a four-year "veteran" of the underground press now working with *University Review*, a radically oriented publication concerned with literature and the arts, and Thomas Ritt, executive editor of the *Los Angeles News Advocate*. The exchange shows also that a distinction is being made between the underground press and what is coming to be called the "alternate" press.

Raskin wrote that he had made a thorough survey of several underground papers. There were many good papers, he determined, carrying important and useful stories relating to students' and women's groups and offering service information about demonstrations, clinics, community centers and cultural activities. But he also found gaps:

> The underground press reflects the nature and depth of our political activity. It can only be as good and as strong as the movement as a whole. At the present time [January 1972] the underground press portrays a movement where there's local organizing going on in colleges, high schools, work places, jails, but no national organization, little national focus, and confusion about ideology, strategy, and tactics. It seems to me that most newspapers lack an overall unified perspective. Theoretical grounding and ideological framework are missing.

Raskin noted that publications of specific radical political parties had their clear ideology, but he did not think that was the solution for the underground press: independent newspapers ought to develop a "coherent politics" which would make the papers "less random and less erratic." At present, he said, there was "little sense of imperialism as a system, and little revolutionary strategy. . . . They do not emphasize that the whole imperialist society has to be overthrown, that we have to build a new communist society which serves the needs of the people all over the world."

There was an obvious contradiction in Raskin's presentation: his statement that the underground press could be only as good and as strong as the movement, and then his insistence that the press in effect become the movement. This rhetorical flight was brought gracefully down to earth by Editor Ritt of the *News Advocate*. He and his staff had also been reading a lot of the underground lately, he wrote in February 1972, and enjoying it less:

> In most cases, unfortunately, we were disappointed, primarily because most undergrounds are not newspapers; they, like their establishment counterparts, use graphics, pix, and words to write biased and distorted stories. Many, for example, do not bother with either an editorial or an op-ed page where opinion and statement have a legitimate place. As to "overthrowing" and reaction to "pig" raids, the language itself is inflammatory and even counterproductive. Radical and revolutionary pieces must be written in such a way

as to inform, not in a style that alienates the very people who must be moved to meaningful action.

Ritt then made a "subtle distinction" between the underground and alternative press. The underground, he said, was marked by "sexism" (accepting degrading ads making sexual objects of women) and "rampaging rhetoric" unrelated to the facts. An alternative newspaper, he said, had to be an alternative to the underground as well as to the establishment. The underground press, he found, "panders to sleazy advertisers" on the ground that they cannot survive without them. The *News Advocate* was going to make an effort to prove them wrong: "We believe the people will support a radical newspaper, providing it is also responsible." Ritt concluded:

As an alternative newspaper obviously oriented to the left, we at the *News Advocate* are ever conscious of the need to engage all of the people in the struggle for a truly humane society. Accordingly, we print the views of the totalitarian left in spite of their infallible or omniscient dogma. Concurrently, however, we believe, with many others, that the importation of foreign "heroes" and their views is neither good tactics nor is it politically practical. We have our own revolutionary tradition—and we should use it without becoming élitist or nationally chauvinistic. Mao and Castro work in underdeveloped countries. The United States, whatever else it may be, is technologically far superior to Cuba or China. This fact must be recognized by those "turned off" by the System here. It is time for radicals and revolutionaries in America to begin the arduous task of differentiation: the System and the democratic process are not one and the same. In fact, they may be antithetical.

Ritt's comment reflected a new awareness generally among young radicals that if a serious effort was to be made to change the world "out there," the first step would have to be acknowledgment that radicals were a part of that world; that such an acknowledgment might be made without yielding a single principle. Richard Harrington, a staff member of *Quicksilver Times* of Washington, D.C., put it thus: "We realize that it's not enough to print radical ideas if their style alienates people; and radical ideas remain radical even if they are put into a largely middle-class style"—which is to say, simple and good English.

It may produce a snicker in some circles to spell "America" as "Amerika," but it is at bottom an exercise in adolescent semantics. "Balling a chick" may be understood by the inner circle as bedroom gymnastics rather than a barnyard chore, but it still is sexist. It may produce a certain measure of exhilaration in some groups to advocate "offing the pig," but it is not the vocabulary of 99 percent of the reading population—and even at that, some cops are young, black and even human. Thus, to class all cops permanently as porkers may be both a political and a sociological error as well as futile jargon.

A documented article with cogent argument, written in language clear and understandable to all readers, is a far more effective political and social weapon than the mindless use of four-letter words. If the writers and editors of the underground press come around to this point of view—as they seem to be doing—they will help many more people "out there" to an understanding of the basic problems confronting the nation, rather than to a misunderstanding of the semantics of the problems.

Despite its failures, the underground press has had therapeutic value for its own audience and has shocked a complacent communications industry into an awareness that it was being shunned by a vast young audience. And as has so often been the case with movements for change, the media moved to exploit—profitably— the superficial aspects of the underground movement. Thus several newspapers instituted a weekly "youth page" in which features of the underground press were imitated. Pseudosociological surveys began to blossom in the weekly magazine sections, generally with such titles as: "How did the nation's young get turned off? Where did the straight world go wrong?"

Advertisements for women's fashions, a survey[3] reported, "have appeared in the total-impact style of overall design and dazzling color so familiar to readers of underground newspapers." The practice was carried over into television advertising and programming, and into the singing and musical commercials on radio, where the rock motif was adopted by purveyors of deodorants, detergents, breakfast foods and remedies for hemorrhoids.

---

[3] Gaye Sandler Smith in the International Press Institute Report (301969).

New magazines, making their appearance as the formula-bound mass-circulation magazines folded, sought their readership among a free-swinging young audience. The approach, in some cases, has been financially successful, but has missed the mark entirely in understanding what the rebellion is all about—if it ever sought to understand. Some nonradical critics of the press with a sense of history and a clear understanding of the responsibility of the media got the message, however, and sought to warn the owners and managers of the aboveground media.

William L. Rivers,[4] a professor in the communications department at Stanford University, declared in an article entitled "Notes on the Underground" *(Columbia Journalism Review,* May/June 1971):

> This much is certain: there is a growing awareness that a vast distance stretches between conventional dailies and important segments of their potential audience. In the time when many newspapers served small publics an editor spoke directly to the central interests of his readers. But as papers became larger—in part by swallowing their rivals—the editors tried to corral even larger audiences, which meant that they could neither appeal very strongly to one group nor offend another. The marketplace of ideas began to look more and more like a common denominator, and irreverent thoughts were replaced by the same conventional wisdom. A change there is, and it would be stupid to ignore the underground press in searching for its cause.

In the *Saturday Review* (November 13, 1971) John Tebbel, journalism historian and professor at New York University, wrote:

> At its best, the "underground" has justified that word, in a sense, by its investigative reporting . . . and to date this has been the chief influence it has exerted on the Establishment press. There is a great deal more of this kind of reporting now in conventional newspapers, and one reason for it is that the alternate press has been digging out the kind of facts that the Establishment papers should have been

---

[4] He is the author of two sound books on the communications industry, both published by Beacon Press of Boston: *The Opinion Makers* (1965) and *The Adversaries* (1970).

doing. Their work has reminded the better papers that too often they have been bland or unseeing in their reporting of American society, particularly American government. The alternate press takes the general attitude that politicians are the natural enemy of the people, who have mistakenly elected them, and that political systems are not designed for the public good, no matter what they proclaim themselves to be. If that sounds too radical, one must remember that it was substantially the attitude of some of the greatest nineteenth-century editors. Charles Anderson Dana, for example, who made the *New York Sun* one of the best newspapers in history, flayed every President and administration in Washington from Lincoln to the end of the century with a biting cynicism and contempt that equaled if not surpassed much that is written today.

The prospect is that the alternate press may be much reduced in size and may change in content and tone, but it will survive. And that is a good thing, because the diversity of the press in a democracy is one of the best guarantees of the system's good health.

The communications arm of the system at present, however, seems determined to restrict even further the diversity that could guarantee its good health, and by the same token to validate the need for an alternate media.

CHAPTER XIV

THE LONG ROAD

THE exposition, analysis and problems laid out in the preceding pages suggest formidable obstacles in charting an enlightened course out of the great American communications wilderness. Yet I believe an attitude of realistic optimism is warranted. Realism is always advisable; optimism is in order because of the circumstances and events which have moved the media to the center stage of national scrutiny as never before and have stimulated unprecedented discussion about the media. Out of this scrutiny and discussion some basic questions emerge:

If, as seems to be the case, the fundamental issue is improved access to the media by the public, how can this be accomplished?

Is a public television network financed by government (that is, public) funds a partial answer? If it is, what are the guarantees that a "fourth network" will not become an agency of government just as unheedful of the public as the existing media?

Granted that the First Amendment is a noble bulwark for the press against governmental encroachment: how can the protections and privileges of the First Amendment be extended to the staffs of newspapers (against encroachment by their employers) and to the public, which today is effectively denied meaningful access to the media by the monopoly control of its operators?

Is it possible for national, regional or community newspapers and listener-sponsored radio stations to maintain themselves economically and culturally—given the reading and listening habits of the public, and the remunerations and blandishments offered by the commercial media?

Finally, in the face of conglomerate power, how can idealistic political and social groups direct the thinking of the public toward the positive alternatives of decentralization and diversity?

As answers are sought to these questions and sensible discussion mounted, the most heartening fact is that despite years of governmental repression and deception, despite decades of journalistic distortion and omission—despite all these things, the effort toward an enlightened public opinion has never ceased, inside and outside establishment institutions. Within this framework, an examination of some possible solutions to the problems is appropriate at this point.

Considerable excitement was stirred in 1967 by the report of the Carnegie Commission on Educational Television which served as the basis for the Public Broadcasting Act of 1967, enacted by Congress with remarkable speed during the administration of Lyndon B. Johnson. The act established the Corporation for Public Broadcasting (CPB) as a nonprofit, nongovernment corporation to promote and help finance the development of noncommercial television and radio at a series of regional production centers. Financing was to be through federal and private funds.

Arthur L. Singer, who was a key figure in initiating the Carnegie Commission, said that the commission had considered the advisability of a "fourth network" but had rejected it. "The report," he said,[1] "was a plea for pluralism, a plea for localism, a plea for an escape from the ponderousness and the pedagogy that had afflicted most of Educational Television."

Soon after the creation of the CPB, the Public Broadcasting Service was established to maintain the "interconnection" concept of the Carnegie report between the CPB and the local public outlets in the National Educational Television sphere. Hartford N. Gunn, Jr., president of PBS, saw the job as follows: "How best to distribute these programs so as to provide for choice and diversity in programming while insuring the maximum insulation from possible dictation of content by the source of the funding

---

[1] In a speech to a public broadcasting conference in Boyne Highlands, Michigan, in July 1971. The text of the speech was prepared with Stephen White, who wrote the Carnegie Commission report.

—whether it be Congress, a foundation, or another source." This was a cumbersome way of saying: no censorship, please.

It was a problem indeed, because Congress was doling out funds meagerly on an annual basis, the Ford Foundation was continuing as the major source of foundation funds, and corporations such as Mobil Oil were giving annual million-dollar grants to demonstrate their concern for the culture of the nation, in return for which their commercial identity was stamped (visibly) on the noncommercial programs being presented.

The Carnegie report did foresee some national network programs, mainly journalistic in nature, but its main recommendations were for "grass roots" television, with local or regional subsystems providing local programming and locally determined network programming. "They were radical proposals," Singer said. "Then or now there is no hard evidence that they can be made to work."

There are seven public broadcasting production centers (New York, Boston, Washington, Pittsburgh, Chicago, San Francisco and Los Angeles) serving 212 public TV stations. Of these, Boston and San Francisco have been particularly innovative. But today these two centers and all the rest are unhappy about the control exercised by CPB, which grants approval of the limited funds, and about PBS, which rules on the content of programs distributed to any of the stations. Contrary to the Carnegie recommendations, the trend is toward more centralized control and direction. Emphasizing this aspect is a National Public Affairs Broadcast Center in Washington being built with 500,000 dollars allocated by the CPB. The regional production centers envisage further centralized control and greater reluctance to present controversial programs. Singer had some strong views on all this at the Michigan conference:

Public television has cast itself in the mold of commercial television. It is divided into networked and non-networked programming. The networked programming is every bit as centralized as the networked programming of CBS or NBC. The non-networked programming is local and parochial. And this is exactly what the Carnegie Commission did not have in mind. The public television system has assumed the posture of a fourth network, with what are really insignificant variations, and is now operating exactly the way it was assumed, a few years back, a fourth network would operate.

The present system is not pluralistic. It is dominated by the Corporation for Public Broadcasting, the Public Broadcasting Service, and the Ford Foundation. What goes on the air in the system, as distinct from purely local production, is what these institutions approve.

There has been ample evidence of growing PBS timidity that has caused disputes with producers of documentaries at the production centers. One case involved the program *The Banks and the Poor*, a study of discriminatory practices by the country's banking institutions. The producers objected to having their work scrutinized in advance and resented particularly an invitation by PBS to bankers for specially arranged previews. Representative Wright Patman, chairman of the House Banking and Currency Committee, commented:

In Washington, the American Bankers Association received an opportunity to view the show some days prior to its appearance on any channel. It is interesting that these channels decided that it was important to have only the bankers invited to view the show prior to its release. The very title of the show, *The Banks and the Poor*, indicates that there were at least two sides presented in the film, and it is surprising that only one side—the banks—was invited to these special previews. This would indicate something less than an objective view of the issues raised in the film by the various program directors of these noncommercial channels.

In April 1971 its producers proposed that *The Banks and the Poor* be submitted as an entry for the annual awards of the Academy of Television Arts and Sciences. PBS rejected the proposal. There also was censorship by PBS of a program concerning FBI informers in the radical movement and of skits in a show satirizing "the selling of a President" in a future election. The candidate bore too close a resemblance to Richard Nixon.

The hierarchy of CPB and PBS follows closely the model of the corporate setup at the commercial networks—including salaries for executives and star performers lured from the commercial networks. The executives decide what is to go out over the

national network. The regional managers are no longer origi-
nators: they are petitioners.

Compounding this situation was the introduction in January
1972 of the Agnew syndrome in public broadcasting. In an election year, the White House was reported to be incensed by the
hiring of Sander Vanocur, formerly with NBC News and known
to be less than cordial to the Nixon administration, as a key figure
in a new PBS news program emanating from Washington. Further, with Nixon's keen appreciation of the uses of television in
election campaigning, even an impartial presentation of the
1972 campaign would be regarded by the White House as hostile,
particularly with some of the funding governmental in origin.
The administration view was presented almost without disguise
by Clay T. Whitehead, head of the White House Office of Telecommunications Policy, a new and personal Nixon watchdog
agency:

> There is a real question as to whether public television, particu-
> larly the national federally funded part of public television, should
> be carrying public affairs, news commentary and that kind of thing,
> for several reasons. One is the fact that the commercial networks,
> by and large, do quite a good job in that area. Public television is
> designed to be an alternative to provide programming that is not
> available on commercial television; so you could raise the legitimate
> question as to should there be as much public affairs, as much news
> and news commentary as they apparently plan to do. . . . When
> you're talking about using federal funds to support a journalism
> activity, it's always going to be the subject of scrutiny. The Congress
> will always be watching closely. The press will always be watching
> it very closely. It just invites a lot of political attention.

In the last analysis, the composition of the board of directors
of the Corporation for Public Broadcasting should have set at
rest any concern that CPB would venture far from the straight
and narrow world of communications policy. The chairman of
the board is Frank Pace, Jr., Secretary of the Army in the Truman
administration and later chairman of the board of the General
Dynamics Corporation, the largest defense contractor in the
country. He is at present a director of Time, Inc., and Colgate-
Palmolive. The vice-chairman is James R. Killian, former presi-

dent of the Massachusetts Institute of Technology, who in 1959 became chairman of the board of the Mitre Corporation, specialists in missile rocketry and radar homing devices. He is a former director of the Foreign Intelligence Advisory Board, which supervises the work of the CIA. CPB's president is John Macy, Jr., a government and military personnel manager, and chief assistant to Pace as Secretary of the Army. There are 13 members of the board, mostly from industrial corporations, corporate law firms, banks and publishing houses. Nixon has made four appointments—a banker, an oil man, an undertaker (Hollywood's famous Forest Lawn) and a State Department showcase black woman. He was scheduled to make four more appointments in 1972 for an effective "Nixon board" majority.

"The issues are clear," said the *New York Times*'s television critic John J. O'Connor on July 11, 1971, in an article discussing the increasing centralization of public television.

> Does the country need a "fourth network," with all the usual pressures for conformity placed on any network? Or does it need a stronger regional "interconnection," with its potential for greater diversity and perhaps greater "mistakes"? It would seem profitable for everyone concerned to bring the debate to a public forum—maybe even to public television.

But that is only the tip of the issue. The problem below the surface is the emasculation of the hope of public television altogether. If the forces set in motion are allowed to operate unimpeded, public television as envisaged in 1967 could be already doomed. What may be left will be an occasional token controversial program, *The French Chef* (an original Boston production) and *The Forsyte Saga, The First Churchills* and *The Last of the Mohicans,* all British Broadcasting Corporation imports. It may also be the last of the fourth network as an attraction for Americans surfeited with commercial TV. And perhaps that's what the Corporation for Public Broadcasting is all about.

Variety (January 19, 1972) saw a "shred of optimism" in the work of the House Subcommittee on Communications and Power, headed by Representative Torbert Macdonald of Massachusetts, which has been seeking to resolve the seeming disagreement between the CPB and the White House. It quoted Macdonald:

> I think the government should have no part in deciding what form, or what programs, or what emphasis should be given by public broadcasting. The Congress and every other branch of government should just look and see as to whether or not the public broadcasting system has done what it was set up to do, which is to bring superior programming to the American public.

But the authors of a pamphlet entitled *The Fourth Network*[2] were less sanguine. They had asked to testify before the Macdonald committee in 1971, in support of Macdonald's expressed desire to keep the programming clear of political pressure. They received a written invitation to appear, but it was rescinded a few days later. The reason offered was "lack of time." It is conceivable, however, that the views of the authors of *The Fourth Network* had a lack of sympathy among persons behind the scenes in public television. In an article in the *Nation* (March 13, 1972) Gregory Knox, one of the authors, wrote: "A broadcasting system that is established, funded, staffed, managed, and directed by the government is, if only in the most literal sense, a government network." He concluded:

> Until the public is more aware of, and more concerned about, the profound way in which telecommunications affects individual life and shapes the communal environment, efforts to promote an alternative will meet the same rebuff which the Project met at the subcommittee hearings. Those who currently control the government network do not want to hear how their power can be decentralized. They are ignorant of the price of their own insulation from the public. They do not know what they have done, what they are doing, or what will be the consequences of their future actions, and the public knows less. The price paid by the Congress for its ignorance is merely millions; the price paid by the people might be calculated in terms of democratic survival.

---

[2] A comprehensive study of the public broadcasting system by a group of young scholars based at Columbia University (but unaffiliated with the university). It may be obtained on request from: Network Project, 102 Earl Hall, Columbia University, New York, N. Y. 10027.

One small network that does understand the price of survival is the Pacifica Foundation, listener-sponsored radio operating in New York, Berkeley, Los Angeles and Houston. In November 1971 Pacifica's New York station WBAI-FM[3] invited the Network Project to present a series of eight broadcasts based on its study of television, public and commercial.

WBAI has been operating since 1960 as listener-sponsored and -supported radio and, like its sister stations, refused to accept grants from the Corporation for Public Broadcasting and invitations to join the CPB's radio network. "The prospect of receiving additional funds was very tempting," says WBAI's general manager Edwin A. Goodman. "But we felt that, inevitably, these monies would undermine our listener-support base, which is truly the liberating mechanism of Pacifica Radio. We also perceived the danger of having a single noncommercial audio network which would be federally funded and therefore subject to federal pressure."

Pacifica feels other pressures in startling fashion. The Houston station was bombed twice and forced to close down for a period of several months in 1970–71. The first dynamiting smashed the transmitter completely (damage was 25,000 dollars). The FBI came into the case only after a public campaign forced it to act— and three suspects (who had been arrested and released once before) were apprehended, allegedly on their way to another dynamite job at Pacifica's Los Angeles station. Senate committee hearings on "Communist affiliations" of Pacifica executives have been held, and the Federal Communications Commission has on several occasions delayed decisions for months on license-renewal applications for WBAI.

The FBI has ample reason, in its own fashion, to be hostile to Pacifica. In 1962, all four Pacifica stations broadcast a devastating two-hour exposé of the inner workings of the FBI by a former agent, with special emphasis on the despotism of Director Hoover. The agent, Jack Levine, reported that he had offered his story to the *New York Times* and the wire services before approaching WBAI in New York. All turned the offer down. After the broadcast, the *Times* and the wire services published long articles

3 The others are KPFA Berkeley, KPFM Los Angeles and KPFT Houston.

based on Levine's story. A few weeks later came subpenas to WBAI personnel to appear before the Senate Internal Security Committee, headed by Senator Thomas J. Dodd of Connecticut. License-renewal requests following the FBI broadcast were not approved until January 1964.

Pacifica again was under investigation early in 1970 by the FCC, the Justice Department and the Congress for permitting alleged obscenity on the air. "We have no desire to cuss and swear on the air," said Larry Josephson, who conducts an early-morning music and talk show, "but the use of so-called objectionable words has become absolutely central to a certain kind of dissent. If political polarization continues to get worse, as it probably will, the time will come when we will broadcast something that will be deeply offensive to a lot of people. If it comes to a court test, though, I'm optimistic. All the Pacifica stations have tremendous support in their communities, and one of the most sacrosanct principles of the FCC is that a station must reflect the community it serves. We do that, God knows."

Pacifica was cleared of the obscenity charge, but only after another license delay of several months for WBAI. *Variety* commented:

> As this paper surmised, behind the charges no doubt were political considerations as regards WBAI's thorough coverage of the Moratorium [against the war in Vietnam in October 1969] and other recent peace demonstrations, which included a number of news bulletins on restrictive actions by FBI agents against the movement demonstrators in Washington.

The support received by KPFT in Houston following the bombings is an indicator of a change in mood toward intimidation among both the public and the media. When Pacifica was in trouble following the FBI broadcast in 1962, there was little public support and almost no editorial support in the media. In 1970–71 there was support for KPFT from CBS, the National Association of Broadcasters, *Broadcasting* magazine, the *Houston Post* and the *Houston Chronicle*. The *Post* offered a reward of 1,500 dollars for the arrest and conviction of the dynamiters.

Robert Lewis Shayon, television critic of the *Saturday Review*, once called the Pacifica stations the "intellectual pony express."

While they may be faulted on occasion for esoteric flights, these lapses are nothing compared with the superb public service rendered by the stations. Shayon's intellectual label is no longer applicable: the stations are down to earth.

Pacifica has presented outstanding programs and live coverage of the antiwar movement and testimony by returned veterans about atrocities in Vietnam, the various trials involving radicals, legal guidance, women's liberation activities and racial news. Its shortcomings have been technical rather than artistic, because of lack of funds. The staffs draw minimum wages (often delayed) and much of the work is by volunteers. WBAI has 22,000 listener-sponsors who pay 24 dollars minimum for a program folio, and the listening audience is estimated at five times that number. The San Francisco and Los Angeles stations have about 8,000 sponsors each, and the Houston station about 3,000.

Most of the sponsors if not the listeners are liberal or radical, but all Pacifica stations maintain a policy of regular programming and access to all points of view. For example, the program folio of Houston's KPFT states:

> KPFT is an open enterprise, and Pacifica has no ax to grind other than insuring that its microphones are open to every point of view. If you know of something we ought to broadcast, please write us about it. We are likely to respond by asking you to help or advise on production of the program you suggest; in such cases, the station's materials, equipment, and workers are available to any organization without cost or obligation to them.

Early in 1972 WBAI found itself once again in trouble with the authorities. The matter involved the station's refusal to turn over to the New York's District Attorney Frank Hogan, on demand, the tapes of 30 hours of broadcasting by WBAI during the rebellion of prisoners at the Tombs prison in New York in October 1970. The district attorney sought the tapes in preparation for prosecution of seven inmates who were being charged in the rebellion—although no hostages had been hurt and Mayor Lindsay had pledged that there would be no reprisals. WBAI's refusal was based on New York State's "newsmen's privilege act" protecting a reporter's sources and on the First Amendment privileges for the press. A Criminal Court judge ordered station manager Edwin A. Goodman to turn over the tapes and, when Goodman refused, sentenced him to 30 days in prison. Bail was denied pending appeal and Goodman spent a day in jail before a federal Court of Appeals judge ordered him released. Again demonstrating the increasing sense of uneasiness among media people, more than 500 signed an *amicus curiae* brief in a period of three days in support of Goodman and WBAI, even though many had misgivings about the legal grounds for the station's refusal to turn over the tapes. Some felt that since the broadcasts had, of course, been public, they were in the public domain; but WBAI contended that the act of surrender and the possibility of tracing the voices—some of them live phone calls from in-mates—would jeopardize the persons involved and cause the sources to dry up. The *amicus* brief said in part:

> If Edwin Goodman is required to remain in jail as a condition precedent to litigation of the privilege claimed by him, the concept of the judicial process as a tool of constitutional law development is destroyed. If the rest of the newsmen in this nation are to be taught by a decision in this case at this stage that Edwin Goodman is to be denied his freedom while the privilege asserted is determined, which of us will ever again be sure of his or her own courage to publish an item which might invite a subpena, which might invite a jail term if its validity is to be contested? Which of us will ever dare refuse to comply with the demand of any prosecutor, investigating committee, or other arm of the government, no matter how outrageous that demand may be deemed by us to be if the price of resistance is jail? Will not such a price tag upon the assertion of constitutional rights not only discourage their assertion by reporters or other news people, but also encourage abuse of process by overzealous investigators or prosecutors? Will not the existence of such threat eventually cause the more timid to steer far clear of the threatened zone by avoiding all discussion and report of controversial subjects? Will not others among our ranks be compelled by such procedures to yield and become unwilling adjuncts of state prosecutorial and surveillance systems? The distinction between press and the state must be maintained.

When he was released on a writ of *habeas corpus*, Goodman was asked his reaction to being in jail. "It was a radicalizing experience," he said. What had it been like? the reporter pressed. Goodman replied: "Twenty-four hours of radicalization." It is not untypical of the response of other Pacifica personnel. Goodman went back to work.

Discussing the advantages and disadvantages of joining National Public Radio—which Pacifica had rejected—Goodman cited NPR's potential for disseminating an alternative broadcasting voice around the country. But he also perceived the problems of governmental control—problems which moved Pacifica to embark on a network of its own—the Pacifica Program Services Division servicing stations affiliated with but not operated by Pacifica. In 1970 there were 12 such affiliates; the following year there were 30, and the number is increasing.

Thus Pacifica, harried by government and law-enforcement agencies, pressured by lack of money, hampered by inadequate equipment, perseveres as genuine alternate radio. While its scope is small in comparison with the commercial outlets, its influence is strong in critical areas, and it stands as a model of courage and principle.

Despite the vision of facsimile newspapers oozing out of a Xerox-like aperture in a television set in the living room, media dissenters—and dissenters in all areas of public life—still maintain a measure of faith in the printed word purchasable at newsstands or through mail subscription. For underground publishers and small community newspapers, such technological phenomena will in any case not be realizable, and they proceed without the year 2000 in mind. A recent survey, for example, reported 42 papers published by various factions of the Women's Liberation movement alone—from *Lysistrata* at Slippery Rock State College in Pennsylvania to *Goodbye to All That* in San Diego. And the underground press has spread even into the corporate world with the appearance in the last two years of unofficial employee papers at the headquarters of giant industry.

Contents of the corporate underground newspapers (the *Met Lifer* at the Metropolitan Life Insurance Company in San Francisco and the *Stranded Oiler* at Standard Oil, for example) range from grievances about class discrimination in company restaurants to complaints about the use of computers at Met Life made

by Honeywell, on the ground that Honeywell also makes frag-
mentation bombs for use in Indochina. Most of the papers are
a mix of fact and satire and occasional schoolboy pranks, and
their chief effect has been to add a note of irreverence and
skepticism to the dehumanized atmosphere of corporate mauso-
leums. Corporate executives publicly minimize the effect of the
underground publications, but there has been evidence of
snooping to identify the perpetrators, and even of dismissals.

The movement has spread into government also. The *Rainbow
Sign*, published by members of the Vietnam Moratorium Committee at the National Institutes of Health and the National
Institute of Mental Health, circulates about 6,000 copies. In addition to antiwar articles, it publishes serious commentary about
problems of employment in the vast government bureaucracy,
and social issues such as conditions in the prisons. Unlike most
of the corporate underground editors, the *Rainbow Sign* editors
are known to officials. Government employees have greater protection, through civil service and unions, than their vulnerable
brothers and sisters on the corporate firing line.

In the area of general circulation, dissenting weekly and
monthly newspapers operate from a base within the establishment
(like the *Village Voice*, with a political position of Democratic
reform politics and wide-ranging social and cultural coverage),
or at the edge of the establishment (like Bruce Brugmann's
the *Bay Guardian* in San Francisco). Others fall somewhere in
between: publications such as Ronnie Dugger's *Texas Observer*
in San Antonio, and *Boston After Dark* and the *Phoenix* in Cambridge, Massachusetts. All of them find their rationale in the
neglect of investigative reporting and advocacy stands in the
general press. Perhaps the most exciting and interesting newspaper in this category—and pointing the direction for similar
papers in other areas—is the *Bay Guardian*.

Bruce Brugmann is a Nebraskan who went to the Columbia
Graduate School of Journalism after editing the campus paper
at the University of Nebraska. He joined the Army, served as
editor of *Stars and Stripes* in Korea, then worked for a short time
at the *Milwaukee Journal*. Intent on starting his own newspaper,
he headed for San Francisco ("because the newspapers were so
bad"), and in 1965 raised 35,000 dollars to start the *Bay Guard-*

ian. He adopted as his motto "We print the news and raise hell," borrowed from the slogan of Wilbur F. Storey of the *Chicago Times* in 1861. Brugmann has lived up to his motto. Starting from the premise that a crusading newspaper must assume an adversary stance toward all institutions, he has taken on the San Francisco city administration, the Chase Manhattan Bank and the Ford Foundation; cracked the code of the supermarkets indicating the freshness of food, and campaigned against the growth of high-rise buildings in San Francisco. An exposé of unrepresentative grand juries won for the *Bay Guardian* a prestigious award from the San Francisco Press Club; so did a muckraking article on the economics of the "hip culture." Shortly thereafter the rules of entry for the awards were changed effectively to exclude the *Bay Guardian.*

Brugmann charged that the Pacific Gas & Electric Company, whose monopoly in the San Francisco area has been a continuing target of the *Bay Guardian,* had pressured the Press Club to alter its rules (a PG&E public-relations man was chairman of the club's awards committee at the time). In a speech on the Senate floor in August 1970, Senator Lee Metcalf of Montana agreed with Brugmann. He noted that the *Bay Guardian* "has criticized PG&E's love-in with the major San Francisco dailies, and, finally, it has recently advocated municipal ownership of PG&E's local electric distribution system."

When hearings were held in 1969 on the Newspaper Preservation Act (formerly called the Failing Newspaper Act) in Washington, Brugmann presented 24 pages of documented testimony to demonstrate that the act was designed to preserve existing monopolies—specifically arrangements in 24 major cities under which newspapers shared printing facilities and advertising and subscription revenues, plus other production and business facilities. San Francisco was a prime example. The new law, while giving lip service to the principles of competition and independent editorial voices, in fact guaranteed that there would be no competition and little diversity of opinion. The hearings were almost entirely blacked out by the nation's press, and the act was signed into law in July 1970 at a ceremony that went as little publicized as the debate about the act. (Even the news of the signing was not reported for three days.) The *Bay Guardian* has filed suit against the *San Francisco Chronicle* and the *Examiner* in an attempt to break up their profit pooling and other joint arrangements. It is a major test of the Newspaper Preservation Act, whose cosmetic name conceals antitrust blemishes of scandalous proportions.

Brugmann is explicit in stating his purpose:

> I aim my derringer at every reporter and tell him, by God, that I don't want to see an objective piece of reporting. But this is not dishonest journalism; it is "point of view" journalism. Our facts are as straight as we can make them! We don't run a story until we feel we can prove it or make it stick; we always talk with the adversary and try to print his side as part of the story; he always gets the chance of reply in the next issue (rarely do they, even when I offer in letter or by phone). We run almost all the critical reaction we get to stories; but the point is we don't run a story until we think it is in the public interest to do so.
>
> How do you talk about our major stories, environmental pollution, Vietnam, the Manhattanization of San Francisco, saving the Bay, unless you do some "point of view" reporting? We're not just covering meetings. We're not just checking with the official sources. We're going after stories, hopefully before they become certifiable facts. Along with this come different forms of the new journalism, letting participants write their own stuff, using experts with special knowledge, more literary writing, the use of irony, poetry, impressionistic writing—everything, really, that has relevance, and merit, and readability—and goes for the jugular.

The jugular most often reached for belongs to what Brugmann calls "SuperChron," the newspaper-television monopoly—one of the most powerful in the United States—controlling the *San Francisco Chronicle*, the *Examiner* (a Hearst newspaper), radio stations KRON and KRON-FM, KRON-TV, and cable TV franchises, in addition to the Hearst interests throughout the world. This monopoly, Brugmann contends, has brought San Francisco journalism "to the final stages of arteriosclerosis."

By January 1972 Brugmann had attracted enough support to enable him to redesign the *Bay Guardian* into a handsome 32-page tabloid, with added contributors and expanded cultural coverage. He announced a shift from monthly to bimonthly publication, aiming at eventual weekly publication. The SuperChron behemoth does not disconcert him. He says:

> A good metropolitan weekly, starting small, but speaking with integrity, can soon have influence in inverse proportion to its size. There is nothing stronger in journalism than the force of a good example. The *Bay Guardian* can succeed, despite the galloping contraction of the press in San Francisco, because there are many of us who still feel that the newspaper business is a trade worth fighting for. That is what this newspaper is all about.

Across the country, in Washington and Boston, others believe in starting big, with a very old dream—an independent national daily newspaper. The project is the *Morning News,* and the initiators are Walter Pincus, a former investigative reporter for the *Washington Star* and the *Washington Post,* who had also worked as a staff investigator for the Senate Foreign Relations Committee; and Dun Gifford, a lawyer and real-estate executive, who had been on the staff of Senator Edward M. Kennedy of Massachusetts. Gifford (now in Boston) and Pincus had been friends in Washington and had begun as far back as January 1970 to plan the *Morning News.* They are laying their groundwork very carefully.

The plan ultimately is to produce a morning newspaper based in Washington and published simultaneously in four or five cities. The stress is on investigative reporting, more imaginative use of graphics and an approach similar to that of *Le Monde* in Paris— that is, the emphasis will not be on objective reporting but on in-depth reporting by journalists who are experts in specific fields and will express their opinions based on this expertise. The goal, roughly, is a livelier version of the *Wall Street Journal* aimed at persons who would read the *New York Times* if it were available to them in their city each day.

Like *Le Monde,* the *Morning News* had adopted the "society of editors" format of ownership and control. Staff members own 35 percent of the stock and vote as a bloc. The owners receive income from the stock, but cannot sell it. The remaining 65 percent of the stock is held outright by the original incorporators and the staff, with a portion held in reserve by the company. Thus, control is in the hands of the incorporators and the staff, and the experiment marks the first time that the *Le Monde* system has been introduced on a newspaper in the United States.

A four-week trial period was to be followed by some months of follow-up surveys and market analysis. If the reception was favorable, the interim months were to be devoted to raising the rest of the estimated 4.5 million dollars required to operate the newspaper for two years. If all went well, regular publication would then start.

In addition to the control plan, the founders planned the *Morning News* with the most advanced American technical and marketing methods. The design is by Samuel J. Antupit, one of the most innovative designers in the country, among whose products are the *New York Review of Books,* the New York journalism review (*More*) and the *Antioch Review.* Associated with Pincus and Gifford are the owner of a string of newspapers on Boston's North Shore, a Wall Street investment banker and a leading media consultant. National advertising firms have been engaged.

The pages of the newspaper are to be composed in Washington and page negatives flown by air courier to publishers with modern plants in major metropolitan areas who will print and distribute the paper each day, inserting their own pages of local news and advertising. The plan is for five-day publication, and the 16 pages from Washington are to be augmented by four to eight local pages, adhering to the graphic design and advertising rules established in Washington. Page one will contain short news summaries and a full feature-length article. Overseas news is to be obtained by reciprocal arrangement with *Le Monde* and the *Sunday Times* of London. There are to be no regular editorials (although a brief one may appear on important occasions), but an opinion page will deal in depth each day with a single issue. Regional correspondents will report once or twice a week.

The ratio of news to advertising copy is 60 to 40 percent, the reverse of most American newspapers. Pincus believes that most newspapers in the United States have fallen into a "technological impasse" in their effort to gain more and more advertising in an ever-larger package. "They have forgotten that people don't have more and more time to read the paper," he says, "and that the larger the paper gets, the less it is read." Many well-known journalists have been approached to join the *Morning News,* and the number and quality of those willing to leave their well-paying jobs on prestigious publications may indicate the chances of success or failure for the *Morning News.*

In the planning stages, the stress of the incorporators seemed to tend toward making the *Morning News* a financial success—a goal not much different from that of ordinary newspapers. Whether this emphasis will clash with the paper's admirable journalistic prospectus, of course, remains to be seen. Technologically the plan is radical, the composition of the board of incorporators markedly less so. But if the *Le Monde* model is adhered to, and the editors are determined to operate with more regard for publishing a newspaper of quality than for the balance sheets, the public will have the opportunity to pass judgment on a new and welcome kind of journalism.

The national daily newspaper experiment is being watched with keen interest by newspaper people deeply concerned with their function and responsibility as staff members of the general daily press. One who fits this category is David Deitch, who came to the *Boston Globe* in 1968 as a commentator on financial and economic affairs after service with the *New York Post* and the *New York Herald Tribune.* He is in his late thirties and, like Arthur Alpert and others of the "swing generation" between old and new left, has gone through an intensive period of personal evaluation. Deitch classifies himself as an independent radical, and his columns reflected his views. As they attracted more and more attention and comment, the *Globe* began to place them frequently on the Op-Ed page. In a sense, Deitch had created for himself the kind of job that was rare on any other major newspaper. His work resembled in many aspects the *Le Monde* approach, in the sense that he was a highly qualified and knowledgeable journalist allowed to express himself with great latitude.

When I spoke with Deitch in the summer of 1971, he had just published a series of Op-Ed page columns about the responsibility of the press in the publication of the Pentagon Papers—articles which went far beyond the questions of the government's interference, legal proceedings and self-congratulatory editorials about freedom of the press. He was much more concerned with the role of the journalist himself and his vulnerability in the situation. He noted that several journalists were liable to federal prosecution for their part in the publication of the Pentagon Papers, and even though they were "laying their lives on the line," they had little or no voice in the process of deciding whether the papers should be printed and how they should be dealt with. Where the process was shared to a degree—as it was on the *New York Times*—it was an isolated case, and the final decision always remained the publisher's. For Deitch it was "the broad idea that is important: the point is that newsmen and women are told to do certain things and are substantially excluded from the decision-making process —and that seems to me to be a large contradiction."

In that case, I said, how did Deitch account for the lack of consciousness by staff members as to the dangers involved? Could it be attributed to their faith in the publishers, or rather to a lack of political awareness? Deitch replied:

I think it is the latter, no doubt about it. But it is a manifest also of alienation. They don't feel connected to their work. They don't think very hard about their role in society; in a way, they are anti-intellectual to a distressing degree. It seems to me that they are in an occupation extremely important to our society. The kind of responsibility they have, and the impact, are great. Yet the discussion about their role is minimal.

It was clear that Deitch had thought a great deal about his own role as a journalist, in relation both to society and to his own superiors, and in the latter area he had some strong views:

I don't think my superiors should have the right to censor my work. Just because they represent the publisher's authority does not make them any more qualified than I to judge my work. Consultation and discussion are another thing. The criteria which they use to censor and suppress seem to be spurious. First it was objectivity, then fairness, and responsibility; but these terms, in the context of the chain of command, are intellectually bankrupt. I have come to understand the political meaning of what they do, and the political meaning of the criteria they use. All it means is that they are the instruments of control. They have to establish their firm control over everything that goes into the paper. They have a specialized and narrow concept of freedom of the press, which they don't admit to the public. They seek to identify the public interest, and the reporter's interest, with their own. In their interpretation, the First Amendment has nothing to do with me: it is a private property consideration.

How then would he go about enlarging the First Amendment to make it public property, as its framers intended it to be? How would he go about educating the journalists themselves as a necessary first step? Deitch said:

This is going to happen through an enlargement of the contradictions that are inherent within the newspapers themselves, through the effort by workers to gain more control in the operation of the newspapers. The other is the movement toward what I would call a "community-controlled press." They are parallel movements which influence each other and, sooner or later, a synthesis is going to take place.

. . . The incipient movement toward worker control is already underway here—without exaggerating its progress. And it is not going to be achieved until the contradiction I spoke about before is enlarged, and taken advantage of—the gap between what a reporter can do within the decision-making process, and the liability he may suffer as a consequence of these choices not being open to him. Some accommodation must be made. He can go to jail; and if some reporters do go to jail, it may be an enlightening thing—just to expose the ridiculous state of affairs in which the proprietors and editors exercise complete hierarchical control over the editorial function.

The parallel movement to workers' control, as Deitch sees it, is toward a community-controlled press. There the first step is to force the publishers and editors to engage in public dialogue with the community about every issue of significance to the community. Implementation of such a program has been the subject of study (in which Deitch has participated) by the Cambridge-Goddard Program[4] in cooperation with community-based organizations in the Boston area.

---

[4] Under the auspices of the Cambridge Institute, a radical "think tank," and Goddard College of Vermont—combined in a graduate program offering master's degrees in social change.

There would be tremendous resistance to such dialogue by the publishers, I suggested. What pressure could be applied to force them to engage in it? Deitch replied:

The editorial hierarchy is not going to agree to anything voluntarily any more than society in general will agree to certain changes. And they are going to try to take over this movement if they can. What is going to force the hierarchy to engage in public debate is the politics inherent in the situation. But that may sound too abstract. There is more immediate action that can be taken, and we are doing it in the form of a Boston Area Media Project, designed to work toward decentralizing the media hierarchical structure in the following ways:

By publishing a critique of the press written by the community rather than by journalistic "experts." Community groups thus would begin to see themselves as a "constituency" lacking guaranteed representation in the media. Publication of such a community-written and -controlled journal would result in the compilation of a list of "grievances" or deficiencies perpetrated by the establishment press. This list might be used in legal action against the metropolitan newspapers.

By demanding legislation or an expansion of the constitutional guarantees to protect journalists from management censorship and suppression.

By creating the conditions that would make journalists responsible to the "constituency" they serve rather than to the owners of the press.

By working toward the ultimate goal of a community-controlled press, and how it might work in a pluralistic society.

The project, of course, raises sensitive questions. A newspaper staff member under the Boston Area project would in effect be responsible to "the community" rather than to the newspaper. This clashes with the insistence of publishers that they have the sole right to determine what goes into their newspapers and therefore control over what a staff member may choose to write. If a staff member persists in seeking greater access to the paper for a community-based organization, the publisher can fire him. Deitch's response to that is that if the community groups achieve enough power, they can act in concert to prevent the firing. If they succeed, it will encourage other journalists to take a stand

and make demands. This, in collaboration with the workers' control activity, will form a "pincers movement" against the media hierarchy.

For himself, Deitch said: "It seems to me that the only protection I have now is that I do relate to the community in certain ways. If I was fired, some kind of fuss would be made. I don't know how large, but they would have to think twice about getting rid of me. They have to think about their liberal image."

Eight months later, Deitch's words of the summer of 1971 had a prophetic ring: he became the first test case of his own theories. In the first months of 1972 the *Globe* management moved Deitch's column off the Op-Ed page back into the financial section. Then they asked Deitch to undertake general assignment reporting of financial news—assignments which would make it impossible for him to have time to research and write his column. Deitch refused, on the ground that he had been hired as a columnist and that the management's move was a violation of its agreement with him. (The *Boston Globe* operates with an employees' association; it has no contract with the Newspaper Guild.)

When word reached the community organizations, they rallied behind Deitch, wrote letters and sought meetings with the *Globe*'s editors to persuade them to permit Deitch to continue his respected column. Pressure was exerted by union groups, political organizations and social agencies. The editors called Deitch in for new sessions, and it became clear that the basic issue was management's traditional prerogative and authority, and Deitch's challenge—in effect, denial—of that authority.

In the summer of 1972 the confrontation and the stalemate remained fixed. Deitch regards the action by the *Globe* as a validation of his analysis of the newspaper hierarchy theory. The incident, he feels, proves beyond doubt the need for the Boston Area Media Project. What was happening to him, he says, was an incident in the continuing rebellion in the media.

There have been setbacks in this rebellion—frustrations, rebuffs and tangential flights by sometime rebels who can take just so much rebellion. But there has been remarkable progress, too—sufficient, I believe, to justify my realistic optimism.

The struggle for honest journalism goes on, inside and outside the establishment media. The rebellion, like all movements for progress, has a long road ahead, but, as Bruce Brugmann put it, "there are many of us who feel that the newspaper business is a trade worth fighting for." And the most heartening element of that fight is that it is based on a fundamental concern for freedom. That, in the last analysis, is its strength.

APPENDIX A

JOURNALISM REVIEWS

Following is a list of journalism reviews produced by journalists being published in the United States:

Buncombe, A Review of Baltimore Journalism
2317 Maryland Avenue, Baltimore, Md. 21218
(Bimonthly; single copy 25 cents.)

Chicago Journalism Review
192 N. Clark Street, Chicago, Ill. 60601
(Monthly; one year, $7; foreign, $8.50; airmail, $13.)

Hawaii Journalism Review
53-133 Kamehameha Highway, Punaluu, Hawaii 96717
(Monthly; contributions only, no subscription fee.)

Journalists Newsletter
Box 1174, Postal Annex, Providence, R.I. 02903
(Quarterly; one year, $5.)

(More)
Box 2971, Grand Central Station, New York, N.Y. 10017
(Monthly; one year, $7.50; two years, $12.)

Philadelphia Journalism Review
1001 Chestnut St., Room 915, Philadelphia, Pa. 19107
(Monthly; one year, $5.)

Point of View
2150 Rexwood Drive, Cleveland, Ohio 44118
(Bimonthly; one year, $5.)

Review of Southern California Journalism
6101 East Seventh Street, Long Beach, Calif. 90804
(Quarterly; one year, $2.50.)

San Francisco Journalism Review
Box 3451, Rincon Annex, San Francisco, Calif. 94119
(Bimonthly; one year, $6.)

St. Louis Journalism Review
Box 3086, St. Louis, Mo. 63130
(Bimonthly; one year, $3; foreign, $5.)

The Unsatisfied Man, A Review of Colorado Journalism
Box 18470, Denver, Colo. 80218
(Monthly; one year, $6; U.S. airmail and foreign surface mail, $8.50.)

Thorn, Connecticut Valley Media Review
Box 1040, Holyoke, Mass. 01040
(Issued periodically; one year, $5; foreign, $10.)

Twin Cities Journalism Review
Box 17113, St. Paul, Minn. 55117
(Bimonthly; one year, $3.)

APPENDIX B

CABLE TELEVISION

Cable television is a system which distributes a television signal via a coaxial cable about the size of a telephone wire. The system was first devised for communities unable to receive conventional (through-the-air) TV signals because of an obstruction, such as a mountain. A typical system requires a receiving tower (on top of the mountain) and wires running to customers' homes, hence Community Antenna Television, or CATV, as cable television is known. It is, of course, a system of "pay television," as against the present "free television," and two arguments for its implementation have been advanced: one, that it provides a better signal and the potential for greatly diversified programming because more channels are available; two, that a cable system, like the telephone, permits electronic signals to move both ways.

In an interview with the *St. Louis Journalism Review* (March 1972), Nicholas Johnson, a member of the Federal Communications Commission, expanded:

A two-way cable system means that the customer at the receiving end could become more than just a passive consumer of whatever happens to be "on the air" when he turns on his set. It is technically possible for him to "order" special programs or information. For example, it might be possible to search a library's card catalogue and request that a book be sent to your home—or to read the book from the screen. Newspapers might be "delivered" that way in the future, with an attachment that permits subscribers to make a "hard copy" of what is being shown on the screen. There are innumerable potential uses, such as shopping and ordering via the cable, not to mention that it would be possible for public-opinion researchers to take an instant electronic poll of cable viewers.

There are a number of questions, Johnson said, about the future of cable television that remain unresolved at present, "questions that go beyond the issues—important as they are—that have been debated by the FCC in Washington." He said:

There are a variety of opinions about who should be able to own cable systems and what level of government should regulate them. As matters stand, cable franchises are granted locally and regulated, to some extent, locally, but they are also under the jurisdiction of the federal government and some state governments. One factor in this discussion is that there are several established interests which see CATV as a threat, including existing broadcasters and the national television networks, some elements of the sports business, and movie theater owners.

For the broadcasters, cable immediately reverses the situation that has characterized television since its inception—that is, a scarcity of channels in any one area. Cable can create an abundance of TV channels. For sports and movie theater owners, it could mean a whole new way of marketing their product.

Then there are questions of public access; that is, given a number of available channels—not all of which are necessary or even useful for selling soap, aspirin and deodorant—who will be able to use those channels, what will they show, and what will they cost? Will community groups—say a neighborhood association, for example— be able to get on cable TV? And if so, what will they be able to do or say? Should government regulation of cable encourage that sort of thing, or should it be left to the marketplace? These are just a few of the questions.

Some of the questions raised by Commissioner Johnson, and additional ones, were explored in a summary article in the New York Times *of December 19, 1971, by the* Times's *television critic John J. O'Connor, whose comments follow.*

Cable television is important. Just about everyone is agreed on that single point. Communications is power, the modern theory goes, and its power may eventually replace that of even the dollar. Cable television, its present and future, represents an entirely new communications complex.

Granted that point of agreement, the rest tumbles into disagreement and downright confusion as to how cable TV might best be developed. Its potential benefits to the general public are widely recognized by the experts but hardly comprehended by the public itself. Technical, social and cultural studies on the subject are scattered over the landscape, offering formidable challenges to the serious student.

For the present, moreover, the conflict-of-power arena is dominated by the professionals. The future is being argued by small and large cable operators, over-the-air TV operators, the networks, program producers and various government agencies.

The arena is being broadened, however, with the publication of reports and studies geared to the enlightenment of the public. And one of the more impressive efforts is *On the Cable: The Television of Abundance*, the report of the Sloan Commission on Cable Communications. Financed to the nifty tune of 500,000 dollars by the Sloan Foundation, the report involved about 18 months of committee study and it has been published, in hardcover and paperback, by McGraw-Hill.

Overall, the report is cautious. Its predictions are carefully conservative, and its recommendations tend toward compromise. Its basic thrust is clear: Over-the-air television, with its limited channel capacity and its limited radiated-signal abilities, is television of scarcity, economically forced to program for the mass audience and the lowest common denominator; cable TV, with its capacity for 20 or 40 channels and its ability to serve small areas and to devote channels to particular uses, promises a television of abundance.

That promise, covering a wider variety of entertainment, news and services, carries no guarantee. The history of broadcasting is a history of shattered promises. Educational and cultural millennia were clearly sighted with the advent of radio and, years later, of television. The result, with few exceptions, has been a broad band of mass-produced mediocrity, wrapped in the sometimes startling protection of official agencies.

The technology of cable television is not new. For years cable operators have been laying wires underground to bring distant over-the-air signals to outlying areas or to provide a clearer signal in cities where tall buildings interfered with radiated signals. According to the Sloan report, the cable TV industry in the ten years to last January 1 grew from 640 systems serving 650,000 subscribers to 2,500 systems serving 4.9 million subscribers. That represents an annual increase in subscribers at a compounded rate of 22 percent.

The report notes:

> These figures include a period, in the late 1960s, when growth was severely inhibited by the entry of the FCC (Federal Communications Commission) into regulatory activities, most of them inimical to cable television. Even during that period, however, subscribers continued to increase at the rate of 22 per cent.

By the end of the current decade, the report predicts, an "interconnected" cable television system will be able to bring as many as 40 channels into 40 percent to 60 percent of all American homes. At present there are more than 80,000 cable TV subscribers in Manhattan.

The cable hookup promises more than television. In a recent speech before the White House Conference on Aging, Hubert J. Schlafly, president of Teleprompter Corporation, ticked off a list of functions that could turn cable into a "personal genie" for the subscriber. Describing the Subscriber Response-Interactive Home Terminal, an offshoot of the basic broad-band cable system, he envisioned a system that, with computers, could check electric power or fuel supplies in the home, could place purchase orders and perhaps eventually could convey personal medical data to a medical center.

Some might call it a personal genie. Some might call it Big Brother. In any case, the Sloan report chose to ignore these magical possibilities for cable and to concentrate on the purely TV aspects. Even here, however, the possibilities are impressive. Pay television is undoubtedly a major element. And so is a system of reverse communication, traveling from the home back to the programming center and, using a simple push-button device, allowing practically instant audience surveys.

All of this, of course, is bound to have some effect on commercial and public television as it is now constituted. The report is unimpressed:

> We do not believe that in the short term the structure of over-the-air television is seriously undermined; we believe further that in the long term over-the-air television can adjust to the developing new situation. But in any case, if over-the-air television is to fall victim, in some degree or other, to technological change, it is in no different position from any other enterprise in which investments have been made, and possesses no greater right than other industries to protection from technological change.

The theory is noble. The practice may be somewhat less so. After years of protecting the broadcasters, the FCC finally did come up with a plan a few months ago that would have allowed cable operators the limited "importation" of distant signals. The broadcasters were not pleased. Then, in a "backroom" compromise engineered by the White House's Office of Telecommunications Policy, cable operators and broadcasters agreed to exempt the importation from the "top 50" population markets. The public, needless to say, was hardly consulted.

Still, the cable operators seem ready to accept any plan that will permit expansion. And that presents another problem. The future of cable TV is too important to be left entirely in the hands of the cable operators. While the cable has been around for about 20 years, the Sloan report observes, "only recently has it begun to warrant notice on the front pages of the daily press, and what is perhaps more significant, on the financial pages as well."

The report, being on the side of cable and calling for the relatively unfettered development of the system, evoked no immediate comment from the networks. Cable watchers were a bit more enthusiastic. On the stock market, Teleprompter's stock rose 13 points the week before the report was released; it rose another 13 points in the week of release.

The fact is that the establishment of a national cable "interconnection" will cost billions of dollars. Programming, servicing and ordinary operations will also be costly. If the public is to fully participate, how will the proper elements be able to afford participation?

The Sloan report offers its own broad recommendations and outlines how a 20-channel system might be divided: six for network and local stations, two for service uses, one for public access, one for experimental educational uses, eight for leasing and the remaining channels for the cable operator himself.

Entertainment, serious drama, opera, dance, news, news specials, specialized programs for specialized groups—it's all there in the promise. It was all there in the promise of radio. There are now 41 stations on the AM and FM bands in New York City and, with a few notable exceptions they are all working toward the making of the same profit margin.

If cable TV is to succeed, the public must become involved to protect its own interest. There are encouraging glimmerings in the infant system, but they could quite easily go the way of early radio's "potted palm" music recitals.

INDEX

INDEX

Police:—cont.
Democratic National Convention, 60, 98–100, 148; Glenville shootout, 114; harassment of underground press, 258–61
Pollak, Richard, 108
Polner, Murray, 215
Portland Press-Herald and *Express,* 138–9
Poston, Ted, 135
Potemkin, 204
Powell, Adam Clayton, Jr., 169
Powell, James, 47
Powell, John W., Jr., 245
Powers, Gary, 80
Prendergast, Charles, 44
Press: public skepticism of news, xi; management/staff relations, xiii, 59–60, 98–9, 123–4, 293–6; relations with government, xix–xxi, 31–2, 63; Agnew syndrome of distrust, 14–15; liberal and conservative views, 17–18; subpenas, 20–30, 33, 35–6, 107; confidential news sources, 22–31, 33–8, 284–5; police and government agents posing as reporters, 38–41; press informants, 42–53; military informants, 53–61; cards issued by police, 58; responsibility of press, 63–4, 79–80, 113, 131; reporting on Vietnam war, 66–76; response to Pentagon Papers, 76–9, 83–4, 88–9; response to Cuban missile crisis, 77–9; criticism of, 93–6; union developments, 94–5 (*See also* Newspaper Guild); press councils, 96–8; muckraking journalism reviews, 98–111, 231; in big cities, 101–2, 288; advertising/news ratio, 124; ethics of staff, 137–8, 141; military news in, 217–18; reactions to underground press, 217–18, 224, 260, 264, 273–4; and radical press,

Press:—cont.
240, 242, 248; and U. S. party politics, 245; "alternative" press, 269, 271–4; monopoly with television, 289; Op-Ed columns, 292–3, 296; community control, 294–5; *See also* Blacks in media; Freedom of the press; Journalists and journalism; Journalism reviews; Underground press; Underground press (military); Women in media
Press, Power and Money, 124
The Press and the Cold War, xviii
Press Freedoms Under Pressure, 45
Pride, Armistead, 173
Priest, Roger Lee, 206–8
"Prior restraint," 83–5
Progressive, 73n
Progressive Labor Party, 237
Progressive Party, 238–9, 245–7
Proper Gander, 204
Prouvost, Jean, 125
Public Broadcasting Act (1967), 276
Public Broadcasting Laboratory (PBL), 153–5
Public Broadcasting Service (PBS), 276–9
Public Information Center, 260
"Public interest": television industry, 143–6; journalism, 289–90
Public television, 153–5, 275–80
Puerto Rico, 49

Quick, 126
Quicksilver Times, 271
Quill, 103

Race relations and discrimination, xii, xiv, 20, 104, 240; police informants, 39; Glenville shootout, 114; *Point of View* articles, 114, 117–18; ERCA racist propaganda, 116; and television